Ilyse R. Morgenstein Fuerst is Assistant Professor of Religion at the University of Vermont. Her work has previously been published in peer-reviewed journals and her research deals with Islam in South Asia, historiography and the development of theories of religion. She received a Master of Theological Studies degree from Harvard Divinity School and a PhD in Islamic Studies from the University of North Carolina at Chapel Hill.

D1615771

INDIAN MUSLIM MINORITIES AND THE 1857 REBELLION

Religion, Rebels, and Jihad

ILYSE R. MORGENSTEIN FUERST

BLOOMSBURY ACADEMIC
LONDON • NEW YORK • OXFORD • NEW DELHI • SYDNEY

BLOOMSBURY ACADEMIC
Bloomsbury Publishing Plc
50 Bedford Square, London, WC1B 3DP, UK
1385 Broadway, New York, NY 10018, USA

BLOOMSBURY, BLOOMSBURY ACADEMIC and the Diana logo
are trademarks of Bloomsbury Publishing Plc

First published in Great Britain 2017 by I.B.Tauris & Co. Ltd
Paperback edition first published by Bloomsbury Academic 2020

ISBN: HB: 978-1-7845-3855-2
PB: 978-0-7556-0379-4
ePDF: 978-1-7867-3237-8
eBook: 978-1-7867-2237-9

Series: International Library of Colonial History, volume 24
Typeset in Garamond Three by OKS Prepress Services, Chennai, India

To find out more about our authors and books visit
www.bloomsbury.com and sign up for our newsletters.

for Kevin,
my co-conspirator
(in all the best ways)

CONTENTS

ACKNOWLEDGMENTS

I need to express my gratitude to those colleagues, friends, and family members whose various and divergent efforts have helped make this book.

I have been fortunate enough to enjoy financial support for a bulk of this research as part of my start-up and professional development funding from the University of Vermont, the Small Grants Award through the College of Arts and Sciences, and the Peter J. Seybolt Faculty Fund in Asian Studies. Additionally, the American Academy of Religion's Selva J. Raj Endowed International Dissertation Research Fellowship inadvertently sponsored both the research for the dissertation and this (wholly unrelated) book: while on a break from dissertation-related translating, I stumbled upon the writings of Hunter and Khan, and began the research that would turn into this project. Portions of this book have been presented previously in other forms: portions of Chapter 1 at the 2013 South Asian Literary Association Annual Conference in Boston, MA; Chapter 2 at a 2014 Religion Faculty colloquium in Burlington, VT; portions of Chapters 2 and 3 at the 2014 5th Annual Islamophobia Conference in Berkeley, CA; and portions of Chapters 3 and 4 at both the 2015 American Academy of Religion Annual Meeting, Atlanta, GA and the 2016 Boston College Biennial History of Religion Conference in Boston, MA. The conversations at each conference pushed my work in new — and better — directions, and I am grateful for those opportunities for growth.

Many who have guided and taught me over the years deserve much more than a few meager words of gratitude. Dr. Carl W. Ernst is an invaluable mentor who has pushed me to think about "religion" and "Islam" as categories in need of constant re-thinking; I hope to do justice to his erudition but more importantly to his years of kind guidance and intellectual generosity. My first college professor, Dr. Omid Safi, initiated me into the study of Islam and he has since championed my work, often from the sidelines and without end. In other but equally important ways – through conversations, texts, and even tweets – Drs. Bruce B. Lawrence, Juliane Hammer, and Kecia Ali have openhandedly propelled me from afar as I completed this project. I am grateful to my Fall 2015 Islam and Modernity students, who read a draft of Chapter 3; I had thought I was sharing my work to actively model the revision process of research to help *their* writing projects, but it turned out they were helping me revise and hone my argument. I am indebted to my colleagues in the Religion Department at the University of Vermont, who have welcomed me warmly into our little house on Main Street, listened to me talk often about this project, and helped me to think deeply, sharply, and better.

I am especially fortunate to have colleagues and friends willing to spend hours (and hours and hours) with my writing and ideas. Drs Brandi Denison and Kristian Petersen have offered critical feedback on a number of chapters and have my warmest appreciation. Dr. Gregory A. Lipton has read and commented on drafts of nearly every chapter, some in the very early stages of writing (which always deserves special recognition); while extremely humbled by his critical eye and unstinting reads, I am all the more grateful for our friendship. Dr. Kathleen Foody offered meaningful feedback on the conclusion and has been a constant conversation partner since 2007, for which I am ceaselessly elated. Dr. Megan Goodwin has read every single word of this book, offered bountiful (and often sidesplitting) marginalia, and helped me keep theoretical issues at the fore; her brilliance as a scholar is trumped only by her brilliance as a friend. Despite such a cherished and esteemed cadre of scholars in my margins, whatever errors remain are mine and mine alone.

At I.B.Tauris I was well cared for and advised, first by Azmina Siddique and then by Thomas Stottor, and each offered top-notch support for this project, kind and timely guidance, and clarity. Similarly, I owe Jane Haxby, my copy editor, a tremendous debt of gratitude; her work on this manuscript was impeccable. Yet, support for writing is not limited to the writing itself, of course. I owe much to Carolyn Lewis, who has offered tangible and deeply meaningful support to me in many ways for more than three years. I worked out more of my ideas than I ought to admit while working out at RevIndoor Cycling, so Sarah DeGray and her team have my appreciation. My family – Flo and Lloyd Morgenstein, Karly Morgenstein, and Deena Goodman – comprise the often invisible but omnipresent support network on which I will forever rely.

I want to thank my spunky, smart, and spectacular daughter, Sela. She's gone from incubation to infancy to toddlerhood during the research and writing of this project, and she is now able to ask, regularly, if my book is done yet so I can play pretend and be "less boring." Finally, my husband Kevin has been a true co-conspirator, a colluding partner as we navigate our shared life. This book is dedicated to him for all the ways his loving encouragement makes my work – and daily existence – infinitely, almost unthinkably enhanced.

A NOTE ON TRANSLITERATION

Where appropriate for Islamicate languages, I have followed the transliteration style of the *International Journal of Middle Eastern Studies* (IJMES); the first time I use terms likely to be unfamiliar to readers, I have set them in italic, then in italic or roman according to IJMES usage thereafter. I have followed convention for other South Asian languages. I have not transliterated names of persons or places, and I have marked historical place-names in northern India alongside contemporary place-names when appropriate. I have marked technical vocabulary in italics. In order to preserve clarity and avoid clutter, this does not include, however, words that have become common in English (e.g., jihad); similarly, words that have become common in English-language usage are pluralized, when appropriate, following English convention rather than Islamicate linguistic norms (e.g., fatwas not *fatāwā*). When quoting, I have maintained original spellings and transliterations as applicable. Because this is, in many ways, a book about definitions, most controversial terms will be defined historically, in context, and at length.

INTRODUCTION

Religion is not a thing to be trifled with, and the dullest and most
phlegmatic will be roused to the boiling point of rage and
enthusiasm when it once is affected.

— *Causes of the Indian Revolt, by a Hindu Bengali*,
ed. Malcolm Lewin[1]

On May 9, 1857, soldiers serving in the third regiment of light cavalry
in the Meerut cantonment awaited imprisonment for failing to use
their weapons properly. The newest Lee-Enfield rifles required soldiers
(sepoys) to bite the cartridge, but the sepoys refused — they had heard
the rumors about these new rifles and they were incensed. The cartridges
were greased with lard and tallow, offending the religious sensibilities of
Muslims and Hindus, respectively. After months of growing unrest,
dissatisfaction among sepoys and disquiet among civilians, rumors of a
new rifle sparked the match that lit a flame of mutiny and rebellion.
On May 10, 1857, as the sepoys of the third regiment faced sentencing,
sepoys in other regimens broke rank to liberate their imprisoned
compatriots. Meerut boasted an equivalence of Indian and British
soldiers, approximately 2,357 Indian sepoys to 2,038 British soldiers;
this was a fierce and bloody attack — but the violence was not cordoned
off to the garrisoned walls. Meerut's civilians were not spared. Some
20 British civilians, including women and children, were massacred;
additionally, some 50 Indian civilians perished in the rebellion's first
outbreak. Many sepoys who began the mutiny fled the 40 miles to
garrisoned and protected Delhi during the night, and on May 11, Delhi,

too, witnessed rebellion. Britons – soldiers and civilians – were taken prisoner and many were executed on May 16, 1857. The week in mid-May began a long, terrifying year of bloodshed, rebellion, suppression, and suspicion.

This long year marked – and continues to mark – one of the most important moments in South Asian and British history alike. Scholars of South Asia have amply critiqued such Euro-American historiographies that elided lesser-known examples of resistance to colonial authority.[2] Yet, the centrality of 1857 remains in both Euro-American and South Asian historiographies. One might suggest this is precisely due to the power accorded the initial weight afforded the Rebellion: to suggest it lacks importance or centrality would be a post-colonial resistance to an ongoing Euro-American hegemony. However, one might also suggest that the brutality and scope of the Great Rebellion indicates its position as essential and essentially climactic. The events of the Great Rebellion and its component parts – the initial sepoy involvement, its spread to civilians, its multiple massacres on both sides, the years of famine and deaths that followed, and the brutal ways in which the British regime sought to put down any hint of rebellion in its wake – are no doubt enormously significant in size, scope, and its lasting imprint on British and South Asian popular history and imagination. Despite its overvaluation as *the* example of (ultimately quashed) Indian resistance to British rule, the Great Rebellion is undeniably *an* exemplar of resistance, and moreover, an indelible set of events which fundamentally altered the ways in which India was ruled and how Britons saw the people and landscape that they ruled. There can be no doubt that 1857 marks – perhaps scars – the history and historiography of South Asia.

There is also little doubt that the massive imperial reconfiguration and response to Rebellion fundamentally alters definitions of *religion*. No scholar of religion and its study can afford to ignore South Asia: not only have so many of the field's founding thinkers based their theories on Indic languages, literatures, and racial-linguistic definitions, but as Peter Gottschalk has thoroughly established, the ways in which the British categorized religion in India fundamentally alter how religion is thought about, as a category, well beyond British rule and Indian borders (issues discussed at length in Chapter 1). More topically, however, neither can one ignore how the Great Rebellion seismically reconfigured the ways in which both *religion* and *particular religions* are defined, characterized, and classified. In other words, 1857 marks not only South Asian and British histories, but the history of the study of religion, as well.

A key component of this book is the argument that an oft-repeated (and deeply problematic) formulation that Islam and Muslims are inherently tied to ideas of violence, specifically understood and named *jihad*, is not a new, contemporary categorization. Rather, I contend that the 1857 Rebellion marks a dramatic and palpable moment in which *jihad* comes to signify Muslims broadly and definitionally as religious actors and as (potential) subjects of empire. These are new contributions to the study of religion, empires, and Islam, and I believe them to be vital contributions: as we come to grasp the role and racialization of Muslims in contemporary settings, it is of the utmost utility to trace how that racialization began. This book aims to take the long view and locate these processes not in contemporary memory, but rather as part of imperial formation and global acceptance of the narrative of Rebellion. Just as one cannot understand the history of the study of religion without navigating how India has been portrayed, neither can one comprehend a contemporary relationship between Muslims and *jihad* without first locating its historical correlation to the Rebellion.

On May 9, 1857, disillusioned and disgruntled sepoys protesting the use of (supposedly) greased cartridges awaited sentencing. Many must have anticipated long jail terms, hardships both financial and physical, and humiliation. They perhaps could not have anticipated the violent bloodletting that would follow in subsequent weeks, months, and years. They likely would not have predicted the retaliation of the British that was not merely physical, but imperial: the changes to myriad laws, increased military presence, policies that forced widespread famine, interruptions in daily lives, impositions of definitions of "real" caste, "real" religion, "real" civility. The mutinous sepoys, afraid to lose caste or religion for biting tallow or lard, could not possibly have imagined how definitions of religion would still carry the marks of their actions, many years later, which were essentialized in the wake of 1857.

And yet, how definitions of religion formed in the aftermath of 1857 are major components of the claims in this book. The unimaginable consequences of the mutinous sepoys, acting out of frustration, bewilderment, and anger – acting based upon rumors of betrayals of their religions – included widespread violence and massacres, and also epistemological and ontological (re)categorization of those religious actors themselves. All this — the violence, the bloodshed, the imperial interventions that followed, the reformulation of Indic identities — all this because religion had been trifled with.

Religion, Rebels, and Jihad

This book tells a story of stories: how the memory, history, and historiography of the 1857 Rebellion shape the stories about religion in India, especially the religion of Indian Muslims. It interrogates the 1857 Rebellion in terms of religion asking how religion, as a category, shaped interpretations of the Rebellion and how the Rebellion came to contour conceptualizations of religions and religiously identified people, especially Islam and Muslims. Religion was at the forefront of British imperial thinking in India, which was dominated by fears of rousing the religious sensibilities of the "natives," attempts to recognize, define, and ultimately control religion, and identification of characteristics of religious subgroups. Definitions of religion cannot ignore India or the religions of India; what would become the discipline religious studies begins in India, and it was forged on the British imperial imperative to know its conquered population, as well as, more specifically, on notions that Hindus were not Muslims.[3] The defining of religion — especially Hinduism and Islam — cannot itself be understood without understanding the Great Rebellion.

That the Rebellion came to be portrayed as a *religious* insurrection — and specifically a marker of religious obligation for Indian Muslims — is the central topic of this book. The Rebellion is not important to the narrative of religion in India merely because it is a cataclysmic series of events that reshaped the subcontinent; it is important because the very memory — including history, historiography, and memorialization — of the Great Rebellion *writes* religion in India. It is only after the Rebellion that some of the nascent ideas about Hindus and Muslims, in particular, came to be full-fledged categorical truths, and the Rebellion itself serves as the evidence of those truths.

The 1857 Rebellion had lasting effects for India and Indians of varying religious stripes, but for India's Muslims the interpretation of the Rebellion as jihad shaped subsequent discourses, definitions, and codifications of Islam. *Indian Muslim Minorities and the 1857 Rebellion:*

Religion, Rebels, and Jihad is therefore an examination of the *production* of religion, rebels, and jihad in nineteenth-century India. More specifically, it is an examination of how the Great Rebellion came to serve as the means through which to understand the rebels, primarily in essentialized terms of religion. An exchange between two leading intellectuals, both servants of the imperial regime, serves as a lens through which to read the 1857 Rebellion's construction and reconstruction of Muslim identity in the British Empire. One half of the conversation is W. W. Hunter's *The Indian Musalmans: Are They Bound in Conscience to Rebel Against the Queen?* (1871 (2nd edn 1872)), which was widely published and circulated. Hunter's treatise spurred a lengthy reply from Sir Syed Ahmad Khan, noted and knighted Muslim modernist, Indian Civil Service member, and prominent scholar.

The post-1857 political climate, expressed through Khan and Hunter's interchange, scripted religion, rebellion, and jihad in imperial India. I argue that this confluence produced "Muslims" as a discrete and static category, indelibly marked as rebellious and jihadi. The intertwined processes of minoritization and racialization – theoretical concepts that frame my analysis – played a central role in this cultural and imperial production of Muslims as jihadis.

This book traces the construction of Indian "Muslims." I first discuss religion in India before the Rebellion. I then highlight the theoretically operative conceptualizations of minoritization and racialization in post-1857 India. I argue throughout this book that the minoritization and racialization of Muslims is a direct consequence of the Rebellion. The stories told about the Great Rebellion – histories, memories, poetry, political texts, and more – constitute stories told about religion, rebels, and jihad.

Theoretical Framing

In tracing the ways in which Muslims came to be seen primarily in terms of threat, and how jihad – as we will see, conceived as religious war waged against non-Muslims – came to define authentic Islam. More directly, we will see how the *minoritization* and *racialization* of Muslims after the 1857 Rebellion created a grammar in which to be Muslim meant one was a threat to the empire, and threats to the empire were connected to Muslims. The stories told about the Great Rebellion serve to tell readers and listeners key information about the lead characters; this project is concerned with how these stories tell readers and listeners information thought to be essential (but is deeply essentialized information) about Muslims. Part of the undergirding approach, therefore, is to think through the ways in which Muslims come to be defined in light of essential portrayals of the Rebellion, especially since these portrayals shifted radically after 1857.

Despite the lengthy political rule and expansion of Muslim empires in India, Muslims never occupied a demographic majority – but inhabiting a minoritized position is not the same as inhabiting a demographic minority. Minoritization does not refer solely to the demographic realities of a particular location, but instead to the systematic process by which elites deny power or access to a group through the implementation of power, be that local, linguistic, economic, or political.[4] Minoritization is a process, in this instance, of the solidification of British power *over* former Muslim ruling elites and the demographic, religious constituency they were thought to represent. This was achieved by both *de jure* (legal, economic, and political policies[5]) and *de facto* cultural shifts that included, as examples, the discontinuation of Islamicate and Indic languages and (real or perceived) mistreatment of Muslims.[6]

Despite locating the Rebellion as a crucial rupture in the depiction and conceptualization of Muslims in India, rendering Muslims a political minority did not occur overnight. Rather, as we will see, the act of remembering and retelling the events of 1857–8 created the narrative in which Muslims became both minoritized and racialized. In other words, making Muslims a racialized minority is related to the processes of memory and memorialization, the solidification of a popular and academic narrative of the Rebellion that came to have specific and essentialized characterizations of the lead actors (Muslims, Hindus, and Britons alike). We can pinpoint the Rebellion as the cataclysmic moment in which the shift occurs, but the writing that comes from the decades following 1857 makes this moment palpable. Defining Muslims as a minority – and a dangerous, racialized one at that – was a key goal of a number of the sources we will explore below, including the primary textual focus of Chapter 2, W. W. Hunter's *The Indian Musalmans: Are They Bound in Conscience to Rebel Against the Queen?*

Where minoritization collapses a group into a singularity with both identifiable and marginal traits, racialization marks individuals as having immutable traits because of their membership in a minority group. The concept and construct of race includes essentialization of groups based upon traits imagined to be inherent, hereditary, and prognostic – that is to say, rooted in biology (or pseudo-biology) and therefore scientifically "real."[7] Racialization is the process through which a group is made or marked as a race; it is the process through which individuals are made manifest as both belonging to one cogent group as well as possessing those inherent, hereditary, and prognostic characteristics.

Religions are not races – Islam is not a race – but Islam and its practitioners are *racialized*. As Sylvester Johnson has recently and masterfully demonstrated, assumptions of race as tied to phenotype or biology fail to capture the ways in which power – especially colonial power – invented, assigned, and defined race based upon exclusionary definitions that were *not* tied to specific bodies.[8] In other words, while Islam is not a race, Muslims are racialized and defined racially in large part based upon their relationship to imperial power. After the Rebellion, Muslims in India come to be depicted as possessing inherent, unchanging, and transmittable characteristics. They are portrayed as inherently seditious, bound by both law and intrinsic disposition to violence, and necessarily ill-tempered, incorrigible, and unable to be ruled by non-Muslims. These are decidedly racialized classifications: Muslims cannot escape these traits – they are imagined to be part of the fundamental composition of *what* and *who* is Muslim. To be otherwise, in effect, would indicate that one is *not* Muslim. We will see Britons make claims to the inherent and transmittable characteristics of Muslims in bald-faced statements below; we will also see more obtuse references to supposedly inalienable traits of Muslims in works by both Muslims and Britons.

Racialization and minoritization do not function solely as external labels thrust upon Europe's Others. Instead, they often demand and require the participation of those who have been racialized and minoritized. These are pernicious systems of power, definition, and classification, and with respect to Indian Muslims, they relied on stories told about the Great Rebellion. As we will see below, Britons and Indian Muslims alike told these stories.

Minoritization and racialization are at the heart of the *question* of Muslim belonging – a question posed by Sir William Wilson Hunter and answered by Sir Syed Ahmad Khan in an intertextual dialogue at the center of this book. Works like Hunter's *Indian Musalmans* contributed to the process that rendered Muslims a distinct minority; *Indian Musalmans*, among other texts described below, posited Muslims as a distinct problem to be solved by the ruling elite. They come to be portrayed as an inherent threat on the basis of racialized characteristics that stem from interpretations of Islam. Further, as we will also see, even Muslims arguing against these characteristics perpetuate the idea that Muslims stand as a unique, cogent group, and thus participate – albeit asymmetrically – in the processes of definition, racialization, and minoritization. Ultimately, I argue that the Great Rebellion is a catalyst for the minoritization and racialization of Muslims, and that in its wake Muslims in India emerge permanently differentiated along these lines as a result of the epistemological and physical violence of imperialism.

A Note on Language

Accounts of 1857–8 India have an almost bewildering set of titles: the Great Rebellion, the Sepoy Mutiny, the Uprising of 1857, the Sepoy Rebellion, the Indian Mutiny, India's First War of Independence, the Indian Rebellion, the Indian Revolt, the Sepoy Revolt, and, tellingly, the Mahomedan Rebellion. Each moniker represents a vantage point and interpretation of the tumult – each tells a story about how the stories of 1857 were told. These titles indicate the operations of power and control not only during the events, but also and more importantly, in historical narrative itself. In the years immediately following the conflict, British authors preferred the term "mutiny." A mutiny indicates insubordination, which assumes instantiated leadership; this word choice reflects an understanding of official and properly established power against which a group of soldiers acted. Most Indic authors, on the other hand, preferred "rebellion" or "revolt" in their discussions about 1857–8. These, too, indicate a rejection of an established authority but more readily communicate *resistance*, a term itself laden with symbolic and semiotic meaning an imperial context. Further, where "mutiny" necessarily communicates disobedience against an authority, usually within an army, "rebellion" suggests noncompliance vis-à-vis the entire ruling elite. "Revolt" similarly suggests an impetus to fully upend the status quo and end the current authority's reign.

Language expresses power, and many scholars have suggested that all communication is merely the exchange, establishment, and negotiation of power.[9] I do not aim to rewrite – or unnecessarily rethink – how terminologies and categorizations of these events support, negate, or obscure historical and relational power dynamics. I aim instead to justify my near-exclusive use of "rebellion," and occasional use of "mutiny" and "revolt," to refer to the events of 1857–8. In all cases, I maintain the language used by the primary source in question. One expects to find "mutiny" in the official records of the East India Company and writings of British imperial agents; similarly, "mutiny" appears often when I highlight authors of popularly available articles as well as various tracts and treatises printed in South Asia and the United Kingdom. "Rebellion" and "revolt" most often correspond to sources written by Indic authors, though occasionally to works by critical Britons as well.

I almost exclusively use "Great Rebellion" and "the Rebellion" for a number of reasons. The first is that for many years historians were quick to dismiss the Great Rebellion as a chaotic, haphazard war, and while the events of 1857–8 were not masterminded by a military strategist or one centralized commander, it is important to see them in terms not of military history, but of purposeful resistance to imperial might. "Mutiny" smacks of a particular insubordination that communicates a lack of development, a hasty attempt. When "mutiny" is paired with "sepoy" (i.e., soldier) – as in the popularly used Sepoy Mutiny – it communicates a definitional militaristic defiance (soldiers taking up arms against commanders) and belies the participation of civilians and other non-sepoy actors (a central fear and fixation of policies after the Rebellion and later British writings about 1857). Confusing how events unfolded with what they came to signify is problematic, and "mutiny" renders Indic actors as immature or impulsive. The bloody events of 1857–8 were not, ultimately, a result of sepoys' fears of guns smeared with cow and pig fats; they were anti-imperial revolts that did not merely scare Britons on the ground in that moment, but rather shook the imperial machine to its core, spurring cataclysmic global change that had lasting effects especially for Indians, as we will see below. I want to express the gravity that is better communicated in "rebellion," so as to do better justice to Indic actors, but also to better represent Britons' fears of those actors. The *fear* of Muslims as provocateurs of such a serious, terrible set of events was a real outcome in the aftermath of the Great Rebellion – so if a mutiny is localized and a rebellion widespread, the latter term better captures the historical imagination that is investigated here.

A further introductory note on language and vocabulary: alongside the political terming of "rebellion" are the fluid terminologies – and spellings – for what we render today as "Muslim." I follow the lead of my sources, and thus "Muslim" is sometimes rendered as "Musálman," "Muhammadan," "Mohametan," or "Moslem." I have retained their uses not only to maintain the integrity of the original works, but also to highlight the mercurial natures of terminologies, definitions, and meanings; I am concerned, in other words, with how seemingly static terms have radically shifted, especially with reference to particular historical events in South Asia. In order to visually underscore those shifts, I maintain curious spellings where appropriate. It is no doubt of interest and import that multiple terminologies are used to refer to what nearly all the primary sources claim to be one cogent whole. Multiplicity despite presumed unity underscores the limitations of categories, but more relevantly here, the lexical and symbolic diversity in terminologies for and about Islam and Muslims is directly located alongside an ideological and stated homogeneity *of* Islam and Muslims.

Chapter Outline

In order to sketch how Muslims came to be branded as uniquely and challengingly disloyal after the Rebellion, it is imperative first to approach how various facets of religion and Islam were seen in the period leading up to it, as well as how the events of the Rebellion themselves were seen as having religious underpinnings. While religion had been a preoccupation for Britons at home and abroad, the Great Rebellion solidified threats to Empire imagined to be the singular purview of religious actors, and especially Muslims in British India. The first chapter, "The Company, Religion, and Islam," outlines the historical context of the nineteenth century, and addresses how "religion" as a category was regarded and policed in India. It also attends to issues of how the Rebellion was remembered by both Britons and Indian Muslims.

Chapter 2, "Suspect Subjects: Hunter and the Making of a Muslim Minority," addresses how the Rebellion produced a Muslim minority. Its central text is Sir William Wilson Hunter's *The Indian Musalmans: Are*

They Bound in Conscience to Rebel Against the Queen? (1871; reprints 1872, 1876). Hunter's answer to the titular question was a resounding yes — for him, Muslims were *religiously* obligated to rebel, and therefore constituted an inherent threat to the Empire. This chapter elucidates the relationship between scholarly analysis of the Great Rebellion and the production of a Muslim, minoritized subject.

'"God save me from my friends!': Syed Ahmad Khan's *Review on Dr Hunter*" is the third chapter. It primarily attends to Sir Syed Ahmad Khan's written responses to the Great Rebellion and argues that Khan's defensive writing about the Rebellion demonstrates a minoritized Muslim community that was distinctively and uniquely held accountable for the violence of 1857–8. The chapter begins by analyzing Khan's *Causes of the Indian Revolt* (*Asbāb-i baghāvat-i Hind*, 1858), and continues by focusing on *Review on Dr Hunter's Indian Musalmans: Are They Bound in Conscience to Rebel Against the Queen?* (1872). The latter is an academic reply to Hunter that represents both an elite Muslim perspective on the climate of India post-1857 as well as the opinion of a loyalist — in other words, Khan represents a *loyal* Muslim attempting to defend and define Islam *against* British depictions. This chapter, like Chapter 2, attends to the process of minoritization, but takes as a central theme the ways in which Indian Muslims, exemplified by Khan, worked with and against this hegemonic process.

Chapter 4, "Rebellion as Jihad, Jihad as Religion" specifically addresses the use of jihad in the nineteenth century and focuses on how jihad came to inform definitions of Islam and Muslims. It examines Muslims' calls for jihad before and during the Great Rebellion as well as Britons' labeling the Rebellion jihad after the fact; in other words, I take seriously the deployment of jihad as a theological, political, and anti-imperial tactic of Indian Muslims as well as the ways in which Britons come to deploy jihad *against* them. Chapter 4 addresses the relationship between minoritization and racialization, where jihad came to serve as shorthand for inherent, transmitted, violent, and distinctive disloyalty of Muslims. Further, it traces the role of the 1857 Rebellion in both solidifying and manufacturing a particular distrust of Muslim subjects amongst British agents and scholars. I contend that after 1857, rebellion became tied especially to Muslim actors and organizations and to jihad, and, as part of the process of racializing Muslims, that jihad came to serve as a primary identifier of Muslims in British India.

In the conclusion, "Religion, Rebels, and Jihad: Legacies and Ongoing Impact," I briefly revisit some of the major themes of the book, pertinent primary source quotes, and theoretical themes discussed in the preceding chapters. I consider the ways in which these categories — religion, rebels, and jihad — function together after the Great Rebellion of 1857, and I ultimately contend that these categories are indelibly imbricated in the historiographies and memories of the Rebellion. Religion (especially Islam), rebels (distinctively Muslims), and jihad (the unique threat) color not only how the Rebellion was — and is — read, but also how Muslims came to be understood after the tumult of 1857–8, and as the British Empire reframed its rule in the subcontinent. I suggest that understanding the discursive shifts caused by the Great Rebellion is vital to understanding the minoritization and racialization of Muslims in South Asia — an issue that still lingers in South Asia and in South Asian diasporas.

The dialogue between Hunter and Khan exemplifies how Britons and Indian Muslims constructed a memory of the Rebellion that was unmistakably tied to religion, religious groups, and religious actors. Hunter and Khan each weave a narrative that ultimately places jihad as a fulcrum around which Muslim loyalty is addressed; they articulate rather different opinions, to say nothing of their diametrically opposed conclusions, but they each take the theological, textual, and legal category of jihad as a central and real way to think about Muslims as subjects of the Crown. Further, they do this as they think about the primary evidence of seditious behavior — the Great Rebellion. The stories they tell prioritize one trait, imagined to be inherent and shared by one group, revealing a larger, underlying narrative about the category of religion and its role in the minoritization and racialization of Islam and Muslims. After 1857, Muslims come to be portrayed by Britons as always already potential jihadis, as if jihad were an inborn characteristic; even as Muslims argued against this narrative, the story itself became the hegemon, with impacts that continue to echo today.

CHAPTER 1

THE COMPANY, RELIGION, AND ISLAM

The very essence of Muhammadan Puritanism is abhorrence of the Infidel. The whole conception of Islam is that of a Church either actively militant or conclusively triumphant — forcibly converting the world, or ruling the stiff-necked unbeliever with a rod of iron.

— W. W. Hunter[1]

In newspapers, I find the most bitter denunciations against the Mahomedans, who are being freely represented as everything that is vile, treacherous, and contemptible.

— Syed Ahmad Khan[2]

While Hunter and Khan epitomize a particular depiction of Muslims after the Great Rebellion, negative conceptualizations of Muslims and Islam had existed in Europe well before the East India Company came into existence, Britain colonized South Asia — or Hunter wrote a treatise expounding upon the ways in which Muslims fundamentally could not be loyal subjects of the Crown. These preexisting depictions range from portrayals of Muhammad as a fiendish, self-serving, maniacal fraud[3] bent on personal glory, to dismissal of his visions as delusionary, epileptic seizures,[4] to Muslims as lustful, violent fanatics.[5] For Britons in South Asia, the decline of the Mughal Empire meant that no obvious, unified Muslim challenge to their imperial expansions existed; so, before 1857, we do not see a widespread fixation on an *immediate* Muslim threat, nor do we see condemnations of Islam, broadly, to the same degree as we do after the Rebellion.

Before the Great Rebellion, Mughals by and large stood in for Muslims, especially with respect to official or semi-official policies, procedures, tracts, and laws. Britons certainly saw Mughals either as excessive – in their palaces, architecture, and courtly lives – or as despotic, having enacted laws like the *jizya* (poll tax on non-Muslims); more often, they set a self-aggrandizing understanding of British rule in shining contrast to the previous, declining Mughal rule.[6] British commentators often posited Muslims and Hindus as unique and oppositional; in the British imagination Muslims were violent, manly, and fanatic while Hindus were passive, effeminate, and flexible.[7]

The East India Company (the Company or EIC) looms large in any historical account of nineteenth-century India, and especially in those that think through official and unofficial stances, policies, and ideologies. The tracts, treatises, and demographic and cartographic data produced by various levels of administrators – from humble collectors to governor-generals – cannot be overstated in their heft or underestimated in their lasting import. The EIC was famously allergic to religion, deeming interference in religious matters as bad business. Yet, it was also famously attuned to matters of religion, regarding it as central to both sensible business and governance practice. As a result, the EIC commissioned both Indians and agents of the British Empire to research and write numerous tracts about India and its religions. Those varied documents tell us that religion mattered to the Company, and they characterize Muslims in very particular ways.[8]

Before the 1857 Rebellion, many imperial writings about Islam exhibited a missionizing or civilizing tone and seemed rather concerned with what religious deficiencies were left in the wake of the failing Mughal Empire. George Chapman, a Company employee, for example, in a text called *Tracts of East India Affairs* added a poem (in Latin) in which he retells a story about one of the Biblical Magi who is,

> parabolically represented as standing on the bank of the river Ganges, near the city of Calcutta, and bewailing the calamites brought upon his country by the tyranny of its Mahometan conquerors, and their successive and desolating wars: and the angel Gabriel, the benevolent and ancient Announcer of the Messiah, is

introduced as comforting him with the view of general Peace in
that extensive country, and with a prospect of the introduction of
the Christian Religion, in its primitive Purity, under circumstances
highly favourable to so desirable an object.[9]

Chapman represents a particular Christian imagination of Muslims,
and specifically of Mughals: they were despots who conquered India,
tyrannically dealt with its original inhabitants, and then left it in a state
of calamity, which could and ought to have been remedied by the new,
British rulers, who helpfully and happily also brought Christianity with
them. Chapman also presents a fairly typical early nineteenth-century
tract, in which the affairs of the British in India are conflated with either
(though in this case both) the spread of Christianity or of civilization.
Chapman writes that it was by the "will of GOD" that India came to
"obey the KING of GREAT BRITAIN,"[10] later concluding that it was
"by the appointment of Providence, for the purpose of enlightening and
civilizing the blinded and infatuated Indians, and bestowing upon them
the blessings of peace and of the *Christian Religion*."[11]

However, unlike Chapman, who called for conversion and religiously
sanctioned rule in India, many imperialist agents explicitly criticized
religious connections between Britain and the Indian subcontinent.
Many East India Company officials vehemently opposed conflating
Christianity – by way of missionaries – and their own presence in India.
In fact, until 1813, missionaries were not granted permission to work or
travel in India. A number of East India Company officials thought
missionaries, in their roles as promulgators of Christianity, would
damage the relationship between Britain and India. Sir Henry
Montgomery (d. 1830) warned that widespread, unrestricted activity
of missionaries in India would encourage feelings of suspicion and
rebellion in India.[12] The Honorable Frederick Douglas (d. 1819) added
that the EIC ought to tolerate but not encourage missionaries.[13] While
these men, among others, wanted to support Christianity and religious
and civilizational change in India, they saw the work of missions as
counter to the financial and administrative work of the Company – and
to the tenuous peace it held over zealous natives.[14]

The East India Company was originally a joint-stock trading
company, meant to solidify Britain's financial and political holdings in
Asia. It was not necessarily conceived of as a religious force for native

peoples; almost immediately upon its founding, the EIC functioned as a company-state, establishing not only trade routes, partners, and products, but also functional and self-sufficient governmental apparatuses, like tax collection, armies, and other civic institutions.[15] In 1813, Parliament passed the Charter Act, which formally and fundamentally altered the Company's and the Crown's relationship to South Asia. The Charter Act expressly established the Crown's sovereignty over India and, significantly, ended the East India Company's monopoly on trade.[16]

During the official hearings for and about the Charter Act, religion – especially Hinduism and Islam – was fiercely discussed and debated. Members of the Houses of Commons and Lords alike cited the "natures" of Hindus and Muslims as part of the rationale for expanding British presence in South Asia; they debated what sort of market it would be for various goods; and they considered at length the role of missionaries and the merits of purposefully seeking to convert Indians to Christianity. They were particularly concerned with the possibilities of disorder, of threats to British power, and, ultimately, of revolt or rebellion.

Lieutenant Colonel Sir John Malcolm (d. 1833), a long-serving and high-achieving member of the East India Company's army, was called as an expert witness before both Houses of Parliament during the examinations on the East India Company's charter. When questioned by a member of the House of Commons about the Indian population and the possibility of stable, orderly rule, Malcolm stated: "That our territories in India contain a great number of seditious and discontented men, there can be no doubt."[17] During the same exchange, when asked to specify between Hindus and Muslims, he plainly asserted that the majority of the Hindu population was "contented," but "the Mahomedan part may not be so much contented."[18] He added that "I certainly conceive that the attachment of the Hindoo population of India is the chief source of our security in India," but that "our authority could not last a day" if Hindus and Muslims united in rebellion.[19] Others during these hearings suggested the same: rule in India was to be maintained by virtue of a sleepy, submissive Hindu majority, but Britons ought to worry about Muslims disrupting the calm.[20]

Sir Charles Warre Malet (d. 1815) echoed Malcolm's assessment and concerns. Malet was another long-serving and decorated officer of the East India Company who was questioned by the Select Committee of the

House of Commons on the issue of the East India Charter. Like Malcolm, Malet was asked specifically – and at some length – about the trustworthiness of Indians, the ways in which Muslims and Hindus interacted, and how those interactions might shape unrest. He stated:

> India is a country of vicissitude and revolution; I think it not at all improbable that some great genius, some extraordinary spirit, might arise, that could combine the present floating spirit of discontent in the Mahometans into one mass; in which case I think, notwithstanding the general amicable disposition of the Hindoos, that spirit might be dangerous and difficult to subdue.[21]

India, Malet attested, was a country of revolution *despite* the majority's amicability. He placed the possibility of rebellion upon the shoulders of a charismatic, dissenting leader who could mobilize the discontented Muslim masses and then excite the otherwise-agreeable Hindus. For Malet, only Muslims held the potential to set alight the rebellion, despite the majority Hindu population's general compliance.

Malet thought that Britons were the root cause of Muslim distress and dissatisfaction with British rule. He testified that "the hostile spirit" was "produced by any indiscretion or violations of the manners on the part of our countrymen," and suggested that "only power and opportunity would be wanting to effect the suggestions of any indisposition which might have been created."[22] Others, too, believed that British religious policies and missionary activity in India brought about rebelliousness, especially in retrospect: after 1857, many pointed to British policies and events as having led Indians toward rebellion. Salahuddin Malik, a contemporary scholar, notes that "many Britons regarded the excessive missionary activity to be largely responsible for the uprising in India."[23]

We ought not dismiss anti-missionary pronouncements lightly. The Great Rebellion came to be portrayed as a *religious* rebellion, and both Indians and Britons cited the Charter Act which allowed admission of missionaries and enacted broad and formal changes to the Britons' religious policy toward native Indians, as a seismic shift and precursor to the Rebellion itself. In our contemporary moment, where post-colonial and decolonial studies of religion, the (former) Commonwealth, and India have successfully challenged historiographies of empire, it may seem unlikely to us that missionaries were problematic for the EIC. Certainly, missionaries and missions played a tremendous role in myriad expressions of colonialism, imperialism, and governmentality in South Asia. But before the Charter Act of 1813, the EIC was remarkably careful about allowing them access and permission to operate in India.

Salahuddin Malik notes that:

> A cursory glance at the history of the rise to power of the East India Company would reveal an extremely cautious and conservative policy followed by them with regard to native religions, customs and conventions. There was a time when the Company's government would not let a missionary set foot on their territory, obviously for fear of offending native religious beliefs. Every conquest, every annexation and every occupation was invariably followed by a solemn pledge of non-interference and observance of complete neutrality in religious affairs.[24]

Claims to neutrality do not actually vouchsafe it; and, as other scholars have noted, missions and missionaries, in spite of restrictions, operated with relative safety and freedom in South Asia well before 1813.[25] However, the Company's formal reluctance to allow missionaries, its policies – even if lip service – of noninterference, and its track record of denouncing missionaries should not be overlooked. Taken together, these earlier policies demonstrate what a fundamental change occurred with the Charter Act of 1813, reactions to which largely engendered both later hostility toward evangelizing Britons and a popular memory of unrest attributed to British disregard of native religions leading up to the Great Rebellion.

The East India Company's policies do not indicate a secularist ideal of equality of religions. Instead, they communicate real trepidation about the Company's ability to control a populace and represent a pragmatic attempt to mitigate Indic concerns about foreign rule, forced conversion, and the appearance of invasion. Some observers flatly commented that "Asiatic" or "Oriental" people – and especially Muslims – were known for their religious zeal, and controlling zealotry became a strategic device to maintain order. These commentators found all religious people in India to be swayed by emotion, especially religious emotion, but they reserved fears about fanaticism, and fanatic revolt, for the Muslim population of India.[26]

For example, during the East India Company Charter Hearings of 1813, Thomas Sydenham stated that Muslims, across time and space, were well noted for their "bigotry and fanaticism," and that the "very considerable body of the Mussalmen inhabitants of India" posed a "considerable danger" to British control.[27] Warren Hastings (d. 1818), the first governor-general of India who was infamous for being tried for (though acquitted of) corruption, likewise testified on the East India Charter before the House of Lords Select Committee. Despite a reputation for hardness vis-à-vis indigenous Indians, he strongly argued against a heightened British presence in India, calling such an influx of "foreigners" both "ruinous" and "hazardous."[28] With regard to Muslims, Hastings insisted that arrivals of more Britons – which would certainly include missionaries and Christian officers – would yield "religious war," because he could imagine that Britons "might speak in opprobrious epithets of the religious rites" of both Brahmins and "Mahometans," adding that such behavior would no doubt "excite the zeal of thousands in defense of their religion."[29]

In 1813, as part of a debate about the nature of the East India Company before the Houses of Parliament in London, officials suggested that Muslims were predisposed to religious war against British rule, and that this predisposition should influence how Parliament proceeded with respect to the Charter Act. All of the men cited above had illustrious positions and careers in India and as part of the EIC, and all – among others – advocated cautious fortification of Britain's presence in India on the basis of the religious nature of Indians generally and Muslims particularly.

While some scholars have held that the Company remained resolutely cool toward introducing missions and Christianity in imperial India, others have convincingly argued that over time, these two facets of empire warmed to each other and found common cause in missionizing vis-à-vis either Christianity or "civilization." Historian Ian Copland notes that, especially between the passing of the Charter Act in 1813 and the Great Rebellion, the Company and the Empire "eventually developed a fruitful and at times even intimate relationship, based in part on their shared faith, and in part on their common interest in providing Western education to the country's elite," adding that "this honeymoon did not last" and "after 1858, both sides came to re-evaluate the benefits of partnership in the light of new theological strategies and changing political imperatives."[30] The relationship between missionaries and the EIC was ever-changing, though after the Charter Act, each side seemed gradually to see the other as helpful in their various aims.

Nevertheless, between 1813 and the Great Rebellion in 1857, real changes that stemmed from religious ideologies (like evangelism) and were based upon definitions of religion and religions came into being and affected Indians. The full-fledged allowance of missionaries after 1813 did not simply permit Christian men and women, individually seeking converts, to roam freely in British-controlled areas. Instead, it sanctioned the establishment of institutional structures, including mission schools, printing presses, and centers for materials distributions, that could support missionary activity and foster a long-term set of plans for the safeguarding and promulgating Christianity in India. Further, these institutions relied on fundamental changes to laws and their application. Still, these changes did not happen readily, as even though the Charter Act passed, it could not change the EIC's longstanding ethos of avoiding religious matters.

For example, in 1821 the Anglican bishop Thomas Fanshaw Middleton, who was appointed by the Crown per the Charter Act and financed via Indian revenues (making him an officer of the State), suggested an ordinance that would forbid "the employment of native artificers on Sundays."[31] The ordinance was refused, as the governor-general and his advisory council feared that such a policy would "do violence to the religious habits of Muslims and Hindus" and thereby damage the reputation and standing of the Company. Lest we imagine offense was a primary concern, in their refusal the council added economic concerns as well – such as losing 52 Sundays of work.[32] Even though this ordinance did not pass, it exemplifies the sort of structural change made possible by the Charter Act: before it, missionaries and missions were at the sole discretion of the EIC, and generally frowned upon, but after it, the EIC was obligated to entertain their suggestions, and, in a slow, case-by-case manner, address them. Other ordinances and policies passed across the regions and presidencies, including those that established mission schools.[33] As we will see later, mission schools, which openly used Christian scripture, enforced attendance through truancy laws and then attempted to convert children while their parents were elsewhere; they became sources of deep contention, anxiety, and anger for many Indians.[34]

Structural changes required both institutional support and on-the-ground reinforcement. As but one other example of the effects of the Charter Act, by 1830, laws set by Mughal rulers and local ruling elites on the basis of *shari'a* (an idealized Islamic law[35]) and *fiqh* (jurisprudence) had already seen formalized changes. At a hearing before the Select Committee of the House of Lords, part of an inquiry into the state of the East India Company, attorney Courteney Smith testified that "Mahomedan criminal law has, to a great extent, been altered by the Regulations [of the East India Company]."[36] He stated that these laws had been modified, citing that:

> Mutilation has been put an end to, and some rules of evidence have been modified; the rule about female evidence has been modified. The Mahomedan law of evidence requires two women for one man; but according to our practice, a woman is thought as good as a man for a witness.[37]

Well before the Rebellion, changes in legal code with specific reference to Islamic law had taken shape. Laws around conversion had similarly changed: in the district of Bengal, the noted stronghold of the Company, making conversions to Islam (or "Mahomedanism") could be ruled illegal, finable, or jailable *if* a judicial official found the conversion to be "forcible." In 1832, two such cases were tried and prosecuted with success.[38] Mechanisms of the Mughal Empire – an empire ruled by Muslims, though one that would be challenging to term "Muslim rule" – were stripped as new rulers carved their own space, informed by their set of missives, and these posed distinctive challenges to Muslim life in India. Yet, however great the challenges to Muslims became as Britain increased its authority and control, none would be as great as those that would follow the Great Rebellion of 1857–8.

Religion before Rebellion

In order to make sense of the Rebellion's influence on the depiction of religion, it is worthwhile to first briefly sketch how scholars conceived of religion prior to 1857. "Religion" as an academic field relies on the

history and culture of imperial India. Many pioneers of the nascent field
were Indologists, some employed by imperial agencies.[39] The effect of
colonial, missionary, corporate (i.e., East India Company), and imperial
documentation of religion, religions, and the religious[40] in South Asia
has direct impact on the field of religious studies. We cannot and should
not study the history of religion without engaging South Asia, yet few
nonspecialists attend to the unique role India has played in the
construction of religious studies.

Britons invested in ruling India before and after 1857 fixated on the
role that religion and ethno-religious identities played in governance.
The British Empire's emphasis on religious distinction – based on
creed, sacred text, and ritual – weighed heavily upon official and
unofficial imperial policies.[41] For many, the Rebellion clarified the
relationship between politics and religion: Indians would constitute
either a controlled population or a horde of religiously justified
insurrectionists.[42] Before the Great Rebellion, during that tumult, and
well beyond into the twentieth century, Britons portrayed Muslims as
an especial concern – a nuisance before 1857, and an outright threat in
the period after the Rebellion.

Religion before the Rebellion inhabited a space of interest to Britons
in their ruling, trading, and civilizing aims. Sometimes these aims
competed with each other, sometimes they complemented each other,
and other times still they were wholly absent from conversations about
India. Yet religion – and the British construction, maintenance, and
ongoing classification thereof – was roundly (and problematically)
understood to be vital in understanding India.[43] At hearings about the
East India Company, its charter, and its dealings in South Asia and
beyond, members of Parliament routinely asked questions pertaining to
the religious spirit of "Hindoos" and "Muhammadans."[44] In popular
recountings of the Great Rebellion, religion sparked the events of
1857–8 and demonstrated the dangerous power religious belief and
affiliation presented to the Raj. Britons imagined religion to bear
dangerous weight: to offend religious sensibility or to impede upon
religion at all would enrage even the "dullest and most phlegmatic"
Indians,[45] and for many Britons, avoiding enraging the integrally
wrathful Muslims was an ongoing and pressing concern.[46]

As scholar John L. Esposito has incisively observed, Muslims
represent a threat, both political and theological, to Christian empire

and in Christendom's imagination from the medieval period onward.[47] Further, because the British had wrested power from the Mughal Empire, a dyad of political and theological threats seemed very real. Britons may not have feared the decrepit remnants of the Mughal regime, but they recognized the powerful significance of displaced Mughal elites, their potential to incite revolutionary zeal, and the theological precepts that rebellion might intone.

British imperialists saw Muslims both as former rulers of India and as politically and theologically dispossessed. Britons also considered Muslims uniquely violent and intolerant to non-Muslims – both able to incite rebellion and religiously required to do so. They were a double threat before and after the Great Rebellion. While attitudes toward religion and Islam changed over the course of British interventions in South Asia, these broad strokes painted Muslims rather consistently across fluctuations in rule and region. The specific concern about and fixation on Muslim rebelliousness increased dramatically in the wake of the Great Rebellion, but it is vital to explore precursor imaginations of religion and Islam, formal and informal, so as to properly contextualize later conflations of Islam and rebellion, Muslim and jihadi, and jihad and rebellion.

The project of defining and delimiting religion as part of European imperial expansion marks a complex matrix of political agendas, relational inflections, and various expressions of domination (across race, ethnicity, color, gender, mother tongue, and so forth). This process attended to more than religion;[48] however, the relationship between the British company-state and indigenous people in India, elite and subaltern alike, in many ways rested on religion or an understanding of local practice as a function of religion. Britons were concerned with religion as it related to their rule, as it affected their profits, and as it demanded correction – all issues in the multifaceted historical moments leading up to (and shaping memories of) the Great Rebellion.

Categories constructed and observed in India were also communicated back from the colony to the metropole, with lasting effects. Historian of religion Peter Gottschalk observes:

> Since the fifteenth century, a system of knowledge has been in development in Europe that would form a matrix of interrelated disciplines used not only by Europeans to understand, exploit, and

control non-Europeans, but also by non-Europeans to understand and control their own societies, and by others while resisting European power. This matrix formed, and continues to represent, a keystone in the Western hegemony that exists today, albeit in an altered form. Not only was this matrix instrumental in establishing Western-originated disciplines in non-Western societies, but it also served to globally communicate information about those societies and their cultures generated by imperial and colonial practitioners of those disciplines.[49]

What British observers reported about India and Indians served to communicate truths received as objective about both India and Indians, and, as Gottschalk explains, that are maintained in both Western and non-Western disciplines.

The categorization of Muslim and Hindu traditions has influenced far more than colonial practices during imperial control; these definitions have lasting legal, political, and societal consequences.[50] Religious categorization has undoubtedly shaped the ways in which observers came to write about the Great Rebellion; portrayals of Muslim rebels as jihadis (as will take priority in the fourth chapter) have as much to do with a scientific classification of Islam, its component parts, and its systematic structures as with witnesses' reports, attitudes, and biases. Put differently, the Great Rebellion – like other historical events – came to be read through the categories and lexicons available. Those categories and lexicons, both distinctly imperial and distinctly religious, in turn came to be read back onto the Great Rebellion, making definitions of Islam and Muslim both theoretical interesting and historically vital.

While Britons may not have singled out Islam or Muslims to define, exploit, or control them, the Empire held Muslims in different esteem than other religious groups, notably in terms of threat. It was widely thought that Hindus would not rebel, for a variety of reasons, unless Muslims agitated them to do so. Before 1857, Muslims occupied a position of suspicion different from that of their Hindu counterparts, and were seen in terms of a unified whole, capable of whipping other religious groups into a revolutionary frenzy – even when these groups (namely, Hindus of varying castes) normally would be seen as incapable of revolution when left to their own devices. The concern about Muslims and Islam is fear of an inherent and rebellious contagion – Muslims in this definitional landscape are a threat because of their capacity not merely to rebel but to incite rebellion.

The agents of the British Empire, both before and after the Rebellion, had a keen interest in their Indian subjects across religious affiliation, and one could certainly argue that British agents paid greater attention to the demographic majority (Hindus) than to the largest minority (Muslims). Britons also worried about Hindus and their loyalty in the wake of the Great Rebellion. I submit, however, that their concern about Hindus was subsidiary to their capacious preoccupation with Muslims; many Britons in official capacities, ranging from governor-generals to members of the East India Company army, saw the threat of Hindu rebellion as definitionally tied to Muslim actions. Hindus obviously comprised a major part of the 1857 Rebellion, India's demographic majority, and a governmental concern. However, because of the imperialist focus on Muslims as instigators of rebellion, I have largely omitted portrayals of Hindus before, during, and after the Rebellion; I focus specifically on the imperial processes of racialization and minoritization as they relate to Muslims and the Rebellion, its aftermath, and its historiography.

"Watershed Moment": the Great Rebellion

However often its import is repeated a year cannot exist on its own. 1857 was, of course, preceded by 1856, and historical imaginations that take seriously the apparitional nature of the Rebellion fail to properly contextualize those events or to interpret the historiographical contexts in which 1857 was written as a watershed. It was not the first time Indians had rebelled, fought, or dissented against colonial regimes.

"Watershed" is a favorite term of a number of scholars for describing the chaotic events of 1857–8 in South Asia.[51] Watershed, here, refers to the perceived radical change to the flow of history in India. Prior to 1857, a decrepit and depleted Mughal Empire still existed, albeit in titular capacities that barely echoed the imperial might of prior eras; Britons colonized India largely through the sanctioned actions of the East India Trading Company, but the relationship between Empire and Company was complicated, and imperial power functioned and flowed differently across the various regions of South Asia. After the Great Rebellion, however, the flow of power changed – many mark this moment as the difference between the colonial and imperial experiences in India, though I would argue this terminological difference, while historically accurate, does not fully encapsulate lived realities in South Asia or the complex transitions from Company to Empire both before and after 1857.

Yet 1857 remains a watershed for scholars in the twenty-first century as it was for elites in the mid-nineteenth and early twentieth centuries. It is the oft-repeated, oft-blamed, and oft-cited source of changes that ranged from the final demise of the Mughal Empire to the solidification of linguistic identities to sweeping legalisms and legal reforms. For our purposes, the interpretation and emphases placed on the Great Rebellion in terms of religion and, critically, Islam, will be the primary concern. Before delving into these imaginations of 1857, and their effects upon definitions of religions and religious people, we must examine the Rebellion itself, and the concomitant depictions of religion in this historical moment.

While the Company had official recognition and permission – as far as Britain was concerned – to operate in India as early as 1600, most historians regard the Battle of Plassey in 1757 as a decisive blow to indigenous rule in the colonies. Plassey is an Anglicized rendering of Palashi, a city approximately 150 kilometers north of Kolkata in the Indian state of West Bengal. In 1757, the region was under the dominion of the Nawab of Bengal and Murshidabad, which was subordinate to the Mughal Empire. Mirza Muha Siraj ud-Daulah (d. 1757) was the Nawab at the time, and he attempted to stop British expansion in Bengal, partly through an alliance with the French East India Company (*La Compagnie des Indes Orientales*). However, the leader of Siraj ud-Daulah's armies, Mir Jafar (d. 1765), betrayed him and collaborated with the British invaders in return for promises by the British East India Company of financial and political favors.[52] Despite the treason of their commander, the armies of Siraj ud-Daulah, in collaboration with the French, were still a force to be reckoned with, and Robert Clive (d. 1774), the British commander, resorted to extreme violence (which came to light only well after 1757) to quell them. This was not, as was sometimes romantically relayed, a kingdom without leadership, nor a fantasy of savage natives without any governance.[53]

While the Battle of Plassey stands as the temporal demarcation of British dominion in India, it did not inaugurate a time of peaceable control over what would become British India. As historian and theorist Ranajit Guha notes, "India was not conquered in a nine-hour battle on a single day."[54] Indeed, it took EIC troops years to secure Bengal, even after the Britons had declared Plassey a decisive victory.[55] Expansion happened gradually and was accompanied by battles, skirmishes, and their related resistances. Britons sometimes classified these as battles, sometimes as protests, only rarely as rebellions.[56] Regardless of classification, the resistance to expansion demonstrates – perhaps commonsensically – a resistance to British dominion writ large. As South Asian historian Kamaluddin Ahmed demonstrates, resistance to British rule was active after 1757; he specifically traces Muslim and Muslim-affiliated movements, actions, and outward revolts that indicate a pattern of active anti-British campaigning in the years between the Battle of Plassey and the Queen's proclamation of sovereignty over India in 1858.[57]

The century between the Battle of Plassey and the Great Rebellion was marked by a number of protests against, skirmishes with, and complicated victories for the British East India Company. That the Great Rebellion took Britons by surprise indicates not – as our sources attempt to claim – a vast conspiracy that opportunistically reared its head, but rather a system of privileging certain voices and information. Much as British media reported definitive victories in 1757 despite the hard-won (and lost) realities of conquest in South Asia, smaller movements of resistance went unmarked or were written off as unorganized, dislocated protests. Some of these were coded as minority expressions of discontent or peasant rebellions. This may have mirrored class politics in Europe, and had the effect of annulling native sentiment; further, Euro-American historiography and European eyewitness accounts alike branded peasant rebellion as unimportant, local, and limited. As Guha notably observes, this history failed to fully appreciate either the scope or scale of peasant uprisings, of which there was no short supply from the beginning of British control in South Asia.[58]

The disregard for peasant uprising is evident even before the Great Rebellion. Many contemporary observers were shocked by the violent events of 1857, which demonstrates a failure to connect the Rebellion to other movements in northern India at the time. The Rebellion was contemporarily held over and above other, smaller examples of resistance, and historians have replicated this lacuna by assuming functionally narrow foci on 1857, the sepoy (soldier) involvement therein, and the bloodshed that followed. The real context belies those foci: in central India (Khandesh, Dhar, and Malwa), the Bhils, an Adivasi people, rebelled in 1852; Santhals, another scheduled tribe typically located in north-east India and Nepal, rebelled in 1855–6; and Savaras of Parliakhemedi revolted in 1856–7.[59] Likewise, despite adamant claims to the contrary, Bengal saw the Indigo Revolt begin in 1859, which complicates the neatness of the Great Rebellion's impact, duration, and finality, as well as the claims that Bengal was a "zone of peace" at that moment.[60] Moreover, ongoing protests dotted India's map well after 1857, right up until Independence/Partition in 1947, though none were characterized by the extreme violence or overtook popular imagination as did the Great Rebellion.

In 1857, the British – via the East India Company – controlled approximately two-thirds of the Indian subcontinent's land, and about four-fifths its population, maintaining influence over the remainder.[61] In May 1857, sections of the East India Company's sepoy (from the Persian *sepāhi*, meaning "cavalryman") army began to rebel, first at Meerut and then across northern India. The revolts spread from sepoys in cantonments to civilians, and some historians note this shift from disquiet among soldiers to full-scale civilian uprising linguistically: the distinction between Sepoy Mutiny and Indian Rebellion or Great Rebellion becomes less of a marker, as we saw earlier, of power, and more a historic demarcation aimed at clarity.[62]

As revolts spread, many Britons, including men, women, and children, found themselves quickly outnumbered and isolated in unfriendly or hazardous environments. Infamously, some were killed in massacres at Delhi and Cawnpore. Others fled private homes or family compounds, some taking shelter in forts and mass residencies that were also besieged (as in Agra and Lucknow, among other places).[63] Stories of atrocities, especially those committed against women and children, quickly and freely circulated in the British press in India and the United Kingdom; the defilement and murder of women, and murder of children spurred particularly ruthless calls for vengeance.[64] While they pale in comparison to today's instant and immediate digital news cycle, communication systems in the mid-nineteenth century had vastly new technologies and improvements, making the British (and European) public well aware of the Rebellion's spread and viciousness.[65] Scholars

Andrea Major and Crispin Bates note that the Rebellion marked the "first experience of 'total war' for the British [. . .] in which British civilians were seriously caught up in the front line of conflict alongside officers and soldiers."[66] As such, Britons across the Empire – in India, at the margins of rebellion, and safely at home – not only called for retaliation, but also experienced deep anxiety and fear about their personal status in India and about the status of the British Empire in India.

While history favors the victor, and many British commentators certainly assumed victory, this outcome was not always so assured. As the Rebellion progressed, it was clear that the outnumbered Britons did not necessarily expect to win. Reinforcements needed to be called in to ensure security and to replace lost sepoy (i.e., Indian) infantrymen, who were no longer seen as trustworthy. Some socially marginal whites – whom scholar Sarmistha De calls "low Europeans" – were drafted into the EIC armies; these included English working-class men, poor Scotsmen, and Irish peasants.[67] The desperation in British calls for retaliation and desire to suppress the revolts indicates the depth of fear and uncertainty caused by the rebels. When the British regained control, though it was imperfect, there was no uncertainty in their actions.

Brutality was not limited to the massacres in Delhi and Cawnpore, and Britons quickly answered the call for retribution. As others have noted, the British doled out retribution not just to active rebels but also to women, and, as historian Arshad Islam demonstrates, particularly to women affiliated with the former ruling Mughal elite were heavily targeted in the wake of the Rebellion.[68] Concurrent to the Rebellion, Parliament passed Act XIV, which instituted martial law and allowed British officials to try native officers and soldiers in the sepoy regimes for actions against the army and state.[69] It is unclear, however, if all who were tried were actively engaged in rebellion or mutiny. In fact, in the moments immediately after the Rebellion, as British forces sought to regain and maintain authority, they summarily executed vast numbers of rebels. In addition, under a "scorched earth" policy, they left wide swathes of the landscape in utter ruin, which both induced and added to the already-extant widespread suffering of Anglo-Indian society.[70]

In light of famine, murders, sensational (if largely discredited) stories of rape, and viciousness on all sides, the Great Rebellion became imprinted on the collective memories of Britons and Indians alike.

Many have debated the "true" or "authentic" causes of the Rebellion, with numerous contemporary eyewitnesses and commentators pointing to religious fervency, ethno-racial inclinations to fanaticism, and, ultimately, an inescapable irrationality. Anxieties around religion and religious (in)sensitivity permeated initial reports about the "mutiny" and continue to bear weight today. While the Great Rebellion cannot and ought not be characterized as a singular moment without precedent nor aftershocks, it is nevertheless uniformly understood as a watershed – if not *the* watershed – in modern Indian history. 1857 looms large because of the depth and scope of the Rebellion, its unprecedented violence, and the resultant reinforcement of British authority. Its effects continue to be manifold: the machinations of Rebellion, in the imperial record and in native responses to it, shaped religion, religious definition, and especially the portrayal and conceptualization of Indian Muslims by both imperial and native agents.

Greased Cartridges and Chapatis: the Anxiety of Religious Conspiracy

If the Great Rebellion is the watershed for South Asian history, then the harbingers of that climactic event are greased cartridges and passed chapatis. These two – the former more than the latter – figure immensely in the narrative of the Great Rebellion and contribute especially to its inherent religious undertone. Many have disputed the actuality of these events. Others have discredited the notion that these limited occurrences could have sparked such widespread and long-lasting bloodshed. Still others place these events within a complex matrix of other events, policies, and shifts. Despite these efforts, the narrative stands: rifle cartridges greased with religiously prohibited animal fat caused the Rebellion, and the rebels used chapatis to secretly pass the conspiracy of rebellion from region to region. Religion, religiosity, and fanatic adherence to religious law – law beyond state control, importantly – figure principally in the story of how the Great Rebellion came to be and came to be so devastating. In short, greased cartridges and passed chapatis underscore the widely held belief that religion was a viable and real threat to the Empire, an actual and potential cause for the Great Rebellion particularly and rebellion generally.

No aspect of the Rebellion so captured the imagination of writers, politicians, and commentators as the Enfield Rifle, the updated musket meant to be distributed to the sepoys. It replaced the equally famous "Brown Bess," a smoothbore musket used for decades in sepoy regiments. The Pattern 1853 Enfield rifled musket was more powerful, more accurate, and able to attain better striking distances. The Brown Bess and the Enfield Rifle both required cartridges to be loaded manually. To load either of these guns, the operator had to break open a cartridge of gunpowder by biting it, pour the gunpowder into the muzzle of the weapon, stuff the cartridge case — typically paper coated with some kind of grease or wax to make it waterproof — into the musket as wadding, then finally load it with the ball that would be fired. The act of biting the cartridge, while not a new physicality of sepoy armament, has been credited with sparking the Great Rebellion. Cartridges of the Brown Bess were greased with beeswax. It was rumored that the Enfield cartridges were greased with animal fat — specifically, the fat of beef and pork, religiously prohibited animal products for Hindus and Muslims, respectively. As the popular retelling goes, word of the new weapon's problematic grease spread, causing upheaval; some argued that these reports were merely rumors that conspiratorial leaders seized upon and used to rile up their religious compatriots while working together,[71] though others preferred to see the greased cartridges as the match that ignited the average sepoy's revolutionary zeal.[72]

Rumor, legend, and embellishments typify rationales for the Great Rebellion. Like Colonel George Bruce Malleson's (d. 1898) assertion of a tidy conspiracy story, he (and others) recounted a similar, somewhat fanciful story of the start of the mutiny. He wrote:

It happened in this wise. A lascar engaged in the factory at Dam-Dam asked a Brahman sipáhí to let him have a drink of water from his lotah, or brass pot. The sipáhí indignantly refused, on the ground that his caste would not permit him to use the lotah afterwards if it should be defiled by the drinking of a man of a lower position in the Hindu hierarchy. The lascar, in reply, laughed at him for talking of defilement, when he said, 'You will all soon be biting cartridges smeared with the fat of the cow and the pig.' He then told the sipáhí the method of the new cartridges. The incident occurred when the mind of the sipáhís had been

inflamed, in the manner already recounted, to a high state of
tension. The story spread like wildfire. Thenceforward the sipáhís
were as soft clay in the hands of the chief conspirators.[73]

This story is repeated, nearly identically, in a number of places, and it is
also repeated only to be refuted elsewhere.[74] Many have commented on
the religious underpinnings of the story of the greased cartridge, but
Malleson's observation best summarizes the general theme: "The men
seriously believed that they were about to be juggled out of their
religion by means of cartridges."[75]

Of course, it is both historically irresponsible and flatly incorrect to
suggest that the Enfield rifle singularly sparked revolts. It is absolutely
unfathomable – and unsupportable – that one issue could have caused a
widespread rebellion that entailed small- and large-scale violence,
military action, tribunals, displacements, and months of ongoing
warfare, with vast legal and social ramifications that followed. The story,
however, contains meaningful kernels of broader contexts and schemas of
complex issues. For example, the Enfield was to be – coincidentally –
smeared with exactly the animal fats the two major religious factions
could or would not abide. The rumor was not that the rifle would require
generic animal fat, some of which – like that of mutton – would not be
as offensive or polluting to either religious community. Rather, the story
plays on a commonly known stereotype of religion in South Asia,
Muslims avoidance of pigs and Hindu veneration of cows, lending an
obvious marker of religious offense to the retelling of the rifle story.
Likewise, the tale of how sepoys, and Indians more broadly, came to first
learn of the offensive grease happens in a near-perfect critical fable:
a Brahmin's religious sensibilities are offended – and his religious
haughtiness lampooned – to an audience that both understands the
offense and sees a moral in watching him be humbled.

The greased cartridges often appear alongside a complementary
rumor that leaders of various religious and political outfits signaled
widespread rebellion by way of circulating chapatis, a typical north
Indian flatbread. The passing of chapatis and its evident appearance
of conspiracy, too, became part of the historiography and popular
imagination about the Great Rebellion.[76] Malleson related that the
key agitators of the Mutiny were "Maulaví of Faizábád, the mouthpiece
and agent of the discontented in Oudh; Náná Sáhib; one or two great

personages in Lakhnao; the Rání of Jhánsí; and Kundwar Singh."[77] He referred to them as "conspirators," and he named each as responsible for some aspects of the revolts, but seemed to suggest that their power – and evidence of a true conspiracy – lay in the collective. He narrated the controversy, religious offenses, and conspiratorial narrative as such:

> The practice with the old paper cartridges, used with the old musket, the 'Brown Bess,' already referred to, had been to bite off the paper at one end previous to ramming it down the barrel. When the conspirators suddenly lighted upon the new cartridge, not only smeared, but smeared with the fat of the hog or the cow, the one hateful to the Muhammadans, the other the sacred animal of the Hindus, they recognized that they had found a weapon potent enough to rouse to action the armed men of the races which professed those religions. What could be easier than to persuade the sipáhís [sepoys] that the greasing of the new cartridges was a well-thought-out scheme to deprive the Hindu of his caste, to degrade the Muhammadan?[78]

Malleson summarized the issues neatly: leaders, both political and religious, seized upon a rumor that would surely enrage. He added that when the British and sepoys had trusted each other, no one would have believed that one would knowingly betray the other, but once all trust had been eroded, it was possible to convince sepoys (and, later, civilians) that the British had ill-intent toward them, and that rebellion was appropriate.[79] He narrated:

> The executive council of this conspiracy had arranged, in the beginning of 1857, to act upon the sipáhís by means of the greased cartridge, upon the inhabitants of the rural districts by the dissemination of chapátís. This dissemination was intended as a warning that the rising was imminent. It was further decided that the rising of the sipáhís should be simultaneous, and more than once the actual day was fixed.[80]

The conspiracy was vast, and included an "executive" council, comprised of various leaders; it involved sepoy regiments in a few areas, by way of playing upon religious sensibility; and it aimed to spread to "rural districts" by way of secret messages. Malleson saw in the Great Rebellion a massive network of Indians, raging from powerful to lowly, working together to destroy the British Empire in India.

We ought to be suspicious of the greased cartridges, the passed chapatis, and the mythologies surrounding both. A number of observers and contemporary historians have raised strenuous objections to the idea that new rifles for sepoys caused the Great Rebellion.[81] The offending rifles (which were never issued) and the chapatis (which, while plausible, cannot be confirmed[82]) exist as testaments to a nexus of oral history and legend; their authenticity is relative to its effects, not to its scientific demonstrability. With regard to oral tradition, Peter Burke notes that "what does not meet with general approval is not passed on; in the sense the audience acts as a censor."[83] The rifle and the chapatis are indispensable elements of the Rebellion story.

That these stories persist bears weight in two primary ways for our purposes. First, their persistence indicates a neatness of narrative and resonates as essentially accurate; second, it demonstrates that religious belief – and British offenses to it – was and is seen as a viable, plausible reason for rebellion. The latter demonstrates a number of assumptions: that Britons would, or had, offended local religious custom and order; that Indians, across assumed lines of Muslim and Hindu, would band together in light of religious offense; and that the population could tolerate all manner of the colonial regime's trespasses so long as they did not cross into the sphere(s) of religion.

The story of the Enfield rifle encodes an incredulity at the ignorance or purposefulness with which the British acted in their plan to distribute the weapon. In two of the most cited and standard British accounts of the Great Rebellion, the authors demonstrate, collectively, this encoding: as above, Malleson, in a fairly simple aside, noted what pigs and cows mean to Muslims and Hindus, and, despite suggesting elsewhere that simplistic religion did not singularly spawn rebellion, he intoned that such grave offenses left both groups with little choice but anger.[84] John William Kaye, on the other hand, merely noted that the greased cartridges were to be distributed and did not bother explaining why this might cause offense.[85] The distasteful nature of the greased cartridges is presumed.

Both Malleson and Kaye implied that fat from pigs and cows would be readily and immediately identified as religiously prohibited, so its use in rifle cartridges would indicate either a truly unforgiveable ignorance or a purposeful transgression by the British. Thus, the persistence of the Enfield rifle as a cause of the Great Rebellion encapsulates a British India in which religion comes above all else, and proper control means effective management of religious sensibilities of the two major "sects," Hinduism and Islam. The standard British accounts of the Great Rebellion reveal a critique in which authorities at best failed to know enough *not* to offend, and at worst, knew enough but disregarded how serious a religious offense would be in a heightened religious atmosphere like India. Moreover, the Enfield story similarly implies that the British model of *divide et impera* – divide and conquer – failed in this case because the Britons misunderstood either religion or its grip on the Indian populace. Proper and lasting control relied upon Hindus and Muslims remaining divergent and at odds with each other; only in their unity could rebellious conspiracies take root with measurable effects. Offending both Hindus and Muslims at the same moment violated British philosophies of proper rule in India and made the two groups strange but dangerous bedfellows.

In the immediate aftermath of the Rebellion (and in some cases, even as skirmishes and massacres continued), many commentators suggested that Muslims were uniquely responsible for the rebellion and had persuaded Hindus or others to participate. As seen in the 1813 Charter Act Hearings, Britons represented Muslims as having a predilection toward violence, with a ferocity that was especially reserved for a conquering, non-Muslim regime. During and after 1857, this tableau was exacerbated and used to demonstrate that Muslims, unlike their Hindu counterparts, were predisposed to violence and rebellion, with the potential to agitate the otherwise-docile Hindus into anti-imperial action. This explained the revolts neatly for many commentators.

This explanation is exemplified by the work of W. H. Carey, a British author and compiler for the East India Company, who specifically addressed the Great Rebellion in a book he titled *The Mahomedan Rebellion*.[86] This hurried volume appeared in late 1857, no more than six months after the original outbreak of revolt, as events were still unfolding across northern India, and as British and Indic contemporaries alike scrambled to respond, physically and in writing, to the cascading effects of revolt. Carey's work was shaped by both religious conviction and a Eurocentric sense of history; he replicated religious ideologies about Christian supremacy as well as European ideologies wherein Islam and Christianity were at odds, representatives of differing – even warring – worlds.[87] Carey insisted that the Rebellion was that of Indian Muslims, evidence of religio-political objection to British rule, and proof that deep concerns about Islam in India were justified.[88]

In his prefatory remarks, Carey stridently insisted on the religious nature of the Rebellion. Accusing Indians of "cowardly massacres" and "treachery," and calling them "misguided and faithless miscreants" as well as "hordes of robbers," he attributed British success to a divine hand: "Providence has watched over the Briton, and brought aid at the very moment when most needed – and India continues British India still!"[89] Carey reported that while the general public saw the Rebellion as a vast conspiracy "to exterminate the Europeans in India" that had "been the work of years," his review of documents and records from Calcutta did not provide evidence of a conspiracy.[90] Rather, he saw the Rebellion as a result of Muslims seizing upon British weakness and, importantly, acting on behalf of and in obedience to their religion.[91] In fact, Carey offered a lengthy quote from "the Shah of Persia," and he italicized the portions of it that he saw as supporting – even commanding – Muslims engaged not in a political conspiracy, but in holy war.[92]

In most of his fairly sizeable book, Carey worked from this summation of a document from the "Shah of Persia," which he claimed was recovered "when our conquering troops had fought the battle of Mahamra in the plains of Persia" in a "deserted tent of the Shahzada [. . .] duly signed, but without a date."[93] Carey seems to have mistaken – or collapsed – the concurrent Anglo-Persian wars (1856–7) and the Indian Rebellion (1857–8). The Anglo-Persian wars encompassed a number of battles for control between the British and the Qajar dynasty; regionally, these took place in the greater area of western Afghanistan, on the borders between the expanding British territory in India (and contemporary Pakistan) and the Persian Empire. The Persian Shah did indeed declare jihad, and he did indeed do so during the battles for control against the British.[94] However, these wars were related only in British eyes: they both threatened British control over India insofar as a Persian gain on the borders – with their Russian allies nearby – would pressure Britain in India. Carey's mistakes appear to be based upon an imagined pan-Islamic unity in which a (Shi'i)

Shah of a distant empire would directly sway Indians hundreds (if not thousands) of miles away. Moreover, in his quoted text, Carey reports that the Shah spoke directly to "the people of Heran [Herat],"[95] which is a city in Afghanistan near the contemporary border of Iran. So, even if the Shah directly addressed the Muslims of India, as Carey claims, it is unclear to which Indians either the Shah or Carey refers: are they the *proximate* South Asians, in contemporary Pakistan? Are they Afghani Muslims assumed to be Indian Muslims? Or, are they those Indian Muslims who would, later in 1857, first rebel in Meerut, nearly 1,300 miles away as the crow flies? Are they *all* Indian Muslims? And if so, how did Carey imagine a Persian-language letter would be disseminated, and, once disseminated, to whom?

Carey's assumptions here are vast and go unanswered. Regardless, it is telling that his volume relied upon the Shah's "recovered" letter, the outright declaration of jihad, and an imagined unity among all Muslims. He summarized the letter's most relevant – and damning – passages as follows:

> 1st, that the Mussulmans of India (the Shah proclaims it) had cause for fear in the matter of their religion, from the bad faith and deceitful mode of proceeding adopted by the British invasion and annexation. 2nd, that the war he [i.e., the Muslim] was about to enter upon was a religious war, and that all good Mahometans should arm in defense of the orthodox faith of the Prophet, and slay and exterminate in the cause of God. 3rd, That armies had been equipped and appointed to march on India for the assistance of the faithful residing there. 4th, Combination is recommended and a general rising. 5th, All true believers are informed that this war has been waged for the purpose of taking vengeance on the British for all the injuries which the Holy Faith [i.e., Islam] has suffered from them.[96]

For the Shah, in Carey's summation of his letter, the British had unmistakably overstepped their bounds, not merely as rulers of a political regime, but as arbiters of non-Muslim rule in previously Islamic areas. Less than two decades later, W. W. Hunter's 1871–2 account of the Great Rebellion and its relationship to Muslims and jihad more specifically would replicate Carey's summation as well as his analysis, as we will see in the next chapter. Carey's insistence that his primary sources acutely delineated a religious obligation for Muslims to rise against British rule was neither unique nor limited. Carey not only implied that, but also cited eyewitness accounts that stated that Muslims and Islam were transparently accountable for the atrocities committed during the Rebellion.[97] *The Mahomedan Rebellion* articulated the distinctive relationship between Islam and anti-British sentiment.

Carey represents a vociferous segment of Britons. Historian Salahuddin Malik has written that in major newspapers published across the United Kingdom, it was standard to regard the unfolding rebellion as a Muslim-led revolt.[98] He suggests as well that Britons – and perhaps especially British missionaries – imagined Muslims as doubly-inclined to rebel: first, existentially as Muslims who were imagined as "proud, vengeful, and fanatical;" and second, situationally, as fallen rulers, who bore distinctive animosity toward the British, the newest and formal rulers of India.[99] Muslims were depicted before and after the Great Rebellion as dejected, ousted rulers bent on regaining what they had lost. One commentator in *The Examiner* suggested that it "was a necessity that the descendants of Mahomedan conquerors of India should hate us, and that mingled with this hatred there should be an undying hope of recovering the supremacy they had lost."[100]

British authors reproduced extant stereotypes of Muslims as violent, incapable of being ruled by non-Muslims (i.e., without Islamic law), and with an ingrained despair about having ceded power to Christian foreigners. The background noise of these assumptions was amplified in light of rumors about the Enfield rifle and the related stories of chapati signals. These circumstances, on the whole, proved a fertile ground in which to sow suspicion of a vast conspiracy – one that was notably "Islamic" for some, and for others, merely spurred on by individual Muslims or members of the formerly ruling Mughal elite. In either case, however, accusations and assumptions of conspiracy were tied to Muslim involvement. Anxieties about and evidence for conspiracy speak, in large part, to British concerns about control, but also to the unique nature of religious persuasion in India, especially for (disloyal, warlike) Muslims.

Colonel G. B. Malleson offers a standard example of the British narrative of the 1857 Rebellion, and he was an outright advocate for a conspiracy model. He clearly named chief conspirators, including both

Muslim and non-Muslim actors, citing Maulvi Ahmadulla of Faizabad, Nana Sahib, the Rani of Jhansi, and Kundwar Singh.[101] He most often cited the Maulvi as a key persona and conspirator.[102] Malleson goes as far as to call these four leaders the "Executive Council" of the mutiny, and in the earliest portions of his oft-cited book, attempts to parse how each person contributed to and fostered rebellion.[103] There can be no doubt that he was utterly convinced that a conspiracy existed and that Maulvi Ahmadulla of Faizabad played a central role in it.[104]

Despite identifying these key collaborators, Malleson suggested that "all the active conspirators [. . .] may probably never be known." He proximately contended that there "could be no question" as to the Maulvi's primary role.[105] He then – rather grandiloquently – argued that the Maulvi "was selected by the discontented in Oudh to sow throughout India the seed which, on a given signal, should spring to active growth."[106] For Malleson, the people of Oudh, a vast and influential area of northern India, popularly chose the Muslim Maulvi to incite rebellion. While he offered little direct evidence for this suggestion beyond a possible list of places the Maulvi visited, Malleson forcefully argued that he was not only an influential leader of a great conspiracy but *the* influential leader. Popularly elected to his position, capable of single-handedly sowing seeds of rebellion, and credited with devising and enacting the "*chapati* scheme," the Maulvi appeared as an indispensable and uniquely capable insurgent.[107] Moreover, as Malleson suggested, he represented not only the will of the people of Oudh, who elected him, but also of India, for he was selected to sow seeds of rebellion *throughout India*.

Malleson tidily summed up the Maulvi's power, and his connection to what had already become a standard rationalization for the Great Rebellion, when he wrote:

> The secret agents of the vast conspiracy hatched by the Maulaví of Faizábád and his associates had by this time done their work so thoroughly, had roused to a pitch of pent-up madness of which an oriental people are alone capable, the feelings of the sipáhís and the population of the North-western Provinces generally, that it is improbable that, if the Government had even gone the length of withdrawing absolutely the new musket, and the new cartridge with it, the plague would have been stayed.[108]

In Malleson's imagination, the Maulvi employed "secret agents" and headed a "vast conspiracy" that relied on the story of greased cartridges and newly issued rifles. Malleson stated that because "oriental people" were uniquely capable of hysteria, the Maulvi had no trouble whipping their emotions into a frenzy, regardless of whether the Enfield rifle and its cartridges wrapped in their prohibited animal fats actually replaced the Brown Bess. In the work of one of the most circulated and cited historians of the Great Rebellion, Maulvi Ahmadulla of Faizabad thus represented the essence of a conspiracy; that he was Muslim was not lost on other commentators or on Malleson himself, and speaks to the elision between the events of 1857–8, mutinous sepoys and rebellious citizens alike, and Islam.

Muslim Memories of the Great Rebellion

Despite their overrepresentation and enduring influence, Britons were not the only ones to provide written records of the events of 1857–8. Following their pattern of dismissing the documentation and historical accounts of South Asian peoples, Britons insisted that Indian authors simply did not have a method by which to recount historical events, that they were incapable of making sense of their past with reference to the present. Notably, Romila Thapar has suggested that lingering effects of colonial rule upon Indian knowledge includes the obscuring of autochthonous narrative accounts; she has investigated whether Indians had their own records, methods, or interpretive systems, and found that in fact they did.[109] 1857 is no different. Much of the scholarship neglects local documentation of the Great Rebellion, and when it does, these documents are more often used to support the widely accepted British narrative than to offer a balanced articulation of the events. Further, as Indian historian S. M. Azizuddin Husain estimates, there are some 60,000 documents in Persian and Urdu about the Great Rebellion, stored in a number of libraries and both state and national archives in India.[110] Yet some scholars have claimed that relevant documents dealing with the Rebellion do not exist, are not accessible, or have been improperly stored (and thus are unusable, lost, or deteriorated).[111] Scholar Arshad Islam similarly notes an omission of Indian voices within historiographies of the Great Rebellion, especially with regard to acts of violence.[112]

While ignoring Indic sources, we have seen how Britons characterized acts of rebellion as both distinctively Muslim as well as decidedly religious. For example, in most of the contemporaneous British sources cited above, authors duly outline how acts of rebellion were distinctively those of Muslim actors or inspired by Muslims, as we saw in Malleson and his characterization of the Maulvi. Carey similarly reported various atrocities, both confirmed and alleged – like massacres, rapes, and sieges – as the responsibility of Muslim agitators.[113] Still others, like Hunter, combined both military progress with local effects on civilians, and, perhaps with the benefit of some years' hindsight, offer intellectual analysis of the causes of the Great Rebellion as well as suggestions on how to stem future insurrections. Across these loose categorizations, most Britons explained violent acts committed by Indians by invoking religious parameters; both Carey and Hunter both saw Muslim violence as prescribed and necessarily anti-Christian in addition to being anti-British, for example.

Despite clear understandings of the Great Rebellion as religiously imbued, if not outright religious or holy war, few Britons saw the actions of the British in India as religiously offensive or influenced, even as they called for Christendom's spread. Fewer still identified violence against Indians as religiously inflected. In a particularly telling example of this double standard, accounts by Indian Muslims of the British recapture of Delhi differ in significant ways from the prominent British accounts of the same event. Delhi was an early loss for the British, and a site of great bloodshed, both military and civilian, throughout the Great Rebellion. During the September 1857 British reclamation of lost territory, British forces captured the Jama Masjid, a congregational mosque built in the mid-seventeenth century and the largest mosque in India. British accounts merely mention this factually. Carey, writing contemporaneously, did not elaborate on the recapture (or "fall") of Delhi, but simply declared, "With the fall of Delhi, the successes of General Havelock and the Commander-in-Chief against the mutineers in their strongholds in Oude, the advancement of columns of troops into the most disaffected parts of the country – the rebellion may be said to have ended."[114] Malleson buried the capture of the mosque as one item in a long list of advances made in Delhi on the way to total British victory, and noted the ease with which it was captured. He wrote: "After that success [at the Lahore gate], driving his [Brigadier William Jones] force, he detached one portion up the Chandni Chauk to capture the Jamí Masjíd, the other to gain the Ajmír Gate." Malleson added: "He [Jones] entered the mosque without difficulty."[115]

For Indian Muslim observers, however, neither the siege of Delhi nor the capture of its largest mosque – an anchor of the city's traditional Muslim-majority enclave – was to be mentioned in passing. Nor were these remembered as a simple events. After compiling a number of Muslim-authored sources into one cogent narrative, Arshan Islam recounts the fall of the Jama Masjid as violent, purposefully denigratory, and seared into a collective memory:

> On the evening of 20 September 1857 British and Sikh soldiers danced around a victory fire inside the Jama Masjid. The Sikh soldiers cooked *halva* next to the minaret and the British cooked pork inside the mosque. The whole mosque was turned into a military barracks. Sikh soldiers urinated inside the mosque, and Englishmen's dogs were even allowed to roam in the Masjid.[116]

Two preliminary details merit attention: British soldiers are coded not by their religious affiliation, but by "national" identity, while Sikh soldiers are delineated both religiously and as a unique subfaction of the British regiments in which they served. While this designation of difference replicates official British segregation within the army, it also upholds the axiom that conquering European colonists were considered a neutral, normative body while conquered colonized peoples represented religious bodies.[117] Yet, the thrust of this selection of the narrative is the defilement of the mosque as part of the recapture of Delhi. The commentary, while mentioning Sikh and British offenses equally, includes only one mention of those soldiers acting jointly – together, they danced around a victory fire. Otherwise, they act separately, each participating in a series of sullying activities that included urinating and allowing dogs (a filthy, even *haram* animal for many Muslims[118]), as well as cooking both *halwa* (a sweet with a variety of renditions) and pork – the supposed offending element that ignited the Rebellion in the first place.

The defilement of the Jama Masjid – which was later "returned" to Muslims – highlights a Muslim point of memory ignored by the major and authoritative British histories of 1857. It also supports celebrated anthropologist Bernard Cohn's characterization of the capture of Delhi as purposeful "desacralization" of the stronghold of the (Muslim) Mughal Empire.[119] Undoubtedly, when the British regained control of Delhi, it was a decisive blow to the Great Rebellion and a turning point in the conflict. Its gruesomeness and selective violence affected Muslim authors and observers deeply – whether because the fall of Delhi marked the final blow to the Mughal Empire or simply because of the vastness of the devastation. Many prominent Muslims described the events in Delhi with heartbreak and fear, whether they sided with the rebels or the British.

Mirza Asadullah Khan Ghalib (d. 1869), an eminent Persian- and Urdu-language poet, sometimes harshly denounced the Rebellion and its supporters, calling them "filthy vagabonds" among other unsavory epithets.[120] Ghalib wrote in a number of collected letters, essays, and diaries about the horrific violence he witnessed, listing names of friends, relatives, and neighbors he knew to have been killed during the Rebellion and sieges of Delhi.[121] He expressed a real fear of censorship, exclaiming in a December 1857 letter to Hakim Gulam Najaf Khan:

> I am writing, but what can I write? Can I really write anything, and is it proper to write? This much is true: you and I are still alive. Neither of us should say anything more than that.[122]

Ghalib's personal sense of fear was characteristic of an elite who had previously straddled the space between the East India Company and the declining Mughal court; after the Rebellion, he, like others in his societal strata, attempted to rehabilitate his position by declaring loyalty to the British.[123]

However, this did not bar Ghalib from commenting on uneven and unequal British responses to Muslims in the wake of the Great Rebellion. In a letter to Nawab Ala ud-Din Ahmad Khan Alai, he wrote:

> Surely today every English tommy is Almight [sic] God.
> Now every man going to the *bazar* is panic-stricken;
> The marketplace is become a slaughterhouse, and the house looks like a prison.
> The very particles of dust thirst for the blood of Muslims.[124]

As an intellectual elite and witness to the violence that plagued Delhi during and after the Rebellion, Ghalib's recollections and interpretations speak to issues of Muslim treatment and Muslim perceptions in the wake of 1857–8.

Whether Muslims were loyal to the British during the Rebellion or not, as historian Mushirul Hasan notes, for many and especially for the intelligentsia, "the post-1857 decades were haunted by long memories, some angry, most sickening."[125] And loyalty did not ultimately protect many Muslims from British suspicion or retaliation. Historian Avril A. Powell observes that some Britons – even the famed historian William Muir (d. 1905) – offered evidence that Muslims were not opposed to British rule and, in particular examples, were advantageous allies to Britons.[126] However, she also suggests that elite Muslims, like Sir Syed Ahmad Khan, attempted to demonstrate "overwhelming proof of unquestioning loyalty" with some regularity.[127] This indicates an atmosphere of suspicion in and of itself: a community would not need to regularly assert its allegiance if such a quality were a given.

Much of the British rhetoric around Muslims revolved around issues of Islamic law. Britons assumed Muslims to be indisputably tied to laws – problematically, laws that were not those of Britain. An emphasis (or overemphasis) on shari'a led to British reliance on it in many conversations and disputes about Muslims, as well as to various real legal challenges for Muslims in British South Asia, over issues like personal laws, implementation of long-standing community practices, and definitions of what counts as proper Islamic practice itself.[128] Unsurprisingly, in the wake of the Great Rebellion, and as commentators attempted to get their bearings on the origins of the mutinies and the best strategies to avoid such uprisings again, the place of religion and law took the fore. S. M. Azizuddin Husain's work offers a number of important translations and analyses of 1857 historiography in Islamicate languages, namely Persian and Urdu. His contribution helps make clear that not only is the historiography of the Great Rebellion heavily weighted toward British sources, but it also establishes complex interactions between and among Muslims over time and with respect to political and religious orientations. Of particular note is his observation that primary sources – and especially a letter by Nabi Bakhsk Khan, a clerk of the Mughal emperor – highlight that "both types of people were present in the [Mughal] administration: those who were acting against the law of Islam, and others who were protesting against the violation of Islamic law."[129]

Muslim narratives about 1857 and its aftermath shed important light on the Rebellion. More relevantly, these narratives also give a sense of evolving attitudes toward the British, formalized British rule, and the Great Rebellion, as well as perceptions of British attitudes toward Muslims themselves. The Great Rebellion offered Muslims – especially those of the elite class – an abrupt and pressing reason to define and redefine their relationship to authority in India. Many found themselves unemployed (and even impugned) with the final collapse of the Mughal Empire, and they aimed to reestablish themselves within the British government. This was possible because British agents had long hired local elites to serve in various positions, and in many ways, they merely continued these practices after brutally taking official command in India. Other Muslim elites found themselves in precarious positions after the Rebellion, and scholars have noted the ways in which political, economic, and even physical self-preservation caused some Muslims to shower high praise on British rule where, before, they had been quiet or even critical.[130] Moreover, Muslims were not unified in experience or opinion. As Husain demonstrates, Muslim elites were reviled as members of the fallen Mughals and susceptible to the rebels' violence; but as Muslims and affiliates of the Mughals, they were similarly susceptible to British prosecution after 1858.[131] We will delve deeper into Muslim recollections and interpretations of the Great Rebellion in chapter 3.

Conclusions

After nearly 200 years of operation in South Asia, in 1813 the East India Company saw major revisions to its Charter and thus its writ of operation in South Asia and beyond. The parliamentary hearings for the Charter Act in 1813 not only ushered in a new era of colonial and imperial rule, but also display British assumptions about India's populace – namely that religion dictated nearly all local action and thought, mundane or paramount. Some parliamentarians suggested, for example, that Indians might want, based upon religious mores, Scottish woolen goods, available to them via the trade arrangements proffered in the Charter Act.[132] The Charter Act debate (which centered on the admission of missionaries to India) found members of both Houses of Parliament reproducing conceptualizations of Indic religious actors. Various parliamentarians and expert witnesses depicted Hindus as passive, effeminate, and, though religiously problematic, "good" subjects to the Crown, while they simultaneously cast Muslims as easily agitated, aggressive, and inherently disloyal.[133]

When the Charter Act of 1813 passed, the East India Company lost both its monopoly over trade in India and its right to control missionary activity in the subcontinent. Despite an ongoing connection among the EIC, missions, and the Crown – institutions where the expansion of Christendom or related civilizational machinery were thought to coexist neatly – the development of cordial relationships among these institutions was not nearly so neat. Many Britons, especially those in the EIC and "on the ground" in India, were wary of openly trifling with matters of religion: Britons were concerned that it would take very little to arouse the violent temperaments of Muslims who in turn could and likely would ignite the passions of Hindus. In categorizing Indians as necessarily and distinctively religious, first the Company and later the Empire found themselves rather hamstrung between their warring directives, to carry out civilizational (and Christian) mission and simultaneously to tread lightly, all while enacting brutal imperial control.

As reproduced in the epigraph, Lewin, the editor of *Causes of the Indian Revolt, by a Hindu Bengali* noted that: "Religion is not a thing to be trifled with, and the dullest and most phlegmatic will be roused to the boiling point of rage and enthusiasm when it once is affected."[134] This slim treatise may be meant to represent the ideas of a "Hindu Bengali,"[135] but it implies – as we have seen elsewhere – that Indians and especially Muslims were uniquely assumed to be rebellious, or at least, easily swayed by offenses to religion. Indeed, contemporaneous accounts and later recollections of the Great Rebellion alike repeated narratives that assumed religion and especially Islam to be a key factor in the events. Of course, these assumptions rest upon accepted narratives about Muslims and Islam that predate the Rebellion and even the period in which the EIC (whether begrudgingly or not) found itself closely tied to missions. Nevertheless, the nexus of issues of religion, Islam, and Muslims in India during the mid-nineteenth century produced a climate in which a revolt of sepoys and later of civilians came to be understood as decidedly religious, and especially Islamic.

The broader context of the development and study of religion in the nineteenth century matters here, not only because India was a primary site for such intellectual work,[136] but also because the definitions rendered stemmed from and, cyclically, were applied to its ever-changing landscape. In 1813, as part of the Charter Act hearings, members of Parliament explained that religion was of the utmost importance to Indians, and some expressed concerns about meddling in such personal matters. As few of these parliamentarians had themselves travelled to India, we know that their estimations of Indic norms were assumptions, and from their comments, we have also seen the ways in which generalized conceptualizations – often unflattering at best and racist at their core – dictated high-level governmental conversations and policies.[137] The minutes of the hearings and petitions to sway voting parties do not showcase a uniform British conclusion about religion, but they do establish a consensus that Hindus and Muslims were distinctive, definable groups, and had radically different relationships to their religious texts as well as to Britons and British rule. Some suggested that all Indians were "fanatical," citing Brahmin food pollution mores alongside those of Muslims.[138]

More commonly, however, Britons characterized Indians as religious on the whole, but with the caveat that only Muslims possess the inherent potential for fanaticism that threatened British rule, Christianity, even Britons individually.[139] In the wake of the Charter Act of 1813, missionaries established institutions aimed at properly situating Christianity within the subcontinent, which included rules governing British or Europeans in the EIC and affiliated positions, the founding of schools and orphanages, and the distribution of missionary literatures, to name but a few. In addition to changing the official relationship between the Company and missions, the Charter Act ushered in an era of changing patterns of authority, and it poignantly formalized the relationship of the Company to the Empire, specifically declaring the Crown's position vis-à-vis India.

British characterizations of Muslims as fanatics took the fore during and after the Great Rebellion. We have seen how observers first delineated Indians based upon religious identity, over and above caste, ethnic, regional, or linguistic definition. Carey, Malleson, Kaye – authors of well-documented and standard histories – assumed both unity and cohesion when they used appellatives like "Hindu" and "Muslim." Religion as a driving force is a given in these accounts, even as authors like Malleson offer honest misgivings as to whether individual issues, like the greased cartridges, happened, happened in the way they were rumored to have happened, or affected religious sensibilities evenly.[140] After the Rebellion and its very immediate aftermath, observers increasingly labeled its causes, events, and lingering effects as religious, and many tied these uniquely to Islam.

Hindsight offered Britons a means through which to portray the powerful Rebellion as a purposeful, planned series of attacks by violent natives that was ultimately quashed; their histories were often teleologies that demonstrate the inevitability and "rightness" of British rule over South Asia. Similarly, hindsight for some Indian and Indian Muslim observers offered enough distance from which to criticize both the rebels and Britons with a degree of security; much later, however, the Great Rebellion began to be portrayed by Hindus and some Muslims as the "First War of Indian Independence," highlighting a different teleological interpretation that signposted budding Indian nationalisms.[141] In both cases, however, looking back and reconstructing the history of the 1857 Rebellion – the meaning-making – reified extant notions that religion bolstered, prompted, and promoted revolt. Sir William Wilson Hunter's *The Indian Musalmans: Are They Bound in Conscience to Rebel Against the Queen?* is one such example of meaning-making in light of the Rebellion that fixates on religion, Islam, and innate characteristics of Muslims – and the focus of the next chapter.

CHAPTER 2

SUSPECT SUBJECTS: HUNTER AND THE MAKING OF A MUSLIM MINORITY

For most British observers in 1857 a Muslim meant a rebel.
— Peter Hardy[1]

The Great Rebellion produced "the Muslims" in India — one unified, cogent group. In its wake, Muslims became a singular category in both practice and imagination for Britons. As imperial agents attempted to figure out the causes of the Rebellion in its immediate aftermath and in the decades following, religion maintained a central fascination for Britons. Indians were distinctively religious: religion organized their society, religion ought not be trespassed upon, and, as the East India Company's policies demonstrated, Britons were wary to insult the religious affairs of the locals precisely because they thought this to be a truly unforgiveable foreign intrusion. If Indians broadly were distinctively religious, Muslims particularly were understood to be religiously legalistic, bound unwaveringly and without exception by religious laws. After the Rebellion, Muslims were seen as uniquely culpable for those events and as posing a threat of repeated revolts; observers collapsed differences among the milieu of north Indian Muslim communities on the basis of law binding all Muslims to fight for Muslim rule.

The simplification of vastly diverse Muslim communities into a singular entity is the process of minoritization, the process by which the ruling elite came to perceive Muslims of various and differing religious practices, classes, and castes[2] as a unified collective and as a distinctive problem. Demographic majority has little to do with minoritization: Britons did not turn a Muslim majority into a minority, as Indian Muslims before British control could not be called a demographic majority, although elite culture was undoubtedly Islamicate and, in many places, under the rule of Muslims.[3] Minoritization refers not to demographic reality, but rather to the systematic process by which a ruling elite denies one group access to power through local, national, or, as in this case, imperial politics.[4] Minoritization often refers to the unfolding ways in which a normative majority comes to be recognized – often against a prominent minority. Some have argued that the mobilization and creation of national identities *requires* minoritization.[5] Empires craft subjecthood and establish cogency through this process, either to ensure loyalty or to "divide and conquer" recognizable groups with definitive characteristics.[6] As we will explore in this chapter, Sir William Wilson Hunter (d. 1900), a crucial example, both fostered and invested in the minoritization of Muslims. Making Muslims a minority – outsiders, disempowered, and both unique and uniquely problematic – is a key outcome, if not a stated goal, of *The Indian Musalmans: Are They Bound in Conscience to Rebel Against the Queen?* (1871; 2nd ed. 1872, reprinted 1876).

Indian Musalmans is a fairly lengthy answer to its titular question: would Muslims be required by their religious "conscience" to rebel against the British throne? Yes, Hunter contended, because Muslims are bound by their exclusive and exclusionary religious laws to rebel against any non-Muslim authority. Hunter typifies an agent of colonial apparatus: he served as a member of the Indian Civil Service, working variously as a statistician, compiler of data (firsthand narratives, demography, and histories), and author. He was an influential, respected, and knighted scholar of the Indian Civil Service. Later in life, he became the vice president of the esteemed Royal Asiatic Society. In his official capacity for the British Empire, he wrote many pieces, some in books and others in serials; his work was widely distributed in its day and beyond, and he founded and was a prominent organizer of one of the most important tools for imperial knowledge production, the *Imperial Gazetteer of India*. His most famous and widely distributed work in the *Gazetteer* was *Indian Musalmans*, which went through numerous reprints as both a serial and a bound volume; the second edition, published in

1872 and with a new preface, was the version which was reprinted or reissued frequently, both in part and in full.

W. W. Hunter was a prolific, widely read, and highly esteemed author. Historian S. C. Mittal describes him, alongside other eminent British historians like James Talboys Wheeler (d. 1897) and Alfred Comyn Lyall (d. 1911), as "the official mind of the bureaucratic Victorian historians in India."[7] His work carried gravitas, which led the Viceroy Lord Mayo to ask Hunter to write "his account of the so-called 'Wahabi' conspiracy."[8] Hunter obliged, drawing upon official documents provided for his use by the Home, Foreign, and Military Departments, as well as his own research and experience. *Indian Musalmans*, published in the same year as it was commissioned, was the result of this request. In its conception and execution, *Indian Musalmans* was a project that assumed connections among Indian Muslims, Wahhabism, "conspiracy," and the Great Rebellion. From the outset, it collapsed Indian Muslims into one distinctive category – a group characterized as legalistic, violent, and bent toward seditions against the British.

Hunter's carefully researched book drew upon a broad scope of evidentiary support, including the works of other European scholars and observers, legal statutes and juridical commentaries, East India Company demographies and documents, and Muslim and Islamicate juridical rulings, histories, and commentaries. He tried to offer a comprehensive, objective view of the matter at hand, and while readers today may readily point to his failures, Hunter's contemporaries and some in the subsequent generation lauded his influential work.[9] A number of later authors drew upon Hunter, often reiterating or expounding upon his central claim.[10] At times, his work offered a sympathetic gloss of Muslims' status and position in British India and expressed criticism of both British policies toward and general ignorance about Muslims. However, these criticisms and sympathies were fleeting, and even when Hunter expressed such sentiments or analysis, he typically concluded that Muslims ought to respond better to the pressures of British dominion, rather than that Britons should change their official policies or personal behavior. Hunter unmistakably championed British civilizational models over and above those of the population they ruled.

Hunter contended that Muslims could not ever truly become proper citizens of a modern, secular (monarchial) democracy. Because they possessed their own legal system, he argued, they necessarily stood apart from the British state. In *Indian Musalmans*, Hunter frequently termed Muslims "agitators," "rebels," and "traitors." The Viceroy Lord Mayo was preoccupied with a perception that Wahhabism was spreading rampantly through northern India, and Hunter's expertise was meant to weigh in on this particular threat. Hunter's work often collapsed "Wahabi"[11] and Muslim. It is not entirely clear why he did so, especially since he occasionally warned against such elision; nevertheless, these elided categories dominate his analysis.

Hunter was preoccupied, as were other British observers, with Islamic law, and especially with its relationship to Wahhabism. He contended that Wahhabism was primarily interested in jihad, and he connected Wahhabism to normative Muslim beliefs, laws, and practices. By conflating Wahhabi literalism with normative north Indian Muslim praxis, Hunter depicted Muslims as thoughtful, careful juridical thinkers, but who as such were distinctively bound by laws – laws that, to his eyes, necessarily pitted Muslim subjects against British rulers. Therefore, Hunter advocated for Britons to act carefully and with regard for Muslim law, precisely because Muslims within the British Empire would be bound to rebel. His claims relied on the minoritization of Muslims, on a rigid interpretation of Islamic law and a related conflation between Muslim and Wahhabi, and finally on a belief that Islamic law definitively instructed Muslims to rebel against non-Muslim rulers. In what follows, I will demonstrate how the Great Rebellion of 1857 served to make Muslims a minority and how Hunter's later treatise both reshaped and reproduced conceptualizations of the Rebellion and Muslims' subjecthood in light of it.

Bound to Rebel: Making Muslims a Minority

Eminent historian Peter Hardy notes that for "most British observers in 1857 a Muslim meant a rebel."[12] Similarly, Thomas Metcalf argues that "[i]n the British view it was Muslim intrigue and Muslim leadership that converted a sepoy mutiny into a political conspiracy, aimed at the extinction of the British Raj."[13] The characterization of Muslims as distinctively responsible for the Rebellion developed alongside the events themselves, partially due to preexisting conceptualizations of Muslims as violent, legalistic, and unwilling to be governed by non-Muslims, and partially in light of Britons' characterization of Muslims as one unique and monolithic entity. I focus on Sir William Wilson Hunter's work below in part because his attitudes and conclusions were not aberrations. The ways in which he characterized Muslims as inherently disloyal echo similar concerns held by others and demonstrate a measured approach to the *question* of Muslims under the rule of Britons, especially after the Great Rebellion.

One such example comes from a noted contemporary of Hunter, Sir William Muir (d. 1905), a Scottish Orientalist, scholar of Islam, and British official. He held multiple positions, including, eventually, lieutenant governor of the North-West Provinces. Like Hunter's work, Muir's scholarship was widely cited in its day and beyond, and he held the esteem of imperial agents, scholars around the world, and well-educated elites. His best-known scholarship includes the critical *Life of Mohammad*[14] and *The Caliphate, its Rise, Decline, and Fall.*[15] Muir has been credited, if we may call it that, with contributing to the "myth of the Muslim as always armed with the sword in one hand and the Qur'an in the other."[16] In October 1857, he wrote to his brother about the rebellion and disloyal Muslims: "The Musulmans, while they thought their cause had a fair chance of final success have frequently compromised themselves by flagrantly traitorous acts."[17] He subsequently noted that this was to be expected, given the "singularly close combination of the political and religious elements in the system of Islam."[18] Though well regarded by many Britons, Muir became notorious among Indian Muslim elites as someone whose work specifically and especially misrepresented Islam. Muir garnered the attention of Syed Ahmad Khan, who cited *Life of Mohammad* as emblematic of why Muslim modernists ought to dismiss *all* scholarship from Western or British intellectuals.[19] Muir's characterization of Muslims as traitorous and violent, and of Islam as necessarily tied into the political regime, reproduced Hunter's ultimate conclusion that Muslims were required to rebel.

Others still described Muslim rebels as overwhelmingly destructive, violent, and prone to revolt, or described Muslims broadly as rebellious. Charles Raikes (d. 1885) saw the 1857 events as a rebellion not of a ruled population against its rulers, but rather of Muslims against Christians:

> The green flag of Mahomed too had been unfurled, the mass of the followers of the false prophet rejoicing to believe that under the auspices of the Great Mogal of Delhi [Bahadur Shah II[20]] their lost

ascendancy was to be recovered, their deep hatred to the Christian got vent, and they rushed forth to kill and destroy.[21]

In a June 1857 letter to Governor-General Lord Canning (d. 1862), John Lawrence (d. 1879) comparably noted: "The Mahommedans of the Regular Cavalry when they have broken out have displayed a more active, vindictive and fanatic spirit than the Hindoos — but these traits are characteristic of the race."[22] Both of these commentators saw a characteristic violence in the actions of Muslims during the Rebellion. Raikes unhesitatingly attributed it to religion, especially within a framework of competitive religion — Islam against Christianity, Muslims against Christians. Lawrence conceived of the violence as a consequence of religious fanaticism an inherent attribute of Muslims. In all these cases, despite the particularities of the claims made by Muir, Raikes, and Lawrence, Muslims were portrayed as intrinsically predisposed toward violence and rebellion.

Of course, not all Britons imagined Muslims as uniquely responsible for the Rebellion or even as one homogenous group. Sir George Campbell (d. 1892) nicely represents this counterpoint as he argued that the rebellion was neither Hindu nor Muslim in character, but Hindustani — that is, comprised of previously dominant classes and castes whose fortunes, statuses, and livelihoods had changed for the worse under British dominion.[23] Hardy summarized Campbell's perception of the rebellion as one that "cannot be improved upon," and stated that Campbell's understanding of the rebellion in terms of religion, religious identity, and Islam was simply that, "It [the Rebellion] was not a general Muslim movement against the British."[24]

However, despite meaningful counterpoints like Campbell, the majority of Britons writing about the Rebellion imagined it in terms of religion and described Muslims as a homogenous entity distinctively culpable for the revolts. The Great Rebellion solidified British power, which had previously been present but was ambiguous and amorphous in the earlier half of the nineteenth century.[25] These massive changes to British rule in and Britons' imagination of India demanded formal revision and enforcement of extant policies that stemmed, in large part, from Company procedures. It also meant that relationships among groups would be reshaped and reformed, perhaps especially so between the previous ruling class (elite Muslims and Mughal officials) and the current ruling class (Britons and British imperial officers).[26] In this climate, Muslims found themselves not only a demographic minority, but also an ethno-religious group that came with imported assumptions and characterizations. Muslims became minoritized, in other words, as a result of the Great Rebellion.

Fittingly, a number of scholars refer to minoritized groups in language inherited from the eighteenth and nineteenth centuries, as tracts and treatises on "the Jewish Question" were published widely under developing, liberal governments and during periods of colonial expansion. One significant example is Aamir Mufti, who addresses issues of secular modernity, by linking the so-called question of Jewish identity within post-Enlightenment secularist movements in Europe to the minorities that formed in Europe's colonies – specifically, the British colonies in India. He argues that Jewishness was terrifying to – and that Jews became terrorized by – protestant Europeans,[27] and this formulation of Jewish identity provided a framework upon which "the very question of minority existence" was based, then "disseminated globally in the emergence, under colonial and semicolonial conditions, of the forms of modern social, political, and cultural life."[28] Mufti connects British imagination of Jews, Jewishness, and Judaism to the later imagination of Muslims, Muslimness, and Islam; his careful book charts "how a concern with the particularity of the Jews in a Europe of nations was transformed into a consideration of what the forms of particularity of the Muslims meant for the question of whether India was a nation."[29] He examines the process of minoritization and makes broader connections between a prominent, religio-ethnic European minority (the Jews) and a prominent, religio-ethnic Indian minority (the Muslims).

Mufti observes that the Great Rebellion was a primary catalyst in making Muslims a political minority. He argues, at the very start of *Enlightenment in the Colony*, that the crisis of Muslim identity first became recognized as such in the decades following the events of 1857–8.[30] Later, he elaborates:

> In the decades following the 1857 Rebellion, "the Muslims" come to appear as a group with a paradoxical social existence – on the one hand, as local and particularistic, caught in a time warp outside the temporalities of the modern world, and, on the other, as formed by loyalties and affiliations that violate and exceed the territorial structure of the (colonial) state.[31]

Although documentation demonstrates that Britons, including Hunter, knew that the rebels hailed from myriad caste, religious, and ethnic backgrounds, they defined "rebel" specifically as "Muslim." After the Rebellion, Britons produced robust sets of writing about "the Muslims," as part of their project of systematic comprehension of their (perceived) troublesome minority.[32] The events of 1857–8 – the Rebellion, massacres, and responses – served to mark Muslims as a unique collective, and this marking not only minoritized Muslims, but also obscured the complex, composite cultures of north India. These upheavals changed what it meant to be Muslim in north India, calling into question literary, social, and religious cultures, and often rendering their maintenance impossible. The Rebellion established "The Muslims" as problematic, and responding to that problem engaged not only Britons but also Muslims, Hindus, Sikhs, and others still.

Restrictions upon Muslims after the Great Rebellion varied from region to region. In some cases, they prevented Muslims from joining the subordinate services of the Empire, like collectorships; in other cases, they denied Muslims access to more important arms of the state, like judiciary positions. In his seminal work on the Rebellion, Thomas Metcalf estimates that between 1850 and 1885–7, the number of Muslim judicial posts in the North-West Provinces had declined from a height of approximately 72 per cent to just under 46 per cent.[33] This indicates the effect of official imperial changes in light of the Rebellion, and the specific loss of advantages and privilege(s) enjoyed by Muslims in the North-West Provinces before 1857. Educated, aristocratic Muslim elites were considered suspect by Britons, and consequently they had decreased access to official positions, resulting in a reaction that appeared to be an official inclination toward Anglicization.

Enforced change need not be conceived only in terms of law. Aamir Mufti traces shifts in Urdu literature and culture in the wake of the Great Rebellion, highlighting at some length debates around Urdu as it related to a unified national culture of India.[34] These debates and shifts, present in Muslim Urdu literature – as well as literature *about* Muslims and Urdu – represent conversations about disciplining Muslims and Urdu, and about the delimitation of Indian identity. Other spaces for the *de facto* policing of Muslim identity and the minoritization of Muslims included educational systems, especially those overseen by Britons and purposefully (or titularly) secular.

In short, the Rebellion marked Muslims as a *problem*, and problems entreat solutions.[35] The overwhelming characterization of Muslims as distinctively violent, religiously bound toward rebellion, or ethno-racially predisposed toward both violence and rebellion led to their suppression in the years after the mutiny.[36] In the wake of the 1857 Rebellion Muslims found themselves more regulated and restricted because of concerns about Muslims and their unique threat to the Empire. The Rebellion catalyzed the minoritization of Muslims – even if the ideas and ideologies well predated the uprising. Further, and as we will see below, this process included the recasting of Muslims as jihadis, an idea that crystallized in 1857 and that had real repercussions as Britain claimed full constitutional dominion over the Subcontinent.

Indian Musalmans and Hunter: Author of Empire

Sir William Wilson Hunter was an author of empire who produced knowledge about South Asia's history, inhabitants, literatures, and demography. He was an important contributor not only to what the British knew about India but how they came to know it. Hunter's prolific publications – single-authored monographs, co-authored histories, introductions to other works, numerous bibliographies, volumes of the *Imperial Gazetteer*, a serial, and one comparative dictionary – are distinctive in both their breadth and prolificacy. His work is vital to the history of South Asia, especially as it spans the pivotal transition of Hindustan from a colonized locale to a part of the British Empire. This movement was heralded by the Great Rebellion and followed by British physical and legal force toward India and Indians.

Hunter wrote *The Indian Musalmans: Are They Bound in Conscience to Rebel against the Queen?* in 1871, some 15 years after the Rebellion and in the wake of the still-unfolding transition of power.[37] This seminal book traced the role of Muslims (whom he calls Musálmans and Muhammadans interchangeably) within India, and, as his title suggests, takes loyalty – or assumed proclivities toward rebellion – as a primary concern and point of inquiry. It contains four chapters and a short appendix, which provides English renditions of the primary fatwas he cites as evidence in the main text. The first three chapters address the threat Muslims in India posed to the Crown. The chapters are provocatively titled: "The Standing Rebel Camp on Our Frontier," "The Chronic Conspiracy Within Our Territory," and "The Decisions of the Muhammadan Law Doctors." The final chapter analyses Muslims' grievances toward Britons and British imperial rule, and suggests using education as a means to ameliorate Muslim fanaticism. While this chapter differs from the previous three, it does not suggest that Britons ought to change their behaviors or ruling style, but rather offers suggestions on how to discipline Islam to be amenable to and compatible with British rule.

In 1857, the Rebellion highlighted Britons' greatest fear: in the midst of expansion and solidification of imperial rule on a number of continents, the possibility of revolution was a stark reality. The potential disloyalty of Muslims spoke to a unique concern, however. Because Britain controlled swaths of Africa, the Middle East, and South Asia, its leaders were necessarily concerned with Islam, as many of these areas were, and continue to be, either majority or significantly Muslim. In fact, by the 1920s, British rule directly encompassed substantially more than half the Muslim peoples of the world.[38] We might expect that India's Muslims, as former rulers and with vestiges of power still intact, would hold the imagination of Britons, especially as India occupied a special place within the British imagination of power and control in Asia and more broadly. If Muslims in India could be united under the premise of Islam, or if Islam *definitionally* called for Muslims to hold loyalty to each other or to laws beyond those of the Crown, then Muslims across the still-expanding Empire could be called to do the same. Muslims in India reflected not just a threat to British rule in India, but to the British Empire in its entirety. Hunter's assessment of Muslim attitudes and loyalties was therefore not a limited study and indeed had far-reaching implications.

However, it is worth noting that Hunter's work was neither a polemic against Muslims nor a dismissal of Muslim humanity, decency, or intelligence. His final chapter of *Indian Musalmans*, in fact, is an attempt to systemically address grievances of Muslims, either stated (published or well-known) or inferred (per Hunter's perspective). W. W. Hunter's insistence on including a full (and rather lengthy) chapter delineating Muslim grievances is neither to be applauded nor dismissed out of hand. Hunter was not, that is to say, a post-colonial theorist trapped in the wrong century! In much of this chapter of *Indian Musalmans*, he phrased criticisms, upset, or frustration in terms of the British having moved too quickly or perturbing an irrational populace. He was not critiquing imperialism or colonialism, but rather specific circumstances in which Britons could have carried out imperial practices better, thereby ensuring smoother reign. The places where he sounded sympathetic to Muslim objections, and where he called for British self-reflection, are frankly more analogous to what we might today call a "non-apology" – that is, an acknowledgment that another party was injured, but without any contrition or responsibility admitted.[39]

Hunter openly announced his aim: "The object of this little book is not merely to explain the duties of our Muhammadan subjects to their rulers, but to impress upon their rulers their duty to the world."[40] He added:

> it is hopeless to look for anything like enthusiastic loyalty from our Muhammadan subjects. But we can reasonably expect that, so long as we scrupulously discharge our obligations to them, they will honestly fulfil [*sic*] their duties in the position in which God has placed them to us.[41]

Hunter was willing to engage the idea that British rule had caused harm to Muslims, but he did not advocate for anything beyond smarter rule. His goal for his "little book" (all 229 pages of it) was to outline the problems of rule in India – and of ruling Muslims specifically – to help British rulers either navigate or remedy those problems. Like Warren Hastings, Hunter did not advocate quitting India, but he wanted to help make British rule more efficient and expedient, especially in light of its problem populace. Hunter's remedy for jihad was to outsmart Muslims within the correct bounds of British rule.

To this end, *Indian Musalmans* presents a careful argument meant to survey Muslims as the other (i.e., non-Hindu and non-Aryan[42]) religious group, ethnic identity, and racialized minority in India, because they innately posed a threat to the Empire. The interrogation of Muslim sources was a key part of this survey. Hunter paid scrupulous attention to Muslim sources: he cited, even overemphasized, "Muhammadan legal doctors," as an attempt to demonstrate what "authentic" Muslims said about foreign rule.

Laws, Literalism, and All Muslims: Hunter's Claims

The Great Rebellion demonstrated, to Hunter and others, that British holdings in India were never terribly far from being challenged, if not altogether lost. Elite Britons at home in the metropole worried, seemingly at regular intervals, about their sovereignty in India. For example, the periodic renewal of the East India Charter hearings in Parliament demonstrate a general anxiety vis-à-vis British control over religious actors, especially Muslims.[43] Further, authors featured in serials, gazetteers, and newspapers in the nineteenth century regularly debated the state of dominion.[44] The Rebellion heralded a new era of suspicion and angst, witnessed in all manner of official hearings and tracts, but also in popular literature. Thomas Metcalf estimates that before 1900, some 50 novels about the Rebellion were published, and an additional 30 or so appeared before World War II.[45] The Rebellion figured in institutional and popular imaginations, and many of these depictions rested upon the anger and volatility of religious actors. As the transition of power in India happened incrementally – city by city, region by region, by force on the ground as well as by parliamentary acts passed in London to be enforced on the other side of the globe – Hunter's fixation on threats to power and imperial sovereignty were not abstract, even if they appear now to be rooted solely in overstatements of Muslim identity and ideology.

In *Indian Musalmans*, Hunter located Muslims within a narrative of rebellion based upon his interpretation of their religious obligations, and against the tableau of definitions of and imaginations about Islam and Muslims discussed in the previous chapter. His sustained use of Muslim sources throughout the text is noteworthy. On the one hand, Hunter offered a savvy, knowledgeable, and well-researched set of opinions. In his introduction, he wrote that there was "not a shadow of a doubt" that the Indian empire was endangered, citing papers "by Muhammadans themselves."[46] He did more than merely reinterpret religious and religiously inflected texts (i.e., the Qur'an, *hadith*, *fiqh*, fatwas) and issue broad pronouncements based on a limited interpretation of Islam. On the other hand, however, Hunter foundationally rejected Muslims' ability to apply their own legal histories when it suited his argument, and rather overtly – sometimes bluntly articulating as much, as we will see below – dismissed Muslim glosses in favor of his own, which he presumed to be better researched and reasoned. In this way, while he prodigiously cited Muslim authors, often in their original languages (Persian, Arabic, and occasionally Urdu), he still managed to silence Muslim voices.[47]

Hunter relied heavily on legal rulings, or fatwas, and he overrepresented this genre of text and interpretation because he assumed that Muslims adhered to, held unique faith in, and were unable to argue with (or against) such rulings. Limiting his evidence, Hunter specifically focused on Sunnis, calling them the "Puritans" of Islam,[48] and on Wahhabis, whom he called a fanatical sect but also commented that he would "find it impossible to speak of them without respect."[49] Hunter's reliance on Sunni sources and his emphasis on Wahhabi sources and figures distorts the vast plurality of Islam in India; the emphasis on Wahhabism is telling not necessarily of a reality of Muslim praxis but of Britons' heightened awareness and distrust of this reform and revival movement.[50] On the whole, Muslims across differing times, locations, religiosity, and sects are conflated and collapsed; this is especially noticeable in Hunter's discussions of Wahhabis and Wahhabism.

Wahhabism is an ideological interpretation of its eponymous inspiration, Muhammad ibn 'Abd al-Wahhāb (d. 1792), and it is often categorized as part of eighteenth-century reformist and modernist movements geared toward streamlining Islam, returning to original practices and interpretations of Islamic sources, and purging contemporary Muslim practice of outside innovative additions.[51] Despite being composed and promulgated originally in Najd – a remote, central region of Saudi Arabia with many linguistic and cultural dissimilarities to South Asia – the writing and teaching of 'Abd al-Wahhāb reached India, though accounts differ on how and by whom. Like many of his contemporaries, Hunter imagined Wahhabism in both frightful and laudatory terms; it was, to their eyes, a reform movement bent toward purity and simplicity, but one that jeopardized colonial and imperial projects. Certain Wahhabi Muslims, like those who were part of the Wahhabi Trials,[52] figure essentially as exemplars of legalism and literalism rather heavily in Hunter's analysis. Hunter's read of Wahhabism allowed him to use "fanatic" or "rebel" claims to represent normative Indian Islam. It also demonstrates how his elisions of divergent histories and diverse populations, even within the relatively limited arena of South Asia, both perpetuate and produce anew a universalized Muslim and a totalized Islam.

It is clear throughout *Indian Musalmans* that Hunter considered Muslims a unique group: one with an imagined center somewhere outside the Indian subcontinent and with an imagined legal loyalty to pan-Islamic ideals always located apart from and in antithesis to those of a (non-Muslim) empire. Hunter dissected Indian history, Muslim scriptural sources, and Muslim legal documents and rulings in order to demonstrate that "The Musalmáns of India are, and have been for many years, a source of chronic danger to the British Power in India."[53] In short, then, Hunter ultimately argued that Muslims were, indeed, bound by religious doctrine to laws that both specifically and obtusely demand rebellion.

Hunter began *Indian Musalmans* with his conclusion. The first paragraphs of his first chapter observe, "While the more fanatical Musalmans have thus engaged in overt sedition, the whole Muhammadan community has been openly deliberating upon their obligation to rebel."[54] The entire community is implicated here: the fanatical Muslims were roundly seditious, and everyone else – "the whole Muhammadan community" – overtly discussed how they ought to revolt. Hunter did not discuss the possibility that subjects of any empire might rebel, nor did he contextualize Muslims within a wider landscape of rebellious South Asians – after all, the Great Rebellion was not a rebellion of Muslims, but rather comprised a multitude of castes, classes, and religio-ethnic actors. Hunter instead worried about Muslim subjects in particular, concluding in his introduction that these subjects – both the "fanatics" and, as is implied, their "moderate" or "liberal" counterparts – were *obligated* to rebel. He saw no alternative model for subjecthood, nor did he imagine that fanatics were *fanatical*, which is to say exceptional examples. Hunter concluded that *all* Muslims were bound by laws beyond the pale of British authority.

Hunter foregrounded his argument in the borderlands of the Raj and competing ideologies. Geographically, he drew heavily upon regions of contestation, like the North-West Provinces; similarly, he drew heavily on sites of ideological contestation, like support for and resistance to jihad and the legal status of India. These authorial choices support his conclusions and aims while distorting his depictions of both normative and normalized Islam. Hunter located periods and places of debate and dispute as exemplars of authenticity, and in so doing, he conflated literalism and legalism with what Muslims did in their daily lives, and how they thought about Britons. He also placed heavy weight upon "law doctors" (*muftis*), and many of his particular arguments relied on an assumption that Muslims, because of their "natural" legalism,[55] would necessarily follow anything proclaimed and ruled by muftis.

In his opening pages, Hunter claimed that "Muhammadan law doctors":

> will convince every reasonable mind, that while the more reckless among the Musalmáns have for years been engaged in overt treason, the whole community has been agitated by the greatest state question that has ever occupied the thoughts of a people. The duty of rebellion has been formally and publicly reduced to a nice point of Muhammadan law.[56]

He continued by stating:

> Somehow or other, every Musalmán seems to have found himself called on to declare his faith; to state, in the face of his co-religionists, whether he will or will not contribute to the Traitors' Camp on our Frontier; and to elect, once and for all, whether he shall play the part of a devoted follower of Islám, or of a peaceable subject of the Queen.[57]

These powerful introductory selections demonstrate Hunter's over-arching argument, sensibility, and presuppositions. Muslims, for him, could and would be convinced by legal rule to be treasonous – it was a duty to rebel, and one that would touch each and every Muslim. This is not, however, an argument in the abstract or the hypothetical: to Hunter, Muslims were called to declare their faith specifically by contributing to warfare and rebellion on the frontiers of the British Empire in India. For Hunter, to be Muslim was to declare rebellion against the Crown.

Hunter consequently framed Muslims as having dual allegiances, at best, or outright traitors, at worst. He explicitly called attention to the Muslim masses of people in terms of a source of fear:

> It is not the traitors themselves whom we have to fear, but the seditious masses in the heart of our Empire, and the superstitious

tribes on our frontier, both of whom the Fanatics have again and again combined in a religious war against us.[58]

This short quote packs in many assumptions requiring analysis. Most pressingly, perhaps, are the "Fanatics," a term Hunter used categorically to describe a singular threat. Upon closer inspection, "Fanatics" encompassed a range of distinct and in some cases unrelated groups. The term is occasionally applied to "law doctors," especially those from Mecca;[59] more often, however, he used "fanatic" to refer to anti-British authors, rebels, and, in a few places, populations living on frontiers, be they Muslim, Hindu, Sikh, or "tribal."[60] Earlier in the *Indian Musalmans*, he subtitled a section "Fanatic War of 1857," which he linked to but held apart from the Sepoy Rebellion properly; he claimed that the Fanatic War of 1857 was but the first of such major rebellious acts that demanded retaliation, denoting this event as *the* event that spurred a British response.[61] Fanatic, it seems, functions both as a loose term — those who oppose British rule, a particular British agent, or a specific event with an organizing reference to a religious identity — and most commonly as a particular category for Muslims engaging in anti-Empire ideas or activities.

Hunter was preoccupied by rebellious actions, which is why the 1857 events figured so centrally in *Indian Musalmans*. He declined to outline all of the events of 1857–8, instead stating that the "whole period" was characterized by "fanatics [who] kept the border tribes in a state of chronic hostility to the British Power."[62] He traced the dramatic increase of fighters and the reciprocal increase in a need for British armies.[63] Hunter may have only spent a few pages directly with the specificities of 1857–8, but he repeatedly returned to those events as he explored how Britons might know that Muslims posed a true and unique threat. Further, by tying the Great Rebellion to concurrent and subsequent massacres, insurgencies, and, most importantly, the virulent spread of revolts, Hunter accomplished two things: he made the rebellion catching; and he made it religious and especially Muslim.[64] This equation yields a conceptualization of *Islam* as a contagious revolutionary force.

The virulence of Islam and rebellion in his book speaks to Hunter's focus on the threat of *religious* war. Hunter spent a good deal of space on what he saw as antagonistic, violent Muslim "armies"[65] and the inimitable, religiously articulated threats they posed to the throne. He employed the term "Muhammadan Crescentaders," which suggested a recognizable religious zeal informing these armies, and simultaneously conjured images of a medieval strain of zealotry.[66] The linkages between medieval Crusades and modern threats ought not be read as a mere analogy: this connection played into an ideology of European superiority. In this gloss, Muslims are Crescentaders in their *medieval* religious observance as well as in terms of the threat of armed warfare on behalf of their religion.

When Hunter referenced the physical Empire – "the seditious masses in the heart of our Empire, and the superstitious tribes on our frontier"[67] – he indicated another of his primary concerns, namely, the borders and boundaries of the British Raj. Though they are left specifically unnamed, one can infer that the borderlands in question included the Frontier Settlement[68] of Bengal, where Hunter lived and about which he wrote for a majority of his career. He wrote:

> The truth is, while we have been trying to stamp out the Frontier Settlement beneath the heel of a military force, the Fanatical sects among our Muhammadan subjects have been feeding it with an inexhaustible supply of money and men; pouring oil on the embers which we had left for dead, and nursing them again into a flame.[69]

Hunter raised two issues here: first, that the frontier represented dangerous, contentious space rife with religious rebellion; and second, that the rebels themselves were independently funded, with inexhaustible financial and human resources.

He positioned Muslims as an overwhelming threat. They were also imagined as uniquely connected, supported, and cogent: the fanatical sects, whomever that included (for Hunter or his readers), were actively funding rebellion. Hunter, to reiterate, did not define the fanatical sects – either in name or in an umbrella, categorical manner – and so did not enumerate their collective or specific religious interpretations, presence in the Empire, or the very revenue sources he cited as evidence above. Hunter gave no indication that Muslims might differ in opinion, that the "sects" might differ from one another, or that regional, linguistic, or ethnic identifications might supersede or influence a Muslim one.

We must bear in mind that data was Hunter's primary trade: careful histories, demographies, geographies, cartographies, and geologies form the bulk of Hunter's significant written output. In other words, the data missing in *Indian Musalmans* are present not only in other passages in this text but elsewhere, like *The Imperial Gazetteer, History of British India* (1899), and *A Statistical Account of Bengal* (1875–9), to name a few. Hunter proved himself capable of better specificity, and so his lack of support is notable with respect to these fanatical sects, their outside financial support, and their influence upon other Muslims. This lack speaks to fear but also to Hunter's obvious disinterest in specificity in this case – after all, his argument hinges upon Muslims as a unique and unified entity.

He argued:

> They [Fanatics] preached that the Almighty had withdrawn him from a fainthearted generation; but that when the Indian Musalmans, with singleness of mind, should join in a Holy War against the English Infidels, their Prophet would return and lead them to victory. In all this there was nothing incredible to a Musalman.[70]

The danger of Indian Muslims coming together is foregrounded above, as is the claim that they should – and the implication that they would – join a holy war against the English, infidels by definition. In fact, that Muhammad would return to earth and lead the Indian Muslims to victory, Hunter claimed, is *not* incredible; it is, in his gloss of Muslims as necessarily fanatical, a *typical* expectation held by Muslims. Hunter's claim is not benign, as it linked what he considered fanatic preachers and their lessons to the "average" Muslim living under British rule.

A concern for these "average" Muslims – the ones who would think nothing of their Prophet leading them to victory under the banner of Holy War against infidels (the British) – belied a concern about *good* Muslims. More frankly, this characterization questioned whether a "good" Muslim could be trustworthy. To illustrate, Hunter quoted the Magistrate of Patna, a city in the current Indian state of Bihar on the Ganges River, as saying: "They [Muslims] have, under the very nose and protection of Government authorities, openly preached sedition in every village of our most populous districts, unsettling the minds of the

Musalman population, and obtaining an influence for evil as extraordinary as it is certain."[71] Using the Magistrate's words, Hunter moved his suspicions of Muslims beyond outwardly fanatics, whom he would label bad, "destructive," or "radical," to include those Muslims that the British government *assumed* to be "good."[72]

Thus, there are fanatic, "bad" Muslims who, according to Hunter, actively – with money and armies – sought rebellion and revolution (which he both conflated with and attributed to jihad). The insinuation and overt assertion he made is that even the trustworthy, good, friends-of-the-Empire Muslims were, at their core, not *quite* as good as they would have one believe. Like their fanatical co-religionists, they were bound in conscience to rebel against the Queen, no matter how "good" they appeared at first, second, or third glance. It is this inherent untrustworthiness – the inherent loyalty to rules, laws, and institutions outside those of the British Empire – that marked Muslims in the British Raj as inherently deficient subjects.

Hunter referenced "the treasonist" Syed Ahmed Barelvi (Hunter's rendering was Sayyid Ahmad of Rae Bareili [d. 1831]) as an inspirational Wahhabi for other Muslims; in one place, he called Syed Ahmed a "prophet," noting that this was his term, and not that of his followers.[73] Syed Ahmed had long figured as the link between South Asia and Wahhabism, having reportedly gone on hajj in 1824 and returned from Mecca with a zealous urge to reform his community. Contemporary historians, however, complicate and even refute this well-rehearsed history. Charles Allen, for example, bluntly declares that "the argument that Syed Ahmad picked up his ideas of Wahhabi intolerance and jihad while in Arabia is untenable."[74] Similarly, Harlan Pearson observes: "There is no direct evidence that Sayyid Ahmad Brēlwī was preaching *jihad* before his pilgrimage or that any experience in the holy cities inspired him."[75] For Hunter, however, Syed Ahmed's leadership in bringing Wahhabism to India was both undeniable and cataclysmic: though Hunter explicitly warned against conflating Wahhabis with "traitors,"[76] he also provided numerous examples of Wahhabi and Wahhabi-influenced tracts, fatwas, and pamphlets that announced Muslims' responsibility for rebellion.

As Hunter delineated the specific threat Muslims posed to the British Empire, he explained that Wahhabis "ha[d] developed a copious literature filled with prophecies of the downfall of British Power, and devoted to the duty of Rebellion."[77] Hunter was an historian, and as we might expect of a researcher, did not leave his reader wanting for evidence. He quoted Jama Tafasír in the *Calcutta Review*:

> No true believer can live loyal to our Government without perdition to his soul. Those who would deter others from Holy War or Flight [i.e., *jihād* or *hijra*] are in heart hypocrites. Let all know this. In a country where the ruling religion is other than Muhammadanism, the religious precepts of Muhammad cannot be enforced. It is incumbent on Musalmáns to join together, and wage war on the Infidels. Those who are unable to fight should emigrate to a country of True Faith. At the present time in India, Flight is a stern duty.[78]

Jama Tafasír clearly explicated the duty of Muslims, in one statement and with two possible courses of action: Muslims were unable to be loyal to British rule without betraying their faith. To save their souls, as it were, Muslims were to engage in jihad or hijra – that is, they were to fight or take flight.

For W. W. Hunter, this pronouncement – and those like it – did not represent a limited, sectarian gloss on the religious ramifications of foreign or imposed rule. It did not represent an educated, learned pronouncement, perhaps limited to elite circles, nor did it represent one voice (or even a few voices) making an interpretation within a long, complex, historical tradition of such legal interpretations. For Hunter, it reflected a clear and present danger within the then-expanding Indian Empire. This statement (and those like it) was, in Hunter's eyes, not limited to sectarian, elite, or legal interpretations, and instead, reflected a true crisis. He explained that Wahhabis influence "seditious masses" in four key ways, through: (i) literature of treason; (ii) central propaganda at Patna; (iii) missionizing/missionaries; and (iv) permanent settlements in Bengal.[79] We have returned, then, to the concerns raised by Hunter and the Magistrate of Patna, above: Wahhabis were, they thought, openly preaching sedition and treason to the masses, and because the law is so clear – and Muslims so clearly of one mind – the spread of the requirement to rebel was not to be taken lightly. In this understanding, how could Muslims be anything *but* disloyal?

Hunter did not limit his concern with Muslim sedition, treason, and rebellion to the interpretations of others, or of Muslims themselves. He offered a lengthy interpretation of his own on the nature of the Qur'an, stating:

The plain meaning of the Kurán is, that the followers of Islám shall reduce the whole earth to obedience, giving to the conquered the choice of conversion, of a submission almost amounting to slavery, or of death. The Kurán was written, however, to suit, not the exigencies of a modern nation, but the local necessities of a warring Arabian tribe in its successive vicissitudes as a persecuted, an aggressive, and a triumphant sect. The rugged hostility and fanaticism of the Kurán have been smoothed down by many generations of scholiasts and interpreters; and from its one-sided, passionate bigotry, a not unsymmetrical system of civil polity has evolved. Many of the Prophet's precepts on Holy War have, however, found their way unaltered into the formulated Muhammadan Law.[80]

Hunter conceived a "rugged hostility and fanaticism" as endemically Qur'anic, but which had, over time, been domesticated by the generations of Muslim scholars that succeeded its appearance and promulgation. This domestication did not apply, however, to the arena of jihad: the original harshness of the text remains unchanged, to Hunter's conceptualization and interpretation, when it comes to this particular concept. Despite his almost crass description of the text as hostile and bent toward the fanatical, Hunter held that it was open to interpretation, and he clearly insinuated that Muslims adapted it to modern eras, thereby creating, in his terms, a "civil polity." Put differently, Hunter explained the historical context of the Qur'an, imagined that Muslims had worked to interpret it so as to make it fit an evolving modern era, and yet maintained that Muhammad's conceptualizations of Holy War persisted, without alteration, in contemporary Muslim law.[81]

In light of his various roles as a British subject, "demi-official,"[82] and later official Hunter would be concerned in numerous publications with the potential for rebellions, revolts, uprisings, dissatisfaction, and dissent in the colony and Empire. In the case of *Indian Musalmans*, his roles as historian and statistician of regions undergoing shifts in British control would narrow his vision, and structure his writing, to focus on efficiencies of empire. Similarly, war is a common enemy of rulers, and avoiding it was a preoccupation of British colonial and imperial powers; thus, we may find Hunter's focus on jihad unremarkable as well. However, holy war as a divinely inspired or divinely mandated act of devotion poses a distinct challenge to an author looking, as his dedication, preface, and introduction suggested, to:

> bring out in clear relief the past history and present requirements of a persistently belligerent class – of a class whom successive Governments have declared to be a source of permanent danger to the Indian Empire.[83]

Muslims were a permanent danger, and his work was set up to illuminate courses of actions, what he termed "present requirements." Part of illuminating the problem was to focus, with a clear eye, on holy war – the unaltered words of the Prophet, evidence of Islam's requirement of submission to the point of slavery, and the permanent danger to the Empire.

In his conclusions, Hunter asserted that Indian Muslims held, at their core, religious beliefs that demanded fight or flight responses to foreign rule. And the idea of holy war had a special purveyor: Wahhabis. Hunter commented, "Indian Wahhabis are extreme Dissenters," comparing them to "Anabaptists, 5th monarchy men [...] Communists and Red Republicans in politics."[84] He added that Wahhabis "appeal broadly to the masses, and their system, whether of religious or of politics, is eminently adapted to the hopes and fears of a restless populace."[85] Jihad and Wahhabis – the archetype of a fanatical sect for Hunter – form a gathering perfect storm: religious obligation, religious interpretation, and religious resistance all neatly packaged within an exhortation to revolt.

Hunter again called attention to specific legal reasoning and pronouncements, fatwas. He reckoned that the majority of Muslims would follow the abovementioned legal interpretation – that is, being ruled by infidels demanded that Muslims fight or emigrate. This conviction did not deter Hunter from examining dissenting voices, however. He cited two "distinct sets" of legal decisions that he claimed "have been of late the most conspicuous in proclaiming that they are under no religious obligation to wage war against the Queen."[86] One of these juridical proclamations came from Calcutta, the largest city in Bengal, where Hunter was stationed for most of his career. This important imperial city and trade capital had a thriving Muslim community, and Hunter was keen to examine its interpretation. He wrote:

> The Calcutta Doctors declare India to be a country of Islam [*dar-ul-islam*], and conclude that religious rebellion is therefore unlawful. This result must be accepted as alike satisfactory to the well-to-do Muhammadans, whom it saves from the peril of contributing to the Fanatical Camp on our Frontier, and gratifying to ourselves, as proving that the Law and the Prophets can be utilised on the side of loyalty as well as on the side of sedition.[87]

The Calcutta legal decision cuts against that stated above; rather than finding British rule to indicate a state of infidels and war, *dar-ul-harb*, these legal scholars declared that India was in fact the opposite, *dar-ul-islam*, a country of Islam, of peace. At a glance, the Calcutta ruling would seem to have pleased Britons, as it offered an Islamic pronouncement that supported their (peaceable) rule. Additionally, one might think Britons would be pleased because Muslim elites and leaders sought to stem those Muslims who thought otherwise – the Calcutta ruling ought to have marked these Muslims as loyal supporters, if not outright allies. For Hunter, while the fatwa was a positive sign for the British, its origin demanded a strenuous qualification to its legitimacy: it reflected the opinion of "well-to-do" Muslims, and not, as he continued on to state, "the Fanatical masses," the majority of Indian Muslims.[88]

Hunter chose which Muslim authorities and authoritative texts carried weight and dismissed the very evidence he seemed to seek – and, as a result, he failed to identify the possibility of loyal Muslims. Despite commending this ruling and suggesting it was to be regarded well by his fellow Britons, he forcefully doubted its efficacy and reach. He argued, "It would be a political blunder for us to accept without inquiry the views of the Muhammadan Literary Society of Calcutta as those of the Indian Musalmans."[89] The Muslims who sought out a fatwa seeking to clarify the status of British India in the eyes of traditional Islamic law were precisely the Muslims whose statements and findings were to be interrogated. These elite, learned Muslims could not represent *most* Muslims, let alone *all* Muslims in Hunter's view.

As Hunter suggested the Mohamedan Literary Society maintained only limited appeal and cache, he simultaneously proposed that this fatwa would fall upon deaf ears precisely because it was logical and reasoned. Hunter reasoned, "Extreme zealots of the Wahabi Sect cannot be expected to listen to reason of any sort, yet there is a vast body of Muhammadans, who would be guided by a really authoritative exposition of their Sacred Law."[90] The Wahhabis Hunter both feared and respected represent the power of literalism: in their extremism, they were unreasonable, but in their authoritativeness, they possessed a clarity that appealed to the vast majority of Muslims. The Calcutta decision might be correct, or at least satisfactory, but it demonstrated neither a legal truth nor a solid anti-rebellion strategy, instead providing evidence that elite Muslims might be different from the masses and that the varied religious tradition could be used to either support or refute holy war.

Hunter's work in the remainder of this chapter – and the book itself, for that matter – looked to investigate the effects of zealotry on the *masses*.

> I propose, therefore, to scrutinize the Sunni Decisions with a view to ascertaining the effect which they will have on the more zealous Muhammadans; men with whom the sense of religious duty is the rule of life, and whose minds are uninfluenced either by fear or danger or by habits of prosperous ease [. . .] *For it is no use shutting our eyes to the fact that a larger proportion of our Muhammadan subjects belong to this class.*[91]

The majority of Muslims were fanatics: their religious duties, Hunter argued, ruled their lives, which were therefore unencumbered by fear, danger, or even prosperity. This is how Hunter questioned the motives and authenticity of the elite Muslims who procured a ruling that appeared to favor British rule. Favorable ruling aside, their elite status – their "prosperous ease" – did not guard against the inherent zealotry of their co-religionists.

Hunter's assertions, once again, do not merely represent one Briton's opinion; as Gottschalk and Greenberg point out, he, "like many other

Britons, collapsed diverse Muslim movements seeking divergent goals in disparate parts of India into the category 'Wahhabi.'"[92] Zealotry, in Hunter's writing, became identified with either Wahhabi movements or Wahhabi influence, which in turn were enmeshed with the Great Rebellion − and the lingering threat of insurrection posed by Muslims even after the Rebellion was put down. The proportion of the population with which Hunter was concerned, he insisted, was zealous, "uninfluenced by fear or danger or prosperous ease;" their zealotry relied upon the undue influence and patent appeal of Wahhabi ideology, even if Hunter could not demonstrate what Wahhabis *were*.

The fascination with the potential rebels, the inherent disloyalty, and a religious propensity and obligation toward revolt became the central concern for Hunter as the *Indian Musalmans* continues. Where he had easily pinned Muslims as acting on the basis of religion earlier in the text, he portrayed the British forces as British or English, with more particular references directed toward official positions (e.g., magistrate, registrar). However, as Hunter approached the climax of his narrative, he began to reference Indian Muslims as threats because they were opposed to British, Christian rule; he posited, in other words, a clash of civilizations in the same sections in which he interrogated Muslim legal decisions. Despite having just cited a favorable fatwa, issued by the Calcutta law doctors, he lamented, "Yet the whole country continues to furnish money and men to the forlorn Hope of Islám on our Frontier, and persists in its bloodstained protest against Christian Rule."[93]

He added, "I am sorry to say that the effect of the Decision of the Calcutta Society on this numerous and dangerous class will be *nil.*"[94] The favorable fatwa is meaningless in this conceptualization: it cannot influence Muslims, both because they are dangerous and because the ruling, he later declared, was "erroneous."[95]

Favorable Ruling, Unfavorable Interpretation

The Calcutta fatwa became a fulcrum in Hunter's analysis. He quoted it at length, and then systematically refuted it, often relying upon and preferring his own glosses of texts. The original fatwa was issued because the Mahomedan Literary Society of Calcutta commissioned the decision. While legal rulings are often offered by legal scholars (here, muftis) on critical issues without much prodding, asking a question of a legal scholar is a standard Muslim approach; the vast tableau of Islamic law (shari'a and *fiqh*) has been woven, over time, precisely because Muslims of various standing have sought out rulings as new situations, locations, or innovations arose. This is to say that the Mahomedan Literary Society was not acting strangely, uniquely, or even distinctively in seeking a ruling on an issue facing them in their time. However, it should also be noted that the ability to do so on such a hefty matter indicates elite status, and the publication of these results similarly underscores the relative power and prestige of this organization.

Moulvie (*maulvi*) Abdool Luteef Khan Bahadoor (d. 1893)[96] founded the Mahomedan Literary Society of Calcutta, and he hosted monthly meetings of the group at his home; the purpose of this learned society was to "impart useful information to the higher and educated classes of the Mahomedan community" in "Oordoo, Persian, Arabic, and English."[97] The *maulvi*, like many other elite Bengalis, held various positions within British organizations, including the Bengal Management Council and the University of Calcutta's examination board. The British awarded him two titles for his service and achievements. The first was the title *Khan Bahadoor*, an adopted and adapted titular role customary in pre-imperial South Asia, especially Hyderabad; the second was *Nawab*, similarly a vestige of Mughal reign, later appropriated by British imperial forces and awarded to indigenous subjects of the Crown, much akin to the peerage system in the United Kingdom.[98] The titles themselves are notable, exemplifying how the British maintained and used, for their own purposes, extant titular and honorific systems in order to mark locals as exemplary subjects in vernacular systems that communicated imperial prestige as well as demarcate indigeneity. Abdool Luteef was an elite Muslim, no doubt, but also one whose loyalty to the Crown was noted. Yet, despite Luteef's formal – and positive – relationship with British imperialism, Sir W. W. Hunter dismissed, as we will see, the findings of his society's inquiry.

In November 1870, Abdool Luteef hosted the regular meeting of the Mahomedan Literary Society. The purpose of this meeting was to ask a most pressing question – namely, whether Muslims in India were required by religious law to rebel against the British. In the preface to published meeting proceedings, the anonymous author and meeting secretary noted that such a meeting was held because,

Some time ago a letter appeared in the English Newspapers signed by a Mahomedan Officer of Government employed at Bhagulpore, in which he congratulated himself and the public in having made the discovery that the followers of Islam are not bound by their Religion to rebel against the British Government. It was indeed as if the Mahomedan world were ignorant of that fact before; and that Mahomedans, who had in blindness been hatching treason and rebellion against their beneficent rulers, were to refrain hereafter on behind blessed with this new flood of light.[99]

The Society mentioned not Anglo-Christian Britons who had accused Muslims of being disloyal, but rather, a Muslim officer; the Society's minutes sarcastically declared that, now that Muslims know they need not be disloyal, they could go on living "blessed with this new flood of light."

But while the Society chaffed at the very notion that such a conversation would be necessary at all, scoffing at the Muslim officer's so-called findings, they proceeded to entertain this debate, seemingly so that they could immediately refute it. The author of the meeting minutes commented that the Society felt it "imperative" to hold a "public exposition of Mahomedan Law" in "which it should be proclaimed, that such a question as that which elicited the fatwah was not one which a good Mahomedan in British India should for a moment entertain."[100] The Mahomedan Literary Society moved toward rectifying how Muslims were misconstrued by requesting a formal legal ruling (a fatwa), opting to weigh in on an issue they clearly thought was flimsy and iniquitous.

The November 1870 meeting included *maulvi* Karamat Ali, a Hanafi jurist, and his findings on the issue at hand, namely whether British India was *dar-ul-harb* (country of war) or *dar-ul-islam* (country of peace or Islam[101]), which in turn would indicate whether or not Muslims would be compelled to rebel. He began with the ruling, stating "that, according to Mahomedan law, British India is Darul Islam, and that it is not lawful for the Mahomedans of British India to make Jihad."[102] Karamat Ali added that "ignorant Mahomedans" had posed the question and that he only answered it at the Mahomedan Literary Society's insistence. Even before beginning his ruling, the jurist indicated his low opinion of the question itself, and upon ruling, dismissed its legal premise. The mufti unmistakably ruled that Muslim subjects of the Crown were not permitted to wage religious war upon their sovereigns. Despite this clarity of law and dismissal of the premise, he continued and observed that the conditions for jihad had not been met, citing three primary texts: "Fatawa Alamgeeree" (*fatāwā alamgīrī*, a seventeenth-century text); "Darrul Mukhtar" (*dar al-mukhar*, a sixteenth-century text by Moulana Mahomed Alaudeen Haskafee Bin Shaikh Ali, mufti of Damascus); and "Fusool Imadee" (*fuṣūl imadī*, c. 1254, by Abul Fatah Abdoor Raheem Bin Ali Bakir Bin Abdool Jaleel Murghinanee of Samarcand).[103]

Mere months later, in its original printing in 1871 and in the more widely circulated 1872 edition, W. W. Hunter described this fatwa as deeply inadequate, and not as a dismissal of the necessity of jihad. Moreover, Hunter imagined not only that the ruling of Karamat Ali would be insufficient to sway the "numerous and dangerous class,"[104] but also that it was incorrect.

> Its [the Mahomedan Literary Society's pamphlet] object is to prove that India is a Country of Islam and that THEREFORE Religious Rebellion is unlawful for Muhammadan subjects. Significantly enough, the word THEREFORE is omitted [...] still more significantly, the two most important Decisions, that of the Mecca Doctors and of Maulvi Abu-ul-Hakk, confine themselves to affirming that India is a Country of Islam, and most carefully avoid drawing the inference that rebellion is therefore unlawful.[105]

At first blush, Hunter simply stated that two others, the Meccan and an additional *maulvi* Abu-ul-Hakk supported the Calcutta decision. But, he immediately countered this by adding:

> The truth is, according to Muhammadan law, the opposite conclusion would be correct, and the Mecca Doctors well knew this when they gave their decision. They affirm that India is a Country of Islam, and leave it to the Faithful to conclude that for this very reason they ought to strive, by war or otherwise, to drive out the Infidels who have usurped the Government, and who in a hundred ways have interfered with the practices and procedure, both legal and religious, of the former Muhammadan Rules.[106]

Thus Hunter – a Christian, a Briton – asserted his own preeminence as an interpreter of Islamic law over and above the trained, Muslim expert, *maulvi* Karamat Ali.

He claimed that a ruling in which British India is, in fact, a country of Islam (*dar-ul-islam*) begged action: because the country is *dar-ul-islam* one must fight (presumably, to *maintain* this status). He directly took issue with Karamat Ali's fatwa, arguing:

> The Pamphlet argues that India is still a Country of Islam because it was so under the Muhammadan Rule, and that, although now conquered by an infidel race, yet the three conditions under which it would have become a Country of the Enemy (Dár al-Harb, literally House of Strife) do not apply to it. These three conditions were laid down by the greatest authority of the Muhammadan Law, Abu Hanifa. The Tract quotes them, however, not from one of the older and universally received works, but from the Fatáwi-i-Alamgírí of the reign of Aurangzeb. This latter text materially differs from the earlier works; and it is an unquestionable fact that the conditions, as laid down by Abu Hanifa and by the old authoritative law-books, do apply to India, and that, according to the orthodox doctrine, India is a Country of the Enemy.[107]

These are attitudes that formed a majority mentality of Orientalist scholarship: the quest for origins and a prioritization of the original are hallmarks of scholarship about religion in the nineteenth century.[108] But the fact remains: Hunter asserted that his gloss of Muslim legal and religious texts was more accurate than that of a *maulvi*, a religiously trained expert who had, in fact, been called upon by Indian Muslims precisely because of his proficiency. Inherent in this conceit is, no doubt, the quest for origins and authenticity; perfectly authentic iterations of Islam from within a South Asian milieu simply do not rate in comparison to other "universally received" (i.e., central to Islam, perhaps Arabic or Middle Eastern) works. While other observers have noted the tension between Islam's vernacular traditions and a scholarly and imperial insistence on Arabia as central,[109] Hunter's work is perplexing insofar as it takes Indian Muslims as uniquely concerning as well as distinctive, but still renders Indic texts as inferior, unorthodox, and untrustworthy.

Despite holding Muslims suspect, Hunter deployed Abu Hanifa, "the greatest authority," by his estimation.[110] Abu Hanifa (d. 767) is the namesake of the Sunni Hanafi *madhhab* or legal school, and the Hanafi *madhhab* he inspired still maintains primary influence in Turkey, Central, and South Asia. *Maulvi* Karamat Ali is named as a "Hanafee" jurist in the original publication of the Mahomedan Literary Society.[111] Hunter thus cited Abu Hanifa against the Hanafi *maulvi*. Hunter did not merely offer the comment above, but also demonstrated how he came to such a reading by laying out a side-by-side comparison, of the original text and the text cited by Karamat Ali. Hunter, taking both space and careful explication, laid out key passages from the pamphlet of the Mahomedan Literary Society (Karamat Ali's fatwa), which cited the *Fatáwi-i-Alamgírí* and those found in *"Sirajiyah Imadiyah* and all texts older than the *Fatáwi-i-Alamgírí."*[112] Hunter used the pamphlet's citation of the text from Aurangzeb's era against those texts that were older, highlighting his emphasis on the original as the authentic.

Hunter also offered his own translations and religious commentary as it suited his argument and interrogation of text; we could say that Hunter provided a scholarly and comparative close reading of these texts. He took as an especially meaningful matter the compared lines about when holy war (jihad) is called for based upon whether or not Muslims and recognized minorities (i.e., zimmi or *dhimmī*) enjoyed religious freedoms. He noted that the pamphlet cited the *"Fatáwi-i-Alamgírí,"* which ordains jihad when "no Musalman is found in the enjoyment of religious liberty, nor a *Zimmi* (an infidel who has accepted the terms of permanent subjection to Musalman Rule) under the same terms as he enjoyed under the Government of Islam."[113] He then compared that phrase to one in "an older text" which stated that jihad was ordained "when neither Musalmans nor Zimmis enjoy the *Amán-i-áwwal."*[114] Hunter then defined *amán-i-áwwal* as "religious liberty," following noted Orientalist scholar Henry Ferdinand Blochmann (d. 1878 CE).[115] But, religious liberty, he opined, did not adequately define the term.

> '*Amán*' literally signifies security, and the meaning of *Amán-i-áwwal* is distinctly laid down in the *Jámi'-ur-rumúz* as implying the whole religious security and full status which the Muhammadans formerly enjoyed under their own Rule [...] The *Amán*, or religious status, which the Muhammadans now enjoy, is

entirely dependent on the will of their Christian rulers, and they enjoy it only in such a degree as we choose to grant. This degree falls far short of the full religious status which they formerly possessed."[116]

Hunter focused on the conditionality of religious freedom in defining *amán-i-áwwal*. He argued that under their own rule – that is, during the Mughal Empire – religious liberty would have been a given; however, under British rule, Muslims find themselves at the will of Christians. Therefore, religious liberty is not absolute but qualified. The conditional nature of religious liberty compels jihad.

Hunter then forcefully argued that whether British India was *dar-ul-islam* or *dar-ul-harb* would have little effect on the obligation of Muslims to rebel.

If India were still *de jure* a Country of Islam, this portion of our Musalman subjects would feel compelled to rise against us, and to make it a Country of Islam *de facto*. It is written in all the law books: 'If Infidels press hard or occupy a town in Country of Islam,[117] it is holy incumbent[118] on every Muhammadan man, woman, and child to hurt and drive away the Infidel Ruler.' This is so established a rule that the King of Bokhára was compelled by his subjects to declare Holy War against the Russians as soon as they entered the Country of Islam. Indeed, if India were still a Country of the Faithful, every day some ground of rebellion would arise. Our religious toleration would itself constitute a capital crime.[119]

Interestingly, Hunter cited the annexation and colonization of Russia in Central Asia as a comparative, using the actions of Bukhari Muslims (in contemporary Uzbekistan) to demonstrate plausible actions for Indian Muslims. In this case the king, analogous to the titular Mughal emperor and lesser officials, was "compelled by his subjects" to revolt. This seems to suggest that the king himself was both powerless against the will of the religious mass and inclined to agree that it was religiously responsible to revolt. Similarly, it is notable that Hunter included evidence that implicated women and children, given typical British and Orientalist depictions of women, in particular, as in need of help – these women are not in need of help, but capable and compelled to revolt.[120] It is the final line that demands real attention, however. Hunter asserted that *tolerance* – the gold standard for British rule, civilizational maturity, and even kindness – would itself cause grave dangers. Hunter argued essentially that whether India were a "Country of the Faithful" or a "Country of the Enemy,"[121] Indian Muslims would find legal recourse to rebel, and therefore, even more worrisome, would be under religious obligation to do so.

Hunter continued by stating flatly his concerns with the rulings of both the Meccan jurists and of Karamat Ali, represented in the Mohamedan Literary Society's pamphlet.

> I therefore view with extreme suspicion the decision of the Doctors at Mecca, that stronghold of fanaticism and intolerant zeal, when they declare that India is a Country of Islam, but who, instead of deducing therefrom, as the Calcutta Muhammadan Literary Society infer, that rebellion is *therefore* unlawful, leave it to their Indian co-religionists to draw the opposite conclusion,–namely, *that rebellion is therefore incumbent.*[122]

Hunter cast aspersion on the Meccan jurists and suggested that their ruling only superficially appeared safe and encouraging for Britons, but in reality encouraged rebellion. He based his arguments on claims that the region was filled with zealotry and fanaticism; in such a context, what appeared reasonable – even favorable – must be an illusion, which must, as he suggested, be viewed with "extreme suspicion." Hunter's comments dismiss the Calcutta decision, even as he admitted that some "easy going Muhammadans" would find the "erroneous" decision "acceptable."[123] The easy going Muslims ceased to bear weight in such weighty matters, and in any case, what they found acceptable was roundly declared incorrect. Hunter dismissed not only the Calcuttan decision, but also the opinions of those Muslims who supported it; he made minor their status, influence, religious interpretations, and self-articulation, and he prioritized literal, "fanatic" glosses as authentic and accurate Islam in South Asia.

Of note, as well, is the absent option: flight (hijra). Earlier in *Indian Musalmans*, Hunter discussed the possibility of flight as a legal response to inappropriate governance. He wrote: "The first duty of a Musalmán is religious rebellion; and to those who reply that such rebellion is impracticable under the British Power, they answer that the only alternative is Flight."[124] In the same early section, he quoted the *Jama Tafasír* (1867) as having proclaimed that "Flight was a stern duty."[125] As *Indian Musalmans* focuses more directly on persuading readers of Muslims' clear obligation to rebel, flight drops out as an alternative negative consequence of unwanted rule. I cannot pretend to know *why* this is the case, but I suggest that the conspicuous absence of flight (hijra) supports interpreting Hunter's work as uniformly, problematically focused on jihad. I will return to this fixation – and its implications – in Chapter 4.

Yet, despite appearing to declare India destined for war and rebellion, Hunter hastened to add that because the East India Company had slowly, methodically, and incrementally established power in India, British Rule might be secure, after all. "The truth is," Hunter argued, "that had we hastened by a single decade our Formal assumption of the sovereignty, we should have been landed in a Muhammadan rising infinitely more serious than the mutinies of 1857."[126] Hunter claimed that the incremental process distracted Muslims, it caught them unaware, effectually rendering the change invisible. He wrote: "Before India had passed into a Country of the Enemy, the duties incumbent upon the Muhammadans in a Country of Islam had faded away."[127] The gradual transformation from the Mughal ("Country of Islam") to the British ("Country of the Enemy") rendered British Rule a *"status quo"* that "the present generation of Musalmans are bound, according to their own texts, to accept."[128] Interestingly, however, Hunter added that Muslim acceptance of the British government relied solely on whether the British could "maintain their status (*Amán*) sufficiently intact to enable them to discharge the duties of their religion."[129] Hunter warned his audience – fellow countrymen, officers, administrators, policymakers, and scholars alike – that it was incumbent upon them to maintain a ruling status in which Muslim subjects felt capable of performing their religious duties – or suffer the consequences, i.e., jihad. Hunter thus suggested that it was only through meticulous, wise governance – despite missteps and close calls – that the British were able to govern *without* a major, religiously inflected rebellion. Maintaining this delicate peace in spite of an unruly, disloyal, and volatile population only further demonstrated British prowess and righteousness.

In the wake of the Great Rebellion, Hunter articulated a Muslim minority bent toward rebellion and war. In describing Muslims as jihadis, in conflating Wahhabi or more literalistic Muslims as *all* Muslims, and in making central extreme legal interpretations, Hunter did not describe Muslims in India, but he played a large role in defining what Britons saw as authentic and normative Islam in India. Hunter crafted an Indian Muslim, meant to be consumed in London by Britons, for the purposes of proper, ongoing, and effective imperial rule. And, this writing was well after what many observers agreed was the total demise of the Mughal Empire, Britons still had to establish and cultivate proper imperial rule in the shadow of the great Muslim rulers; they had to wrest power and authority *from* Muslims in order to control them. Britons needed Muslims to become fully minoritized.

Conclusions

Hunter expressed a true fear with respect to the obligations of a religious community whose religion was, according to him, singularly consumed with obligation, submission, and obedience. Hunter's claims to be a "demi-official" are misleading.[130] Although he asserted his lack of a role within the British official apparatus – and even the historical accuracy of that assertion when *Indian Musalmans* was published – it would be imprudent to place his work outside the pale of imperial data, opinion, or knowledge production. He served as a magistrate and a collector in Bengal, he was trained in Indic languages, and he wrote analyses commissioned by and for British use. *Indian Musalmans* itself was written at the behest of the Viceroy Lord Mayo. It is precisely because Hunter had status within elite British circles that his works, including but certainly not limited to *Indian Musalmans*, were treated as serious and accurate assessments of India. When Hunter drew the above-mentioned conclusions about holy war, holy war was accepted by his readers as a logical, factual conclusion, reflecting the utmost danger to and anxiety about ruling colonies and natives from afar.

Indian Musalmans offered solutions to the vexing and still-looming problem of a seditious Muslim milieu. Hunter called specifically for the education of Muslims – especially Muslim elites, those who had previously belonged to the ruling class but now, under British sovereignty, had lost both status and access. He quipped, rather pointedly, that the "former conquerors of the East are excluded from our Oriental journals and libraries, as well as from the more active careers in life."[131] Hunter suggested that education was the way to solve a lack of purpose among this former ruling elite; he called for the establishment of schools, so that Muslims might gain "sober and genial knowledge of the West."[132] But he cautioned that while schools should be amenable to Muslims, the subtle purpose of their education should always be a dramatic decrease in the effect of religion on Muslims:

> Without interfering in any way with their religion, and in the very process of enabling them to learn religious duties, we should render that religion perhaps less sincere, but certainly less fanatical. The rising generation of Muhammadans would tread the steps which have conducted the Hindus, not long ago the most bigoted nation on earth, into their present state of easy tolerance. Such a tolerance impress a less earnest belief than their fathers had; but it has freed them, as it would liberate the Musalmans, from the cruelties which they inflicted, the crimes which they perpetrated, and the miseries which they endured, in the name of mistaken religion.[133]

Hunter bluntly and eloquently argued for education as the solution to fanaticism, for the outside reform of Islam by the virtue and values of the West. He suggested that Muslims ought to be *made* tolerant by being liberated from their own hostility, misery, and histories of mistaken religion. As embodiments of the West, Britons were both poised and uniquely able to foster the development of reform in Islam.

Beyond imperial laws that formally structure inclusion and exclusion, the reign of information on its own contributes to minoritization. Hunter's ultimate inability to see Muslims beyond the mold of rebel, or to see Islam without its dire need for reform by the West, represents the process of minoritization – and its result, as well. In *Indian Musalmans*, Hunter's ultimate claim was that Muslims were bound by religion to rebel against a non-Muslim ruler *if* that ruler did not meet her obligations. He acknowledged that Muslims were "bound by their own law to live peaceably under our Rule."[134] However, he also dismissed the rulings of the Mahomedan Literary Society and concluded that the nature of India – be it a region of peace or war, *dar-ul-islam* or *dar-ul-harb* – mattered little for Britons, as either case could, and almost certainly would, bring about jihad.

Hunter's claims about Muslims and his proposed solutions demonstrated not only epistemic violence[135] born of racialized colonial and imperial projects, but also the ways in which official, demi-official, and unofficial imaginations of Muslims came to bear real legal, social, and minoritizing fruit. Hunter effectively rendered Muslims subject not only to the Crown, but also to the Crown's interpretations of and alterations to Islam, because of Muslims' distinctive (and problematic) characterization. The process of making Muslims – and especially those elite Muslims who had recently enjoyed the perks of being rulers – into a minority, whose agency in public and private spheres was policed and reimagined is both a visible feature and consequence of *Indian Musalmans.*

Hunter placed himself in the role of arbiter and interpreter of Muslim law, and when Muslims themselves offered a legal opinion, he disregarded it by following (his interpretation of) their legal system. By rendering Muslims – and particularly the accounts of the Mahomedan Literary Society and Maulvi Karamat Ali – inept, Hunter ascribed to Muslims a position of inferiority even within their own system. Further, Hunter declared that no matter the system, Muslims would be bound to rebel. His conclusions were clear: Muslims were a problem that demanded a solution, and his solution included educating Muslims so that they would become, in effect, *less* Muslim.

Indian Musalmans stands as a powerful example of the minoritization of Indian Muslims in light of the 1857 Rebellion. In it, Hunter set forth a clear and well-researched argument that judged Muslim subjects to be inherently deficient by virtue of their religion. He insisted that Muslim subjects might be placated should their ability to practice Islam be maintained, but placed emphasis on the placation: on their own, Muslims would not – in fact, *could not* – assent to British authority or rule. Indeed, on their own, Muslims were a dangerous lot, required by religious texts and law to rebel against any non-Muslim government, in any situation. Muslim voices were maligned and rendered ineffectual because even those legal rulings that suggested that loyalty to British rule was appropriate were themselves suspected, as Hunter claimed, of saying one thing but implying another. When Britain quashed the Rebellion and took control of India, finally, "the Muslims" emerged, having been produced as a definable and unified group. As a whole, "the Muslims" came to be understood, as Hunter epitomized, as incapable of living peaceably as subjects of the Queen unless great lengths were taken to ensure a delicate balance of power, authority, and religious praxis.

The Great Rebellion produced "the Muslims" in India – one unified, cogent group, and as Peter Hardy astutely states, for most Britons in 1857, "a Muslim meant a rebel."[136] While Britons may have produced and promulgated "the Muslims," Indian Muslims – especially elites – took it upon themselves to voice dissent and trouble this unified image after the Rebellion. Famously, Sir Syed Ahmad Khan (d. 1898) offered a review of Hunter's *Indian Musalmans*, and in it, Khan challenged Hunter's findings, in scope, depth, and interpretation of sources. He did not take kindly to Hunter's implications, conclusions, or accusations, as will be discussed in the following chapter.

CHAPTER 3

"GOD SAVE ME FROM MY FRIENDS!": SYED AHMAD KHAN'S *REVIEW ON DR HUNTER*

Friend to the Mahomedans, as Dr. Hunter no doubt is, his friendship, as represented by his last work, has worked us great harm. "God save me from my friends!" was the exclamation which rose to my lips as I perused the author's pages.

— Sir Syed Ahmad Khan[1]

Sir Syed Ahmad Khan's (d. 1898) efforts to challenge, criticize, and clarify an "authentic" Islam are evident in many of his writings, including his response to Hunter's *Indian Musalmans*. In *Review on Dr Hunter's Indian Musalmans: Are They Bound in Conscience to Rebel Against the Queen?* (1872), Khan offered a timely rejoinder to Hunter's text. He questioned Hunter's assumptions about Muslims, readings of key fatwas and other interpretations of Islamic law, and estimations of Muslim loyalties. That he stridently disagreed with Hunter may not surprise, but Khan's writing is all the more fascinating in light of Hunter's argument that people like Khan – that is, Muslims both loyalist and modern – might not exist. (Or, according to Hunter, if they existed, they merely inhabited a minority class of Muslims morally and financially above their majoritarian, rebellious counterparts, and were therefore politically inconsequential.) Moreover, Hunter expressly denied the veracity of the very proof-texts Khan relied upon. Their "debate" may well be seen as a one-sided argument, in which Hunter set the parameters and Khan merely participated within those boundaries. Sir Syed's reply, however, echoed in certain communities, English and Indian, Christian and Muslim. Khan did more than participate in a discourse central to the questions of Muslims, identity, loyalty, and the Crown – he helped shape it.

In *Review on Dr Hunter's Indian Musalmans*, Sir Syed spoke directly to Hunter, replicating Hunter's claims while refuting them. In this essay, as in others on the Rebellion and elsewhere, he delineated an Islam that was modern, scientific, and compatible with British rule. These lines of argument often validated his loyalty or his religion, but dismissing Khan as self-interested or as espousing a self-preservationist set of ideologies overlooks the effect of his freestanding writings and direct responses to others in discursive change. Sir Syed Ahmad Khan's contributions to the literature about Muslim identity, loyalty, and belonging more than merit our specific attention. His response to Hunter's impactful monograph stands with statements by other Muslim thinkers as a challenge to depictions of jihad as solely representing their identity, as persons of faith, racially-identified subjects, and as members of a local (increasingly political) milieu.

Khan is most often remembered for his role as a modernist and modernizer in South Asia during the British Raj. Sir Syed, as he is fondly known across South Asia, exemplifies the ways in which the formal transition to British rule affected institutions, religious modernism, and the formation of community identities. He wrote widely on issues of society, religion, and politics. He also wrote about and expressed a deep conviction of the merits of adopting and adapting successful Western educational models; the most tangible example of this dedication to blending Western education, science, and Islamic values is Aligarh Muslim University, the residential college he founded in 1875 as Mohammadan Anglo-Oriental College. Sir Syed's willingness to utilize British practices earned criticism from other Muslims – orthodox and modernist – as well as from political elites, both Muslim and non-Muslim. He was not opposed to British rule, and he had an established pattern of loyalty to the throne.[2] The British formally knighted him in 1888, but Sir Syed's royal title was not a convention or an honorific – nor is it irrelevant: he was knighted for acts of heroism and loyalty, having assisted and rescued agents of the East India Company and British Empire during the 1857 Great Rebellion.

Sir Syed Ahmad Khan is important not only because of his direct engagement with Sir William Wilson Hunter but also precisely because of his support for British rule in India. He managed to both support British rule and critique its methods, its assumptions, and what he perceived to be its ignoble elements. He managed to speak directly against pronouncements like Hunter's that labeled Muslims as inherently violent or treasonous, while simultaneously decrying the effect of British rule upon Muslim identity, practice, and especially education. In fact, much of his work, including the founding of what would become Aligarh Muslim University, centered on religious and cultural practices, ideas, and books, but also attempted to apply scientific assessment to these realms.[3] He was a loyalist, to be sure, but throughout his prodigious writings and speeches he maintained that Islamic learning, Muslim cultural and religious practices, and British rule were compatible. In fact, it could be reasonably suggested that Sir Syed's reply to Hunter served to solidify his argument for an educated elite cohort of Muslims while simultaneously situating himself further from the ruling British elite than he may have been factually.

Positioning himself as more distant from British power than he may have been is, in some ways, an irrelevant observation, however. Sir Syed embraced an imperially defined version of modernity, one that prioritized "small-p protestant"[4] civilizational values, but he did not forego his religious identity, choosing instead to make central this identity – at least in his own estimation.[5] Further, his writing, especially in *Review*, does rhetorical work that transcends his historical context. Khan challenges our assumptions because he refused to fit British definitions of an "authentic" Muslim: he asserted Islamic values and took drastic measures to ensure that they were maintained, while simultaneously asserting and taking drastic measures to demonstrate his support for the Raj. This confounds a conceptualization of Muslims as either "legitimate" – religiously oriented and thus rebellious – or as betraying the ethno-religious community in order to be "legitimate" subjects of the Crown. Sir Syed is thus an interesting study in identity and identification politics, knowledge construction, and rhetorics around minoritization and belonging – he demands and demonstrates Muslim agency while supporting British rule.

Despite remaining a loyal supporter of British rule in India throughout his lifetime, Khan did not indiscriminately support British policies and activities. It is certainly possible to read Khan as an apologist who tried to contort and conform his various identities into acceptable and comprehensible modes for British elites. This would be reductive, however, and may also miss what scholar Faisal Devji, echoing the renowned historian Fazlur Rahman, suggests is a relative gain for Indian Muslims: "apologetic modernity," as Devji terms it, afforded men like Sir Syed the space, time, and relative freedom to slowly and intellectually define and craft "a moral community transcending the particularity of royal, clerical or mystical authority."[6] Sir Syed's loyalism and Muslim modernism were not at odds, and if we take Devji's argument, these ideologies and socio-religious locations uniquely positioned him as an author of a "moral community" bent toward redefining authority.

In this chapter, I examine Sir Syed's analysis of the Great Rebellion and the subjectivity of Muslims in British India. I first explore his earliest writings on the events of 1857, *Causes of the Indian Revolt* (*Asbāb-i baghāvat-i Hind*), to establish his immediate reactions to the Rebellion, as well as his concern that Muslims be unfairly blamed. Second, I closely examine Sir Syed's *Review on Dr Hunter's Indian Musalmans*, a distinctively Indian Muslim critique of Hunter's influential text. His writings highlight the ways the Great Rebellion fundamentally altered perceptions how Indian Muslims were perceived by Britons and Indian Muslims themselves.

Khan's loyalties to the Crown make his work an interesting site of dissent and assent, denunciation and acceptance after and in light of the 1857 Rebellion. While challenging Hunter and drawing British attention to the Empire's mistreatment of its Muslim subjects, Sir Syed simultaneously promulgated British conceptualizations of the Great Rebellion, Muslims, and loyalty. He employed religiously framed debates, arguments rooted in religion, and religious identifications to critique imperialism while maintaining allegiance to the British Empire.

In the immediate aftermath of the 1857 Rebellion, popular sentiment identified Muslims as uniquely culpable; Sir Syed Ahmad Khan's writings reflected this historical and social context while contesting the depiction of Muslims as *naturally* rebellious.

Sir Syed on the Great Rebellion

Khan's rejoinder to Hunter was not his first publication related to Muslim loyalty generally or to the Great Rebellion specifically. In 1858, scant months after the first events of the Rebellion occurred, Sir Syed wrote *Causes of the Indian Revolt (Asbāb-i baghāvat-i Hind)*, which was published in Urdu in 1859[7] and in English in 1873.[8] In the immediate wake of the Great Rebellion, Britons and Indians alike scrambled to explain – often for different purposes – what had happened, who was responsible, and how it might be avoided (or cultivated) again. Sir Syed penned *Causes of the Indian Revolt* in 1858, when some skirmishes, massacres, and rebellions were still taking place across northern India.

Sir Syed's essay is, in this way, a kind of first responder text: what he chose to prioritize in his essay signals not only what preoccupied his personal thoughts, but a conversation in which he was participating and to which he was responding. *Causes of the Indian Revolt* thus suggests a broader conversation than the later 1871–2 intertextual exchange between Sir Syed and Hunter. Though he refuted the implication that Muslims were inclined toward jihad and rebellion, Sir Syed wrote extensively on religiously defined or inflected trespasses against Muslims and Hindus. Khan's writings demonstrated and reinscribed religion – and specifically Islam – as an interpretive framework for the Great Rebellion.

Khan's initial remarks on the 1857 Rebellion, *Causes of the Indian Revolt*, were republished and translated into English within months of the publication of his rejoinder to Hunter.[9] At the center of both texts is Khan's call for Britons' just treatment of Muslim subjects in the wake of the Great Rebellion. In *Causes of the Indian Revolt*, Sir Syed forcefully argued that the Great Rebellion was not jihad and that it did not represent tenets of Islam. He further contended that, while the rebels did not represent Islam, Muslims under British rule had suffered transgressions that might make rebellion appealing. Specifically, Khan critiqued governmental support of Christianity – perceived or real, tacit or explicit – to the exclusion of other religions, especially Hinduism and Islam. Governmental preference for Christianity, Khan argued, had eroded Indians' trust in their Christian, British rulers. *Causes of the Indian Revolt* enumerated a collection of seemingly small infractions that, taken as a whole, indicated two things: first, a palpable shift, tied to the changes set forth in the Charter Act of 1813,[10] in the ways that Britons and the British government treated the population that it ruled; second, that these infractions were undoubtedly tied to religion.

Sir Syed identified religion as a primary cause of the Great Rebellion, but he emphasized that acts of Christians and imposition of Christianity were catalysts. Winifred Sullivan's use of small-p protestantism is instructive once again here: Sir Syed did not locate the problem in Christianity or Christians, but perhaps he did in small-c christianity, which is to say, the acts of a Christian majority in the name of rule, civilization, and proper behavior.[11] Khan believed that the genuine causes of the revolts centered on a series of offenses that threatened Hindus and Muslims. Despite his passionate vocalization of Indians' dissatisfactions, Sir Syed intended neither to defend rebellion nor to justify the behavior of rebels. Yet he adamantly maintained that the rebels' claims and actions responded to vital wrongs that Britons ought to have known about – and correct.

From the outset of *Causes of the Indian Revolt*, Khan maintained that Indians – Hindus and Muslims alike – were dissatisfied, disillusioned, and even affronted by British policies and actions.[12] He remarked that the rebels largely came from disadvantaged classes "who had nothing to lose, the governed not the governing class."[13] He went as far as to suggest that Indians did not despise their foreign rulers, nor even foreign rule writ large. He argued: "we must reject the idea that the natives of this country rose of one accord to throw off the yoke of foreigners, whom they hated and detested," and continued, saying "Hindu and Mussalman, all who have been under English rule have been well content to sit under its shadow."[14] Sir Syed's text first established that *Indians* found themselves impinged upon by British rule, but did not collectively aim to cast off a hated enemy. He contended that Muslims were no different from Hindus insofar as a general sense of disillusionment was concerned, and thus he challenged in his first pages of analysis of the Great Rebellion the conceptualization that Muslims, inimitably, bore the weight of responsibility for anti-imperial revolts.

While Khan linked Hindus and Muslims as similarly disaffected, he also pointed out the distinctive concerns for Britons raised by Muslims. He argued that Muslims were neither distinctively violent nor rebellious and declared: "There are again no grounds for supposing that the

Muhammadans had for a long time been conspiring or plotting a simultaneous rise, or a religious crusade against the professors of a different faith."[15] But, as he further developed the "compilation of causes" for the Rebellion, he contended that "there was little doubt" that Muslims were "in every respect more dissatisfied than the Hindus," and so one might expect to find Muslims "in many districts the greater proportion of rebels."[16] Khan appears to have been sympathetic to British concerns, and aware of some of the initial and numerical claims that Muslims made up the greatest proportion of rebels. However, his sympathies did not shield Britons from critique.

He listed grievances and trespasses against Muslims, committed by Britons individually as well as by British rule epistemologically. Sir Syed cited religion – and specifically Christian religion supplanting "native" religions – as crucially important here, even as he argued that Muslims were not banding together to wage jihad on Christians. He noted that Britons had not taken up religion as a focus of policy in their earlier days of rule, but that it had presently become a grave concern. "Hindustanees," regardless of caste or creed, understood this increased focus on religion – in terms of conversion, and a diminished sense of freedom of practice – to be part of "Government," either officially or unofficially.[17]

A particularly salient example is the actions of Britons and British organizations, including governmental institutions, after the drought of 1837. The drought and its related famine, dubbed the Agra famine, wrought devastating effects on the North-West Provinces. In what he calls a "conservative estimate" based upon extant primary sources, historian Sanjay Sharma reports that by the end of 1838 over 800,000 people had died of starvation or illness related to the famine.[18] Khan documented that in the wake of the drought of 1837, many orphans were taken in by British organizations and reared "in principles of Christian faith," which he suggested "was looked upon throughout N. W. P. [North-West Provinces] as an example of the schemes of Government."[19] This sort of education and assistance to orphans caused great disconcert, as it aimed to undo their *natural* religions. "It was supposed," Khan suggested, "that when Government had similarly brought all Hindustanees to a pitch of ignorance and poverty, it would convert them to its own creed."[20] By centering orphans – paradigms of bodies in dire straits and dire need – Khan highlighted British altruistic programs and placed them within the context of imperial persuasion. If the support of British governance was a system by which "Hindustanees'" religions would be altered, then this seemed not a program of aid but rather one of purposeful destruction. Sir Syed implied that British policies and rule would purposefully impoverish Indians in order to convert them to Christianity from their natural religions.

Sir Syed foregrounded intersections of religion, religious identity, and institutional structures in his explication of causes of the Rebellion. He cited missionary schools in some regions, claiming that they were compulsory in some parts of northern India and that they were ruthless in pushing Christianity upon their students;[21] he enumerated issues around language instruction, pointing toward differences in caste- and religion-affiliated tongues;[22] he brought up the "messing system" at jails, in which Muslims and Hindus were subject to eating food from a singular kitchen and preparation system, rather than having their communities' religious dietary needs met;[23] and, finally, he lamented the British approach to liberties for women, reasoning that such issues irritated Muslims and Hindus alike and inserted Government in the realm of family and religious comportment.[24] Khan listed issues affecting *religious* norms and authority.

As evidence of Indian discontent, Sir Syed cited the perception that British laws meddled in personal affairs, specifically referencing Act XXI of 1850, better known as the Caste Disabilities Removal Act, which altered the ways in which inheritance and taxation on inheritances functioned. Its primary purpose was to ensure that Christian converts still received inheritance and thus aimed to make inheritance laws more equitable.[25] Despite these aims, Khan stated: "This act was thought to have been passed with the view of cozening men into Christianity."[26] The act targeted the standard and religiously articulated practice of stripping converts of familial inheritance rights.[27]

Yet Khan reserved his most palpable rancor for British missionaries. He contended that missionaries were a direct source of anxiety and upset for Indians, writing:

It is commonly believed that Government appointed Missionaries and maintained them at its own cost. It has been supposed that Government, and the officers of Government throughout the

country were in the habit of giving large sums of money to these
Missionaries [. . .] and thus it happened *that no man felt sure his creed
would last even his own lifetime.*[28]

These are deep-rooted fears that not only pointed to culpability of
Britons and the British government, but also expressed a simmering
bewilderment and desperation. Most men, Sir Syed observed, assumed
their religion would perish before they did. This is a terminal prognosis
with Britons as the catalysts to creedal fatality. Britons were implicated
individually, in the persons of officers who donated financially to
missions and missionaries, and institutionally, as the British government
was imagined to support missions.

Beyond their promulgation of Christianity with substantial financial
support, missionaries were particularly upsetting for Sir Syed because they
did not follow the given norms of north India. Myriad denominations
and faiths preached conversion, but in his estimation, those preachers'
audiences were their own communities – fire and brimstone was reserved
for one's place of worship, not the marketplace. For Sir Syed, missionaries,
on the other hand, were supported by the government *and* conducted their
proselytization in public arenas, like "markets [. . .] and fairs where men of
different creeds were collected together."[29] He nimbly wove a critique of
missionaries with one of British rule, reporting that these public displays
of missionizing were often "attended by police,"[30] thus benefiting from
governmental protection to missionaries even in periods when
proselytizing was formally discouraged.[31]

Sir Syed also lamented that missionaries did not limit their public
pronouncements to their own texts, but instead:

> In violent and measured language they attacked the followers and
> holy places of other creeds: annoying, and insulting beyond
> expression the feelings of those who listened to them. In this way,
> too, the seeds of discontent were sown deep in the hearts of the
> people.[32]

Khan brings to the fore the reckless way Britons treated followers of
Indian religions. In the immediate aftermath of the revolts and
massacres, Sir Syed considered trespasses to religious sensibilities to
incite revolutionary ideologies and supporters; he argued that whether

these trespasses were insensitive or calculated, they yielded an insulted populace and courted revolt.

Of course, in *Causes of the Indian Revolt*, he did not ignore "non-religious" factors like economic and political disenfranchisement. Khan cited the "resumption of revenue free lands" as "most obnoxious," specifically mentioning Sir Thomas Munro – whose testimony is likewise cited as part of the East India Company charter hearings[33] – and the Duke of Wellington as perpetrators of these policies and the troubles they wrought.[34] He suggested that these economic policies – taken together with the religiously inflected grievances listed above – stood to prove that the English simply did not understand their subjects. Of course, some of these economic policies were an affront precisely because they impeded upon religious laws or customs, as in the case of inheritance laws. He lamented that no Briton *wanted* to know his subjects, because "almost all look forward to retirement in their native land and seldom settle for good amongst the natives of India."[35] Khan critiqued the problems of repatriation – of Britons never being nor becoming Indian, always remaining strangers in a strange land. Sir Syed concluded his relatively brief *Causes of the Indian Revolt* with an exhortation to better rule: "When by the Divine Will, Hindustan became an appendage of the Crown of Great Britain, it was the duty of Government to enquire into and lessen as much as possible the sufferings of its subjects."[36] Khan appealed to a British understanding of a social contract as a way to exhort his readers to see the Rebellion as a complex web of issues of religion, economics, and politics, and all of the overlapping interactions between these fluid categories.

Causes of the Indian Revolt articulated Sir Syed's reasoned supports and critiques of the British and the Rebellion alike. It was a well-cited essay,[37] and the 1873 English translation contained an appendix of official documents. For example, it included an infamous 1855 letter by E. Edmond, a British missionary stationed in Calcutta, which highlighted official attitudes toward conversion, namely, that the British Empire ought to be entirely Christian.[38] It also contained the lieutenant governor of Bengal's reply to disquiet among Hindus and Muslims caused by missionaries, in which he denounced Edmond's and other missionaries' unsanctioned writings and proclamations and attempted to assuage local unease.[39] In the text, Khan engaged these authors as evidence that Britons, officially and unofficially, were culpable for offending Indians by saying too much, as in the case of Edmond, and by offering too little far too late, as in the case of the lieutenant governor. Unlike Hunter, Khan does not represent the disquiet in a framework dominated by religious pronouncements (fatwas) about the rights of Britons to rule nor did he spend much time on particular theological points, like technicalities of debates about jihad, *dar-ul-islam*, or *dar-ul-harb*.

Sir Syed did in fact write at some length about jihad in *Causes of the Indian Revolt*, more to refute jihad's centrality to the revolt than to identify it as a primary factor. Although he did not specifically address other commentaries on the Rebellion, his tone, the structure of the argument, and the defensiveness of certain positions indicate that Sir Syed was arguing *against* positions that were widely disseminated and well-known. Both jihad and its imbrication with the viability and possibility of Muslim subjecthood are paramount in Sir Syed's writings on the Rebellion. Sir Syed's reflections on the Great Rebellion address both the problems in Britons' definitions and understandings of jihad as well as corresponding conclusions about Indian Muslim subjecthood. In both *Causes of the Indian Revolt* and *Review on Dr Hunter's Indian Musalmans*, Sir Syed maintained that Britons' falsely construed requirement of jihad broadly and as a catalyst for the Rebellion in particular led to the equally false notion that Indian Muslims were inherently predisposed toward rebellion and thus unfit subjects.

Sir Syed bluntly declared all acts committed by Muslims during the Rebellion to be outside the pale of Islam and counter to all its precepts. In *Causes of the Indian Revolt*, he wrote: "The Mahomedans did not contemplate Jehad against the Christians prior to outbreak [of rebellion]."[40] He added:

> None of the acts committed by the Mahomedan rebels during the disturbances were in accordance with the tenets of the Mahomedan religion. The Futwa of Jehad printed at Delhie was a counterfeit one − a large number of Moulvies who considered the King of Delhi a violator of the Law, left off praying in the Royal Mosque.[41]

Khan contended that the fatwa cited by many Britons as evidence that the Great Rebellion was jihad − which Hunter cited later, too − was fraudulent.[42] In his introductory remarks, Sir Syed roundly dismissed the idea that violence inherent in Muslims or Islam played a role in causing the revolt.

Ultimately, *Causes of the Indian Revolt* exemplifies Sir Syed's initial and ongoing evaluation of the Great Rebellion, which foregrounded a sense of native religious subjugation to foreign, Christian power as a primary issue behind Indian alienation and unrest. Although he focused on religious issues, he was keen to demonstrate that issues of religious *war* were not at play. He strongly articulated that jihad was neither called for nor appropriate within authentic Islamic law, even despite Britons' problematic curtailing of religious liberties for Muslims, especially in Bengal and other north Indian provinces.[43] Sir Syed did not disavow British rule altogether in this text or elsewhere, and neither did he offer his support to the rebels. Instead, he presented, in the months following the events of 1857, a reasoned attempt to explain why "Hindustanees" and, of those, Muslims in particular would find motivation to revolt, with the purpose of communicating to Britons what they seemed unable to hear previously.

Many of the religious issues that Sir Syed identified as important causes of the Rebellion spoke to a British ignorance, whether willful or accidental, about the importance of religious mores and norms. These included like the messing system at prisons, which had previously allowed for prisoners to abide by Brahmin, casted food pollution laws as well as by Islamic dietary practices. It also included the conceptualization of proper public religiosity; Khan expressed deep distaste for Christian missionary activities in the marketplaces – not necessarily because of the work itself, but rather because of its location in a shared space. Khan also drew his readers' attention to the more nefarious actions of the British during and after the Agra famine of 1837–8; he implied that British officials failed to act during the famine, and then after it saw orphaned children as an opportunity to rear Indians in Christianity. Sir Syed poignantly acknowledged that both Hindus and Muslims feared that their religions would not last their lifetimes.[44] The 1857 revolts, for Khan, were not religious warfare, but rather the consequence of British indifference to religion in India. His work, geared toward a British audience, demanded that Britons take responsibility for their infractions against Indians and especially Muslims even as it disavowed the actions of the rebels.

When *Causes of the Indian Revolt* appeared in English, many Britons cited it as a particularly helpful view to "native" sentiments, and many suggested that Sir Syed's account was especially valuable because of its reliability. He was well regarded and highly respected by British elites; while British observers did not accept his critiques as assessments as readily as those by British historians and commentators, his views still stood as notable examples of authentic Indian and Muslim opinion. For example, Lieutenant-Colonel G. F. I. Graham – a high-ranking officer and a friend of Sir Syed – later remarked, in his biography of Syed Ahmad Khan, that:

> Although some of us may not agree with Syed Ahmed's 'Causes of the Revolt,' the pamphlet is exceedingly valuable, as giving us an insight into native modes of thought, and as written by the ablest of our loyal Mohammedan gentlemen.[45]

He similarly reported the high estimation of Khan by his fellow Britons, who praised his courage and bravery, his truthfulness, and his manliness.[46]

Some 15 years later, in reply to W. W. Hunter, Syed Ahmad Khan revisited his assessment of the Great Rebellion and reexamined British insistence that jihad was its primary cause and that Muslims might not be able to live peaceably under British rule. His interpretation of 1857's revolts stayed remarkably consistent. This implies other consistencies in Indian and British popular understandings of the 1857 Rebellion: the ongoing characterization of the Great Rebellion as a disproportionately Muslim (or Muslim-initiated) revolt; Muslims as uniquely bound to their religious laws; and Islam as uniquely bent toward religious warfare. These issues – and Sir Syed's refutations thereof – reappear with more vigor and urgency in his *Review on Dr Hunter's Indian Musalmans: Are They Bound in Conscience to Rebel Against the Queen?* (1872).

An Academic Rejoinder to *Indian Musalmans*

By 1872, Syed Ahmad Khan was more than a famous persona; he was a well-established Muslim thinker, having given numerous speeches and lectures, and written widely on issues of modernity and modernism, science and education, religion and governance. In 1872, he wrote a response to Hunter's *Indian Musalmans* (1871), only a year after its initial publication, and the same year its reprint with updated preface – which Khan engaged – appeared. His response was in the form of a review – an academic critique and analysis of what was Hunter's academic work.[47] But this was not a hasty reply, nor was its intent to vehemently invalidate Hunter or his work. Rather, Khan's *Review on Dr Hunter's Indian Musalmans* (hereafter, *Review*) was written to better express "Mahomedan feeling in India" in light of Hunter's work and of "Wahabi trials" and "the murder of Chief Justice Norman."[48] Its audience, it seems, was specifically English: Hunter's text was published in London and in English, and though *Review* was written in Urdu, it was published, reissued, and more widely distributed in English. In it, Sir Syed set about to dismantle Hunter's argument point by point, and he assumed basic familiarity with *Indian Musalmans*. Khan's *Review* followed the organization of Hunter's work exactly, in fact.

In this rejoinder, Sir Syed quoted Hunter at length, and where appropriate, offered differing interpretations of Hunter's Islamicate source material, like fatwas and historical information. His tone is, at once, serious and flippant. At times, the *Review* reads like an impassioned, critical reproach of an influential academic text, and at other times, it is clear that Sir Syed was exasperated with what he found to be outlandish characterizations of India, history, Islam, or Indian Muslims. Despite speaking to Britons as part of his audience, Sir Syed did not shy from addressing their offensive stereotypes of Indians as ignorant, lazy, or stupid. He introduced his review by declaring: "I am aware that many of the ruling race in India are under the impression that English literature, both books and newspapers, seldom, if ever, permeates the strata of native society."[49] He added that "native society" was well informed on matters of "the state of feeling of the English to the natives, religious questions, or matters affecting taxation."[50]

Sir Syed declared that natives were neither uninformed nor unaware, and having established himself and others as reliable informants and critics, he launched his *Review*. He began a thorough critique of Hunter, one that dismantled not only the interpretations and usage of certain texts and evidence, but also the position of power from which he spoke. He argued:

> What books and newspapers enunciate is, by the general native public, believed to be the opinion of the whole English

community – official or non-official – from the veriest clerk to the Governor General in Council – aye, even to the Queen herself!⁵¹

In the preface to the second edition of *Indian Musalmans* (1872), Hunter had used the term "demi-official" to describe the work, and he had carefully attempted to distance his opinions from those of the government, claiming that he spoke only as himself and not on behalf of the British Empire – a disclaimer, as it were.[52] Khan took to task the very idea Hunter put forth that the general reading public, Indian and British, *believed* works like Hunter's to represent the opinion of the imperial regime (with good cause[53]). Hunter represented the Crown whether or not he wanted to, and his work represented the thoughts of the "whole English community," as far as Khan was concerned. Sir Syed thus offered not just a critique of Hunter, but of imperial power.

While taking Hunter's claims of objective, distanced scholarship to task, Sir Syed was careful neither to launch an *ad hominem* attack nor to do anything that might result in being accused of doing so. He wrote that Hunter was a "friend to the Mahomedan," but "his last work [...] has worked us [Muslims] great harm."[54] He was likewise direct about the consequences, implications, and what he perceived as sloppiness of Hunter's often-bombastic language in *Indian Musalmans*. Khan argued that though Hunter "expressly states" he was only writing about "Bengal Mahomedans," the provocative title, along with numerous passages, "gives us the general feeling of Mahomedans through out India."[55] Khan took explicit issue with Hunter's very premise that his claims were limited, regionally specific, and rooted in observation. He added, with characteristic bluntness, a direct challenge to Hunter's work: "I must raise my voice in opposition to Dr Hunter in defense of my fellow-countrymen."[56]

Despite his bold and direct critiques, Sir Syed acknowledged that his personal identity and relationship to Islam would be held against him as he challenged Hunter's claims. He wrote: "The English, who are unacquainted with the general run of Mahomedan opinion, will probably deem me an interested partizan [*sic*], and will pay small attention, or place little reliance on, what I think and write. This, however, must not deter me from speaking what I know to be truth."[57] Sir Syed understood the conundrum of offering his assessment: as a Muslim, he assumed a position of insider knowledge and familiarity with texts and attitudes Hunter had particularly misunderstood, but, also as a Muslim, his very identity rendered him an unreliable interpreter. Nevertheless, Khan specifically addressed the same audience as Hunter, both in and outside India, and in this way, constructed a conversation between two learned elites.

I submit that this was a conversation – unequal in its power dynamic, incomplete insofar as *dialogue* is concerned (after all, these are two freestanding textual statements), but a conversation nevertheless. Its rhetorical power is in the discourse it both represents and propels. Sir Syed noted his minoritized status and pointed out that such a status rendered it nearly impossible to alter impressions made by a member of the powerful elite. Further, he noted that Hunter's assessment of Indian Muslims persuaded the Indian public. He highlighted the ways in which Hunter's work was meant for elite readers – likely elite readers in the metropole – and yet influenced readers well beyond London, including his "fellow countrymen." Sir Syed's *Review* demonstrates the ways in which imperial intellectual products (be they "demi-official" or otherwise) influences the crafting of imperialized identities, histories, and movements. In his *Review*, Sir Syed engaged with Hunter largely on Hunter's terms. Even when denying the efficacy of his arguments, Khan did not fundamentally reject Hunter's proof-texts, presumptions of a pan-Islamic identity, or the heavily textual or literal nature of Indian Muslims.

Khan certainly found many faults in Hunter's work, but *Review* is not a polemical takedown. It is, rather, a complex text that reflects and replicates normative positions on religion, Islam, and Muslims even as it attempts to problematize and clarify assumed misunderstandings about these very subjects. We can productively compare how Khan and Hunter utilized sources, evidence, and terminology to parse Muslims' subjecthood and loyalty. To maintain specific focus on the primary nodes of analysis at work in Sir Syed's *Review*, I do not follow his organizational structure, but instead prioritize his arguments. These include the problematic conflation of Wahhabism with Islam, and the construction of jihad as a central factor in the Rebellion; Khan crafts his chief critiques of these two issues by showing that Hunter's glosses on Islamic texts are problematic, and sometimes incorrect, and by highlighting Hunter's assumption that Muslims cannot be loyal.

This pair of issues in Hunter's work – first, an assumed relationship between literalist Wahhabism and authentic "true Islam," and second, a textual requirement to rebellion or jihad – are not easily separated into freestanding, cogent entities. However, both Hunter and Khan constructed this dyad, and in the process they produced a framework for understanding the Muslim subject. Khan's *Review* attempted to disrupt Hunter's findings, but ultimately it failed to dislodge the inherent assumptions at play in such categorizations. Sir Syed's text successfully dismantled Hunter's assertions, but it fell short of questioning the *question* of whether Muslims could be loyal subjects.

A Legalism of His Own: Sir Syed on Hunter's Use of Islamic Law

Throughout the *Review*, Sir Syed examined – and finally roundly refuted – Hunter's use of Islamic laws, be they specific fatwas or general principles like jihad or *zakat* (charity). He offered line-by-line corrections of Hunter's use of fatwas, specifically in terms of literal meaning and intention. Sir Syed criticized Hunter for misquoting Maulvi Ismail of Delhi's *Sirát-ul-Mustakím* (1818).[58] He argued that Hunter's fixation on jihad, and his catalogs of the instances in which jihad had been legally declared and supported by Muslims, had nothing to do with the British at all, but instead with Sikhs,[59] thereby questioning the specific threat Muslims posed to the Crown – Hunter's titular concern. He offered a reading of *Indian Musalmans* that suggested a fundamental, egregious misread of the issues at stake:

> It appears the learned doctor has mistaken the word *Ijtehád*, which means 'to use one's own reason and understanding,' for *jehad*, and consequently falls into the error of supposing that it relates to entering on religious war.[60]

Sir Syed accused Hunter of mistaking the principle of engaged interpretation (*ijtihād*) with waging religious war (*jihād*), principles represented by Arabic terms that derive from the same root but which have rather different meanings. He effectively accused Hunter of missing the point, and of basing his gloss on such an issue so pressing to his own argument on an error. This is not a benign correction; to my eyes, it is a full-fledged attack on the veracity of Hunter's work.

Sir Syed accordingly assessed Hunter's use of Islamic legal categories, moving to the characterization of *dar-ul-harb* and *dar-ul-islam*, the distinction between countries of war and peace. "It is a great mistake to suppose that a country can only either be a *Dar-ul-Islam* or a *Dar-ul-Harb* in the primary signification of the words, and that there is no intermediate position," he argued.[61] He suggested (as he had elsewhere[62] and as others had similarly attested[63]) that, in fact, India was "both at present."[64] Hunter's fixation on whether the entirety of India could or would be deemed a space in which Muslims would be forced to rebel, on the basis of its status as a region hostile toward or supportive of Islam, did not resonate with Khan's understanding of the legal parameters of such distinctions.

Nor did it conform to Sir Syed's standards of historical facticity: he accused Hunter of manipulating information to prove his point. Hunter used a fatwa by Shah Abdul Aziz (d. 1823), to demonstrate that India was indeed in a state of *dar-ul-harb*.[65] Khan accused him of missing the second part of Shah Abdul Aziz's ruling, however, which defined *dar-ul-harb* as:

> when the power of the Infidels increases to such an extent that they can abolish or retain the ordinance of Islam according to their pleasure, such a country is politically a country of the enemy (*Dar-ul-Harb*).[66]

Khan implied that this qualitative nuance – foreign rule was a nonissue until and unless it interfered with the practice of Islam – had not happened, and thus Hunter's concerns were unfounded. Moreover, Hunter used this fatwa to demonstrate that India could and should be read as a country of the enemy in light of the official shift in 1858 in British rule, which is to say, in the aftermath of the Great Rebellion. Thus Hunter argued for greater vigilance after the British had decisively quashed revolt. Khan, however, did not understand this interpretation, and pointedly stated: "He {Hunter} also forgets the important fact that Shah Abdul Aziz gave out the *futwa*, declaring India *Dar-ul-Harb*, during his life-time, some fifty years ago, when none of the charges owing to which Dr. Hunter says India became *Dar-ul-Harb* had taken place!"[67]

Sir Syed's objections were not limited to Hunter's legal and historical analysis or sources. He likewise found Hunter's logical extrapolations of his own conclusions to be suspect. He wondered how Hunter could assert that India was indeed *dar-ul-harb*. Khan restated Hunter's evidence: Mahomed Wajih and Fazl-ul-Rahman claimed that Muslims had stopped the basic practice of Islam because of India's legal status,

specifically mentioning that Muslims had stopped praying on Fridays.[68]
Sir Syed rather disagreed with these assertions, stating that there were
few requirements to make *jummah* prayers in any state of country, and
cited the Hanafi, Shafi'i, and Wahhabi legal traditions to demonstrate
legal continuity and consensus among these *madhāhib* on this very
issue.[69] Sir Syed fundamentally stressed that Hunter had misinterpreted
what *dar-ul-harb* meant and how prayers – the most basic observance –
functioned. It seems that this lack of logical coherence within *Indian
Musalmans* was jarring to Khan, whose tone in this section noticeably
turned toward derisive.

Sir Syed appeared similarly jarred by Hunter's insistence that in
either case – whether India was *dar-ul-harb* or *dar-ul-islam* – Muslims
could *at best* acquiesce to British rule. In an attempt to demonstrate
Muslims' willingness and perhaps even theological disposition toward
living under Christian rule, he cited the Qur'an. Sir Syed quoted a
passage of which George Sale's translation was offered in the *Review:*

> Thou shalt surely find the most violence of all men in enmity
> against the true believers to be the Jews and the idolators: and
> thou shalt surely find those among them to be the most inclinable
> to entertain friendship for true believers who say we are Christians.
> This cometh to pass because there are priests and monks among
> them, and because they are not elated with pride.[70]

It is worth noting that by utilizing the Qur'an, Khan rhetorically
positioned his argument about the legal and religious wonts of Muslims
over and above Hunter's: Hunter cited only jurists, not the Qur'an
specifically. There is, in other words, an authenticity claim inherent in
Khan's direct use of the holy text.

He then critiqued Hunter and British rule, declaring that:

> Like begets likes; and if cold acquiescence is all that Mahomedans
> receive at the hands of the ruling race, Dr Hunter must not be
> surprised at the cold acquiescence of the Mahomedan community.
> Let us both – Christians and Mahomedans – remember and act
> upon the words of Jesus Christ: 'Therefore all things whatsoever ye
> would that men should do to you, do even so to them: for this is
> the law and the Prophets.' (Matthew, Chapter VII:12)[71]

Sir Syed employed the holy books of both Islam and Christianity in order to demonstrate first that Muslims could willingly and happily live under Christian rule, but second that the "golden rule" applied to all – should Muslims be treated coldly by the British, they were apt to treat their rulers badly as well. Such a move perhaps reflects an intention to compare Muslims and Christians on an equal footing, a comparison that routinely turned inimical in Hunter's text.

Khan seemed repeatedly befuddled, asking his reader rhetorical questions about Hunter's misunderstandings, misreads, and misappropriation of textual sources, analysis, and quotations. It is therefore perhaps counterintuitive that Khan often did not disagree with Hunter's factual assertions even while he eagerly countered Hunter's interpretations of those facts. Sir Syed did not, for example, deny that jihad is a real legal category for warfare; he did not attempt to prove, as some have and continue to, that jihad properly refers to a struggle within oneself, or nearly impossible conditions for producing war.[72] He did, however, strenuously – perhaps incredulously – demand that Hunter account for the supposed conditions in which Muslims' ability to practice their religion had been so limited so as to merit warfare. He wrote:

> Now we Mahomedans of India live in this country with every sort of religious liberty; we discharge the duties of our faith with perfect freedom; we read our Azans [calls to prayer] as loud as we wish; we can preach our faith on the public roads and thoroughfares as freely as Christian missionaries preach theirs; we fearlessly write and publish our answers to the charges laid against Islam by the Christian clergy; and last, though not least, we make converts of Christians to Islam without fear or prohibition.[73]

To back his clear assertion that Muslims in India enjoyed religious freedom, Sir Syed cited tangible and regular examples of praxis, both the masses who so terrified Hunter as well as of the elite Muslims Hunter discredited. Khan's choice to conclude this line of argument with conversion was bold and effective. It is an undeniable demonstration that even the most controversial of religious freedoms – the freedom to add to their numbers, to recruit new Muslims – was safeguarded under British rule.

This powerfully written section of Khan's rejoinder offered an answer to Hunter's titular question – an answer given in a number of ways throughout *Review*. Sir Syed argued that Muslims were not bound to rebel because the legal categories of jihad had simply not been met. He clarified further in his answer to a hypothetical question Hunter posed in a footnote about whether, in the event of a Muslim-led invasion of British India, Muslim subjects would be doubly bound to rebel: first, because they were already bound, and second, because the invaders were Muslim and thus assured to offer a proper *dar-ul-islam*.[74] But Khan allayed this reasoning altogether, and declared that British Muslims would be "sinners" should they rebel against the English and help an imagined Muslim invader.[75] He wrote: "My reply {to this question} is therefore that in no case would it be the religious duty of any man to renounce the Aman {religious liberty} of the English, and render help to the invader."[76]

Khan disputed Hunter's assertion that Muslims were inherently disloyal, bound by religious laws that entailed the obligation to rebel. Instead, he celebrated the religious freedoms granted by Christian, British rule. Hunter saw a necessary conflict with British, Christian rulers who were imposing new laws, regulations, and norms; fundamentally, he saw the very presence of the British Empire within India – and former Mughal India, at that – as an inherent challenge to Islamic law, and thus call to arms for Muslims. While Khan and Hunter agreed on the facts – the British instituted new laws, and their presence caused their new subjects to assess what these laws meant – they did not arrive at the same conclusion. Hunter ultimately could not see past the fact that categories of war, peace, and justified combat *exist* in Islam and, more precisely, Islamic law. Sir Syed not only demonstrated that legal conditions for jihad had not been met, but also argued for and from the perspective of the lived reality of British rule.

Sir Syed noted, however, that despite these freedoms and benefits, hypothetical questions and answers were just that – hypothetical. "I cannot predict what the actual conduct of the Musalmans would be in the event of an invasion of India by Mahomedan or any other power," and, importantly, he wondered if the British were making similar inquiries about Hindu loyalty in the face of imagined invaders.[77] Khan acknowledged a rift – perceived or actual – between Britons' rule over Muslims and their rule over Hindus, pointing toward an understanding of inequality or, at the very least, incongruity in how each religious group related with their government. Lest we assume that he thought the British wholly unfair or unjust, he stated: "It is not to be expected that Mahomedans, who are made of much sterner material than Hindus, will adapt themselves so readily to the various phases of this changing age."[78] Like Hunter, Sir Syed saw Muslims as a distinctive group with categorical identity traits. In Khan's terms, Muslims were "stern" (or at least sterner than their Hindu counterparts) and naturally less willing or able to adapt to British rule.

Nonetheless, where Hunter continually asserted that Britons had both unknowingly and purposefully injured the egos and persons of Muslims, Khan acknowledged these transgressions but denied their import. He wrote: "enlightened Mahomedans are perfectly aware that they cannot expect the same regard for their customs and for their system of education from a foreign government, as they enjoyed under rulers of their own faith."[79] Specifically, Khan mentioned that the abolition of the "Kázis" (Ur., *qazi*, Ar. *qāḍī*, lit., Islamic jurist) was a "grave political error" that nevertheless did not interfere with the faith. He added, "the better class of Mahomedans had but little respect for them."[80] There are classist assumptions at work in this sentiment, and Sir Syed's regal ties perhaps shine brighter here than elsewhere: modernists like Khan often viewed *qazi*s and other members of the traditional Muslim ulama with contempt. However, this does not necessarily capture the general Muslim public who sought counsel from and trusted the legal rulings of the *qazi*s.[81] Khan's insistence that enlightened and better classes of Muslims existed demonstrates a sense of authenticity and real Islam – just as much as Hunter's observations make clear a sense of authenticity and real Islam. In other words, Khan's pronouncements assumed an authentic Muslim who placed little value in the juridical issues raised by Hunter, and they likewise imagined an authentic Muslim community not only of Muslims under British rule, but of Muslims writ large.

Sir Syed asserted that some Muslims did not respect the jurists, and, more importantly, he recognized that a change in rule would have religious, economic, and legal ramifications. Khan's fairly prosaic claim that Muslims might expect less regard for their customs under new, non-Muslim rule appealed to the reason of his (largely British) audience. In making this claim, Sir Syed subtly argued that Muslims ought to be imagined as having a commonsense approach to Britons and British rule, something that Hunter left beyond their grasp.

On Muslim Loyalty

Challenges to Hunter's historical analysis, his problematic glosses of Islamic law, and his over-reliance on Wahhabism comprised a part of Khan's *Review*, but he reserved his most withering critique for Hunter's assertions that Muslims ought to be understood as seditious and disloyal. Sir Syed highlighted a lengthy quote in which Hunter claimed that "fanatical" Muslims had "engaged in overt sedition," but the "whole Mahomedan community has been openly deliberating on their obligation to rebel."[82] He followed the citation with an admonishment: "Now, I have no hesitation in saying that this is one of the most unjust, illiberal, and insulting sentences even penned against my co-religionists."[83]

From this statement onward, Khan focused his critique of *Indian Musalmans* on the events of the Rebellion, as well as the legal issues that followed from it. His analysis of Hunter's inferences about the Rebellion centered on Hunter's misread of plurality, nuance, and what today we might call diversity, in belief, population, and law. Khan ably punctured Hunter's arguments of *totality*, which typifies the conclusions of *Indian Musalmans*: the Muslims Hunter envisioned and produced in that work were categorically and definitionally violent, seditious, and suspect.

Khan's language deviated from fashionable ideals of dispassionate objectivity, and demonstrated anger, frustration, and occasionally exhaustion. In one passage, he described, with increasingly bold language, the ways in which Hunter was ill equipped to speak about Muslims, as well as specific instances in which Hunter had done a disservice to his subject. He wrote about Hunter's inability to take seriously the fatwas issued in light of the Rebellion that deemed jihad inappropriate and undesirable.[84] He argued that Hunter was using his "imagination" to describe history and was "utterly wrong" in his interpretation of fatwas and jihad.[85] Khan added sharply: "the learned doctor [Hunter] has shown little discretion in not sifting more carefully the chaff from the wheat."[86]

Sir Syed addressed Hunter's characterization of the Rebellion as predominately Muslim by addressing the demographic data. After

1857–8, many Indians fled areas in which there had been violence and sought shelter in the safety of the surrounding mountainous regions; Khan and Hunter both pointed to this fact, which others later corroborated.[87] Hunter came to define these people as either part of the "border tribes," original inhabitants of the mountains, or as willing participants in the Rebellion and jihad, especially the followers of Syed Ahmed Barelvi (i.e., Wahhabis). Unlike Hunter, Khan identified them as Muslims and Hindus of varying caste identities, and while neither of our authors suggested as much, we know that those who fled also included non-casted people (those outside the pale of Hindu orthodox categorization) as well as Sikhs.[88]

Khan not only added diversity to Hunter's depiction, he took issue with Hunter's elision of such a plurality of identities. Khan argued that the existence of such a collective, motley band speaks to the problems in conceptualizing the Great Rebellion as jihad: "To assert, as Dr Hunter does, that they were there [in the mountains] for the purpose of making a religious war against the Government – composed, as their band was, of Hindus and Mahomedans of all castes and denominations – is too absurd for belief."[89]

Hunter insisted that Hindus, non-casted Indians, and Sikhs participated in an inimitably Muslim religious war. Sir Syed, in reply, suggested that Hunter's gloss on both Wahhabis and the Rebellion failed to fully account for historical fact. He held instead that the East India Company's "mutinous sepoys" had caused the initial rebellion and instigated further unrest, highlighting the British's involvement and participation in the events.[90] Moreover, he took great issue with the broad strokes Hunter used to portray Wahhabi Muslims, and in turn, Indian Muslims on the whole:

> The border tribes had also a great deal to do with the many raids and cases of kidnapping, burning and plundering of British villages; but to lay all these atrocities at the door of Syed Ahmed's followers, and through them to implicate the whole of Indian Musalmans, is monstrous in the extreme.[91]

As Sir Syed established, the "border tribes" were both a motley conglomeration of refugee Hindus and Muslims of varying castes and denominations, as well as the autochthonous groups who had made their home in the mountains and foothills of the North-West Provinces for generations.

The people of these "border tribes" or "mountain tribes" had a reputation for violence.[92] Sir Syed readily ascribed to that perception. At one point, he even played on English racisms to make a point about these tribes and discredit Hunter's assertions about Muslims:

> Our author forgets the very important fact that these mountain tribes have been turbulent from time immemorial, that they have never allowed any peace to any nation living on their frontiers, whether so-called infidels or Musalmans; that they fought indiscriminately with the Mahomedan Emperors of Delhi, and with the Sikhs in Punjab. Like the Irishman at a fair, it mattered little to them who it was as long as it was someone to fight.[93]

Like the Irish, the mountain tribes were thirsty for fights; like the British with respect to the Irish, Khan and his Muslim compatriots were fundamentally unlike those from mountain tribes. Syed Ahmad Khan thus traded on extant imperial racisms in order to prove his point and, perhaps, to demonstrate his ability to be British – or at least in terms of status, minoritization, and racialization (issues to which we will return below).

Not only did Sir Syed work to establish common ground with Britons by adopting a shared racism, he also highlighted Islamic legal sources, notably absent in Hunter's work, that spoke directly to Christian-Muslim relationships. "Mahomed himself ordered his staunchest followers to take refuge in the Christian kingdom of Abyssinia," Khan wrote, asserting that Hunter's claims were "therefore as untrue as it is uncalled for" to say that "zealous Mahomedans could not remain quietly in British territory."[94]

Hunter thus missed key texts and misused others: Khan specifically argued against Hunter's use of Islamic texts, especially fatwas, in *Indian Musalmans*. He lamented:

> Now, I frankly confess that I am at a loss what to think of Dr Hunter. I can scarcely believe that he intended to deceive or mislead his readers; but at the same time, I can hardly credit him with such gross ignorance as is here evinced.[95]

Roughly halfway into his *Review*, Sir Syed admitted to his readers that he did not know exactly what to make of Hunter's piece. He insisted that Hunter was too erudite to have made such glaring errors in haste or in ignorance, but perhaps too respected and well-known to intentionally deceive his reader. It is equally possible, of course, that Sir Syed here respectfully calls these very appellatives into question: if Hunter was so learned and commanded such cachet, how else might a reader make sense of his glaring errors except to insinuate purposefully false or exaggerated pretenses? Perhaps his confusion was not confusion, but a rhetorical strategy that allowed Khan to question whether Hunter's work should be trusted at all. His fundamental suspicion lingers across the *Review*, as Khan challenged Hunter's attempts at reading law, his stress on Islamic legalism and Wahhabism, and his reading of jihad as necessary and inevitable.

On Literalism, Wahhabism, and Jihad

Sir Syed was deeply concerned with Hunter's conflations of "Wahhabi" with "Muslim," and of "Muslim" with "traitor." Hunter presented a history of Wahhabis in India, notably using language that reflects a Protestant gloss on historicization: he called Wahhabis "reformers," and he referred to their revolutionary writings and actions as "reformations," "noble," and "a practical amendment of morals."[96] He went on to use the term "Crescentade" – an obvious play on "Crusade" – to refer to the spread of Wahhabi ideas and ideals in India, especially under the leadership of Syed Ahmed Barelvi (d. 1831). Hunter read Syed Ahmed Barelvi as a divinely sent leader, and he argued that "Indian Wahábis had claimed for Sayyid Ahmad the title of the great Imam, who should thus precede the final coming of Christ."[97] Hunter imagined the Wahhabi movement as a crusade ("Crescentade") to recapture India and its first leader, Syed Ahmed Barelvi, as a messianic figure. These conclusions – rooted in Christian theology and uniquely dangerous to the political leaders of India – dictated Hunter's read on Islam. Hunter was convinced – or at least argued convincingly – that Wahhabis were reformers bent on (re-)establishing Islam within the borders of India, and that they would do so using jihad, which he rendered "Religious War."[98]

Hunter first appealed to his readers to see Wahhabis as distinct from traitors,[99] then implied and finally stated outright that Wahhabis spoke for and to the Muslim masses, which were, undoubtedly and by definition, religiously bound to rebel.[100] Khan dismantled these claims, focusing on the shift in tone and terminology, and pointed out Hunter's sloppiness in determining who and what constituted "legitimate" Islam. Khan wrote:

> Our author cannot be consistent for even five pages. More than this, however, he brings a charge against the religion of Islam, which, from all that I have proved, is totally unfounded.[101]

Khan, as he did elsewhere in his *Review*, expressed exasperation with Hunter's variations in tone, blatant errors, and incongruous assertions.

In order to demonstrate its pervasiveness and historical reach, Hunter divided Wahhabi history in South Asia into five distinct periods, and Khan addressed each period systematically in his *Review*.[102] Sir Syed questioned Hunter's sources, his historical periodization, and the events and people he prioritized within his schema. He was most critical of Hunter's overemphasis on Wahhabism, as Hunter repeatedly stated that Wahhabi orthodoxy was rampant, a growing problem, and a prime oppositional force in British India. For example, Hunter stated that "Wahabi's [...] orthodox position" spoke to the "great body of earnest Muhammedans" in ways that moderates could not.[103] Khan restated Hunter's sentiments as such: that Wahhabi doctrine and speeches yielded "[their] constant recognition, both in theory and practice, of the obligation to wage war upon all infidels."[104]

Sir Syed simultaneously dismantled Hunter's overreliance on Wahhabism and pointed out his misinterpretations of Wahhabis in northern India. He insisted that Wahhabis encountered marked resistance as well as physical endangerment under Mughal authorities, and that in fact they had only gained extensive access to the public sphere under British rule.

> On the establishment of British rule, however, owing to the English principle of strict religious toleration, the followers of Ahal-i-Hadis again came to the front and preached openly and fiercely.[105]

The principle of "strict religious toleration" to which Sir Syed referred is a set of Enlightenment liberal values and formalized practices, and these took a number of forms in the context of imperialized India.[106]

Queen Victoria's Proclamation of 1858 is a pertinent illustration.[107] The Proclamation states: "none be in any wise favoured, none molested or disquieted, by reason of their religious faith or observances, but that all shall enjoy the equal and impartial protection of the law."[108] As historian of religion and South Asia C. S. Adcock suggests, the Queen's Proclamation encompassed the key components of religious toleration: "freedom from persecution on religious grounds, civil equality with respect to religious affiliation, and freedom of religious practice."[109] British legal and institutional policies of religious tolerance created the space in which all members of minority religions – including Wahhabis – who had been previously restricted found voice and footing within India.

Khan implicated the British in fostering the development of Wahhabi presence and influence: before their policies and principles, the Wahhabi movement had been limited by Muslim ruling elites, the unstated actors in this sentiment, the group to which Khan himself belonged and which Hunter dismissed as ineffectual and unimportant vis-à-vis the fanatic masses. Sir Syed challenged Hunter's sense of Wahhabi history in South Asia, arguing that the blanket acceptance of Wahhabi interpretation by other Muslims, on which Hunter based many of his points, was at least fraught and certainly incomplete.

Similarly, much of Hunter's focus on Wahhabi influence in South Asia relied on his gloss of Syed Ahmed Barelvi's role in history and Indian Muslim networks. Khan disputed Syed Ahmed Barelvi's religious role, stating that he was a "leader of jihads but [...] no preacher."[110] Khan's pointed remark questioned whether Syed Ahmed was a religious figure at all, let alone a proper authority. Yet still Khan did not completely dismiss Hunter's argument. He continued to debate Hunter on his terms, critiquing Hunter's gloss of Syed Ahmed as religious leader and Wahhabi jihadi. Specifically, Khan wondered why Hunter ignored the fact that Syed Ahmed did not pursue jihad against the British at the same time as Syed Ahmed and his followers declared jihad against Sikhs.[111]

Khan asked how one might read Syed Ahmed as a threat to the British if he had not taken up arms against them. Then, to demonstrate, he discussed how Mahbub-Ali did not sign a "proclamation for religious war" but told Bukht Khan "that the Mahomedan subjects of the British Government could not, according to the precepts of their religion, rise up in arms against their rulers."[112] Khan therefore expanded the conversation beyond Syed Ahmed, in whom Hunter had placed such authority. In so doing, he proved two key points. First, that Hunter's reliance on Wahhabism distorted his assessment of Indian Muslims. Second, that Indian Muslim uses of jihad were limited and had not historically been directed at the British – even in instances that might have lent themselves to such declarations.

The literalism of Wahhabi thought that so intrigued and frightened Hunter was related to Hunter's writing goals, that is, to determine whether Muslims were bound to rebel. In Wahhabism, Hunter found what he thought to be ironclad evidence of textual, legal, and historical support for rebellion – simply put, jihad, religiously sanctioned holy war. Sir Syed took these claims seriously and to task, arguing that Hunter willfully misread the very texts he cited. Khan's argumentative thrust was in proving Muslims' loyalty, in unlinking rebellion – both broadly and the specific Great Rebellion of 1857 – from jihad, and in ultimately suggesting that the legal requirements for declaring jihad were nearly impossible to satisfy under British rule.

A major issue for Hunter was the relationship between declaring jihad and the state of British India as part of the world (*dar*), as we saw above. Hunter simplified the problem of obtaining permission for jihad by suggesting that it was only about Muslims being subjected to the rule of infidels; he cited Abu Hanifa, the famed legal scholar around whom the Hanafi legal school emerged, and suggested that other Muslims like Maulvi Karamat Ali had missed the point of these legal texts entirely when they insisted that jihad was not warranted in India.[113] According to Khan, Hunter had, for the sake of clarity of argument, omitted the parts of the fatwa that addressed whether jihad in India was sanctioned due to India's status as either *dar-ul-harb* (a country of war) or *dar-ul-islam* (a country of peace). Discussing whether holy war was permissible and how one might obtain permission, Khan wrote:

> Had he [Hunter] added the words – 'provided that the Musalmans leading the jihad be not the subjects of those Infidels, living under them in peace, and without any oppression being exercised toward them – provided that they have no left their property and families under the protection of such Infidels – provided that their [*sic*]

exists no treaty between them and the Infidels – and provided that the Musalmans be powerful enough to be certain of success' – had, I say, all these provisions been added by our author, his rendering of this doctrine would be correct.[114]

Hunter wanted to show Wahhabism in "its most terrifying form" so he "wisely omitted all these provisions."[115] Sir Syed thus continued his critique Hunter's (mis)use of sources, and he accused him of misrepresentation in ignoring key prerequisites within legal discourses as well as conflating "Wahhabi" and "jihad".

Hunter had argued that while England held power in India, rulers and officials of all ranks would need to constantly and vigilantly maintain Muslims' carefully balanced – but ever threatened – peace. Holy war was sanctioned, according to Hunter, because the British were non-Muslim, a rather tidy argument. Khan's preliminary critique included passages ignored or omitted by Hunter, and thus complicated Hunter's simplistic read of jihad and of the related fatwas that dealt with both jihad and the status of India. But Sir Syed took issue with Hunter's argument not only because it omitted serious and relevant provisos, but also because it overstated Wahhabi influence in South Asia. Khan argued that "Wahabis could not [. . .] preach their faith [under Mughal rule] without great danger."[116] He added that their very name indicated how much Indian Muslims loathed them: their self-given name "Ahal-i-Hadis" (lit., "the people of hadith"[117]) was replaced with the sobriquet "Wahabi."[118]

Hunter, in a section subtitled "District-Centres of Sedition," wrote that Patna, a city and region in the contemporary state of Bihar, in the north-east of India, was particularly "seditious," "rebellious," dangerous, and delinquent.[119] He connected this delinquency to Syed Ahmed's authority and ability to sway the masses toward Wahhabi ideas, including those of jihad. Despite conceding that money and recruits in this period did come largely from Patna, Khan argued that:

It is very evident that not a man of these [recruits] was intended or used for an attack on British India; nor was there the slightest grounds for support during these three periods, that there was a rebellious spirit growing up amongst the general Mahomedan public in India.[120]

Not only did Khan undermine the characterization of Muslims in Patna as overwhelmingly rebellious, he cast doubt on Hunter's claims on the basis of time. It made little sense that Muslims would rise against the British within the periods Hunter had outlined, because these predated the formal annexation of Punjab in 1849, a moment that did invite deep distrust, fear, and even violence.[121] Locating rebelliousness ahead of schedule, to Khan, seemed another example of Hunter's overstatement of Syed Ahmed's power and influence, and, more broadly, of Hunter's basic misread of Muslims in India. Hunter's reading back into history events that could only have been hypothesized demonstrates a teleological bent to his writing and underlines a willingness to creatively reread history in light of the conceptualizations of Muslims he favored. This is a valuable critique, because, as we will see below, a similar process of re-ascribing meaning to the Great Rebellion takes shape around jihad, Hunter's work, and its uses.

Khan highlighted the analytical ellipses Hunter created by focusing solely on religious interpretation of war. He agreed with Hunter that young Muslims were recruited and were leaving their homes, but he insisted that truly devout Muslims, be they Wahhabi or not, had by leaving their homes definitionally "left their families and property in the care of the British Government, and their faith expressly forbids them taking up arms against the protectors of their families."[122] He took an especial affront to Hunter's characterization of these men on the grounds of law – religious justifications for war were, of course, not the only obligations put upon practicing, devout, or pious Muslims.

Sir Syed did not limit his critique of Hunter to historicity and periodization. The next prong of his evaluation centered on Hunter's (mis)understanding of zakat (religious duty of charity). Hunter submitted that because Muslims were required to contribute charitably, Muslim militias would be funded quickly and robustly; further, he suggested that *all* Muslims were conceivably participants in treason and sedition, even if they did not raise arms personally, because they were doubly bound to religious war by zakat and the jihad itself.[123] Hunter was distinctively concerned with the limitlessness of Muslim support, both in terms of men and money, and he tied this concern to the Islamic legal principles of charity and war.[124] He assumed that all charity would funnel toward jihad, implicating even the staunchest supporter of British rule in the mechanisms of anti-British jihadi activity.

On these points, Sir Syed commented, "one has to smile when reading Hunter's accounts" of the Muslim populace – adding, facetiously, that not all people live up to their religion.[125] Having levied a few sardonic jabs, Sir Syed seriously addressed the problem of characterizing zakat as a means to fund rebels or support jihad, obliquely or outwardly:

> So frightened have Mahomedans now become of being accused of aiding and abetting sedition, that in many cases men have abstained altogether from assisting travelers or any one else. Apparently, no Mahomedan can now dispense his "*zakat*" without laying himself open to the charge of aiding a *jihad* against the English.[126]

While he does not support these claims with figures of any kind, the message is clear: in Khan's estimation, many of his Muslim contemporaries had taken to abandoning the religious practice of charity after the Rebellion because of its association with jihad for the British.

Conclusions

Hunter concluded *Indian Musalmans* by offering a set of solutions to the "Muslim question." His paramount recommendation was for Britons to invest in the education of Muslims, with the hope and express purpose of tempering the fanatical zeal he found endemic to Islam.[127] Sir Syed, following Hunter's organization, similarly concluded with a word on education. Perhaps unsurprisingly, he found Hunter's strategy of abominable and thought it would sow seeds of resentment:

> If Government does not deal openly and fairly with its Mahomedan subjects, if it deals with them in the underhand way recommended by Dr Hunter, I foresee much trouble both in our days and hereafter.[128]

Sir Syed championed educational reform, but he was adamantly opposed to those educational reform ideas proffered by Hunter that aimed to interfere with and, if successful, impede native religion. Of course, he is best known for his role as a modernist reformer, and correspondingly for his focus on education as a vehicle for the advancement of Muslims and progress in Islam. While he disdained Hunter's "underhanded" manner of singling out Muslims and educating them in a way that made Islam palatable to Britons, he argued that this educational reform "will certainly come to pass by our own exertions."[129] Additionally, Sir Syed claimed that education ought to speak to "the evils that now exist," which he saw as byproducts of a lack of "union and sympathy between the rulers and the ruled;" he saw Hunter's education as propaganda that would add to the problem, "widen the gap," between these groups.[130] Reform was possible, and for Sir Syed, it was both desirable and achievable through education. Hunter's methods, however, did not read to Sir Syed as genuine reform but rather as specifically hostile to Islam.

Having accused Hunter of recommending underhanded tactics to solve real problems, and of ignoring Muslims who were already working on the reforms he so desperately wanted, Khan concluded by offering an insightful consideration of Hunter's influence and the power of his rhetoric. I include his concluding passage at length below to preserve Sir Syed's tone alongside his primary opinions:

> In conclusion, although cordially thanking Dr. Hunter for the good feeling which he at times evinces towards my fellow-countrymen, I cannot but regret the style in which he has written. I cannot divest myself of the idea that when he commenced his work, he was more imbued with the desire to further the interests of Mahomedans in India than is afterwards apparent in his pages. This Wahabi conspiracy has, I think, influenced his mind as he wrote; and he has allowed himself to be carried away by it. His work was politically a grave, and in a minor degree, an historical mistake. It is, however, hard, as I have already said, for one of the minority to attempt to remove the impression which literary skill like Dr. Hunter's has undoubtedly made on the minds of the Indian public. This impression was as regards the native community, heightened by Dr. Hunter's work having received the approbation of the highest functionary in India. I could not, however, in justice to myself and my co-religionists, have kept silence when such erroneous statements were thrown broadcast over the land. I have striven as much as in me lay to refute the errors published by Dr. Hunter, and although my efforts may have been in vain, I feel that I have done my duty.[131]

Sir Syed finished his *Review* of Hunter's *Indian Musalmans* by dismissing it as erroneous; exhibiting its inherent danger, regardless of its specious nature; and calling attention again to the ways in which his own minoritized status would mitigate his evaluation of the text at hand. Still, he thanked Hunter and acknowledged that Hunter had intended — as indeed he specified[132] — to further the understanding of Indian Muslims. As Sir Syed pointed out, Hunter simply failed in this regard, making grave errors not only in the political arena but in historical scholarship as well. And, Sir Syed drove home yet again his point about Hunter's fixation on Wahhabism and the supposed "Wahabi conspiracy," which profoundly shaped his gloss on India and Muslims writ large.

The conclusion to Khan's *Review* provides crucial insight into the historicity, politics of publication, and import of Hunter's grave misunderstandings of Islam in *Indian Musalmans*. Sir Syed emphasized his own minority status, acknowledging the seemingly impossible task of a minority's argument disrupting that of a ruling elite. Khan also highlighted the influence of Hunter's work on elite readers — likely elite readers in the metropole at that — as well as on readers well beyond London. Hunter's assessment of Indian Muslims also persuaded the Indian public.

Khan described a need to disprove Hunter's characterization of Islam because of its "approbation of the highest functionary in India" — the Viceroy Lord Mayo had solicited Hunter's words, giving them the weight of Empire, as Khan had stated earlier.[133] Sir Syed's closing remarks on the Rebellion and on Hunter's conclusions draw into sharp relief an ongoing academic critique of empire writ large, that is, a critical examination of the ways that empire limits access to the construction of narrative. Khan's conclusion implies that some voices carry inherent power, and some do not. He referred to himself as one in the minority, and while we ought to assume this is a demographic comment, for our purposes and in thinking through the minoritization of Muslims it is a rather telling adjective: Khan was an elite, educated, loyal(ist) Muslim who still feared that, despite a carefully argued *Review*, his words definitionally could not be held in the same esteem as Hunter's. This is a savvy and erudite critique of empire, and one that acknowledges the ways in which many would marginalize his account. In contemporary terminologies, we might say that Khan acknowledged his relative privilege and disadvantage, and that he called into question the power dynamics that allowed Hunter's *Indian Musalmans* – filled with "erroneous statements"[134] – to be viewed as fact, but his critique and subjectivity with suspicion.

Along these lines, Sir Syed's closing critique resonates with contemporary studies that show the lasting scars of colonialism and imperialism on the colonized and imperialized, beyond legal or physical disfigurements.[135] Khan described the indelible mark that authoritative works *about* India came to make *on* Indians. He expounded the ways in which even the erroneous historical assessments of Britons in power affected and altered the conceptualization of historical realities, and in turn, the categories Hunter rendered.[136] He certainly did not make these arguments with the ardor of authors writing in later colonial contexts, like Franz Fanon, who famously referred to the process Sir Syed described as a "colonization of the mind."[137] Nevertheless, Sir Syed poignantly observed the myriad effects of *Indian Musalmans* and works like it not only on Britons' conceptualizations of Indians and Muslims, but on Indian and Muslim conceptualizations of the history and views raised in these works – even of themselves. In short, then, Khan, a staunch ally of British rule, offered scathing critiques of colonial and imperial India.

Sir Syed Ahmad Khan offered a response to Sir William Wilson Hunter, and this response offers us a glimpse at a construction of narrative. Both parties came to define Muslim belonging within British India, and both parties cited religion – religious texts, religious persons, and religious groups – to make their case. Furthermore, both parties highlighted two key legal issues: jihad and when it is justified; and the status of the country, i.e., whether and how a country can be pronounced as safe, appropriate, or accommodating for Islam and Muslims. The two differed with regard to which texts counted, whose words were most accurate, and how the populace might use (or ignore) various texts, pronouncements, customs, or laws. *Indian Musalmans* and *Review*, in short, epitomize a debate about religion.

More relevantly, however, their intertextual construction of narrative is not a remotely perfect dialectical relationship, where the actors exert equal influence over each other or their audiences – as Khan so poignantly articulated in his conclusion. And, he was right: Hunter's work garnered more attention and was considered more valid within the constructs of imperialism and imperial knowledge systems. But it is a relational conversation nevertheless. Hunter's analysis of Muslim religious ideas set the conversation, Khan responded, often having cited the same sources, and together, they stood to define, redefine, and ultimately reify certain characteristics, interpretations, and emphases.

This conversation elicited many responses and assessments, in its time and up to present-day scholarship. A number of commentators declared Sir Syed the winner of the debate while others sided with Hunter's assessment. Lieutenant-Colonel Graham, writing in the later part of the nineteenth century, decidedly thought that Sir Syed Ahmad Khan had offered a "knock-down blow" to Hunter's *Indian Musalmans*.[138] W. A. Wilson, a Canadian missionary, quoted Hunter and clearly supported his interpretations of Muslims; Wilson used Hunter's conclusions as evidence to suggest that Muslims were unambiguously bent on the destruction of the British Empire and Christians. Wilson cited Sir Syed – but only to mark his failures at reforming a religion that ultimately could not be reformed.[139] In the mid-twentieth century, Bashir Ahmed Dar asserted that Sir Syed had triumphed, claiming – though offering no support for this claim – that "[Khan's] was universally acclaimed, and the majority of the Anglo-Indian press of the day agreed with his point of view."[140] Contemporary historian Alex Padamsee evaluates their exchange in terms of what work it did, and argues that Sir Syed's attempts to rehabilitate Muslims in the wake of the Great Rebellion and Hunter's treatise, and to disentangle "Wahhabi" from "Muslim," fell short.[141]

However, assessments that focus on winners and losers do not fully capture the conversation or nuance especially in Sir Syed's work. Nor do these assessments provide insight to the ways in which Khan and Hunter's arguments align. Despite thoughtful and substantial critique, Khan agreed with Hunter's underlying assumptions. Shortly after a particularly harsh set of paragraphs in his critique, Sir Syed remarked: "the purification of our faith and our loyalty to the Government under whom we live and serve are perfectly compatible."[142] Thus, while he criticized Hunter's conclusions, Khan also engaged Hunter's primary concern, that is, the intersections of Muslim loyalty and the possibility of reforming Islam.

Sir Syed both refuted Hunter's assumptions and participated in their proliferation. By reproducing Hunter's concerns, Khan gave them a forum and authority. He certainly took issue with the elisions of Wahhabism with Islam and of Islam with rebelliousness that characterizes *Indian Musalmans*. But, in his criticism, he engaged – and even replicated – the alacrity with which Hunter moved between and among terms like "Wahhabi," "rebel," "Mohamedan," and "Islam." In fact, Sir Syed's *Review* rather ambivalently took up the language of Hunter, criticizing not its use per se, but its interpretation. As Padamsee similarly suggests, Khan implicitly supported Hunter's ultimate claim that British India was a foreign land for Indian Muslims, one that needed to be sorted legally – in terms of both civil and religious law – with great consequence.[143]

Throughout *Review*, Sir Syed referred to Hunter as a friend. And, with friends so ready to disparage and allege grotesque atrocities, both real and imagined, no wonder Khan lamented that this was a friendship from which he – and, one assumes, his fellow Muslims – needed saving.[144] For Khan's part, his *Review* aimed to dismantle the troubling assertions, elisions, and accusations that defined Hunter's *Indian Musalmans*. In many ways, he was successful: his writing in *Review* (and elsewhere) shaped responses to British rule that were, at once, supportive of the Crown and solemnly opposed to some of its disdainful qualities and policies. Khan's *Review* gestured toward ideas that he would later pick up and develop far more fully, including issues of religious and educational reform and a purposeful Indian Muslim identity rooted in modern interpretations of texts, traditions, and the empire.[145] Yet, Sir Syed's implicit affirmation of Hunter's contentions, especially vis-à-vis jihad and the idea of a distinctive Muslim identity, served to reify and sustain a minoritized and racialized Muslim. As I explore in the following chapter, Khan's *Review* helped to solidify the association of jihad with the Great Rebellion.

CHAPTER 4

REBELLION AS JIHAD, JIHAD AS RELIGION

Few concepts have been subjected to more consistent distortion than the Arabic word jihad – whose literal meaning is "striving for a worthy and ennobling cause" but which is commonly thought today to mean "holy war" against non-Muslims.

– Ayesha Jalal[1]

The Great Rebellion crystalized, catalyzed, and mobilized depictions of Muslims as decidedly militant, especially against foreign – that is, British – rule. Sir William Wilson Hunter and Sir Syed Ahmad Khan established which Muslim declarations ought to factor into official (and, in Hunter's case, demi-official) policies and laws. The former adamantly suggested that "puritanical"[2] ideologies represented an authentic Islam, and the latter dismissed this accusation with evidence of modernist, moderate Muslims and their glosses on texts, events, and law. Both engage the concept of jihad – rendered as holy war – as a primary issue. For Hunter, jihad branded Muslims as distinctively rebellious and treasonous, and so was an issue of security; for Khan, jihad was a specific legal designation that was merited neither during the Great Rebellion nor against the British more broadly (even if, as he puts it, some who were "styled as Mouvlies" but who were actually "ignorant and besotted scoundrels" declared jihad legally sanctioned).[3] In the aftermath of the 1857 Rebellion, as Britons searched for explanation and sought procedures to prevent such widespread revolts remain in the future, jihad emerges as both a primary fixation and an obvious culprit. Muslims like Sir Syed were left to defend Islam, argue specific legal points, and discredit other Muslims in order to prove their loyalty – if not individually, then as part of a minoritized, racialized, and unified group.

In the context of the Great Rebellion and in its repercussions, jihad was both a conceptual metric by which to measure the loyalty of Muslims, and, perhaps more importantly, how Muslims came to be known and understood post-1857. It is a key component of the process by which Britons minoritized Muslims, who were then bound by particular legalisms, literalisms, and allegiances necessarily beyond the pale of the British Empire. We have seen how the Rebellion has been cited as a watershed for British colonial history in India, and now we will examine the role of the 1857 Rebellion in both solidifying and manufacturing a particular distrust of Muslim subjects amongst British agents and scholars. After 1857, an imperial understanding of jihad linked – and reduced – Muslim actors and Muslim organizations to rebellion and violence.

Both Hunter and Khan deployed jihad to define the post-rebellion South Asian landscape – most relevantly, to define Muslims and Islam. As such, both participated in a discourse that produced Muslims as minoritized and racialized, even as they disagreed. In fact, Khan refuted Hunter's assumption that Islam sanctioned jihad for all Muslims, while still engaging within his legal landscapes. In this chapter, I return to Hunter and Khan as demonstrations of how jihad became a fulcrum around which the identity of Muslims was written, understood, and solidified as part of processes of minoritization and racialization.

Race is a social construct, not a biological essential. In the nineteenth century, race was a primary way in which communities were imagined.[4] European and American imperialists often grouped – and reduced – disparate people(s) by physical appearance, phenotype, and cultural practices, creating singular and subordinate "races." Sociologist Zaheer Baber argues that in India "religious markers have been deployed historically not just to demarcate ethnic boundaries but also in the long run to initiate a process of 'racialization' of such differences."[5] Race in India encompasses religious and ethnic markers – among others – because of racialization.

Racialization refers, like minoritization, to the process by which one group becomes signified based upon embodied characteristics thought to be inherent, immutable, and hereditary. A number of scholars have defined racialization as a dynamic process that relies on ascribed differences that are vital to social structures, with these differences often imagined in terms of biological difference (i.e., phenotypical traits).[6] Baber helpfully synthesizes leading scholarship on the process of racialization. He writes that:

> most social scientists would agree that race is a social construct that is sustained, reproduced and transformed through its intersection with institutional arrangements, ideologies and discursive formations,

and that therefore:

> the work of essentializing entire groups of people with immutable, inheritable and quasi-biological behavioral attributes contributes to the process of constituting and simultaneously 'racializing' what might indeed be nothing more than cultural differences.[7]

I contend that for Muslims in India, minoritization was concurrent with racialization: as Britons seized control of South Asia, British imperialism reduced Muslims from a diverse range of ethnicities, classes, and castes — including those occupying the cultural elite — under the Mughals to a singular group endowed with "immutable, inheritable and quasi-biological behavioral attributes." Despite vast evidence of a range of Muslim opinions and actions about the complicated legal matter of holy war, jihad became the metric through which Muslims were understood discursively and regulated legally. In short, the production of jihad as the preeminent identifier of Islam is possible because of the minoritization and racialization of Muslims.

For example, after the revolts and siege of Delhi, Indians were expelled from the city. Hindus were allowed to return approximately eight months later in January 1858, while Muslims were banished for an additional year, only gaining permission to reenter Delhi in January 1859. This differentiation in treatment reflects the finalization of the transfer of power from the former Mughal Empire, based in Delhi (albeit in a limited capacity[8]), to the British Empire, but it also signals a fundamental differentiation in the assumed loyalties and culpabilities of

Muslims and Hindus with respect to the events of the Rebellion, in and beyond the city's walls. These disparities rely, in part, on notions of Muslims that collapsed multiple denominational, ethnic, class, linguistic, and casted identities into a singular suspicious minority whose defining characteristics were legalism, fanaticism, and violence.

In this chapter, I trace the ways in which British imperial forces deployed jihad as a defining characteristic of Islam and an immutable quality of Muslims. First, I offer a brief overview of jihad. Then I discuss the ways in which Muslims understood and deployed jihad in South Asia during the nineteenth century. Finally, I suggest that as the Great Rebellion came to be seen primarily in terms of religion, Muslims' religion came to be seen primarily in terms of jihad – a material product of Muslims' minoritization and racialization.

Defining Jihad

"Few concepts have been subjected to more consistent distortion than the Arabic word jihad," noted historian of South Asia Ayesha Jalal insists.[9] Similarly, Islamic studies scholar Shahab Ahmed remarks that jihad "is a word that has acquired a certain centrality in the contemporary Western conceptualizations of and preoccupations with Islam."[10] Use of the word jihad by Muslims and non-Muslims has, in recent years, grown so much that its presence is ubiquitous in contemporary global media, but its history, like any complex and centuries-old concept, does not make its definition as simple as its prominence might imply. Although thus far the majority of primary sources I have discussed have addressed jihad, I have yet to delve into its definitions. This lacuna is purposeful and highlights jihad's contextualized – and fluctuating – definitions in previous chapters as well as across the long nineteenth century. Jihad's imbrication with the Great Rebellion became more evident in the years that followed.

Hunter and other British observers rendered jihad most often as "holy war;" and we still see jihad rendered this way in current media.[11] But this is not literally accurate: linguists, Arabists, and legalists will readily and adamantly insist that jihad translates to "striving." When followed by the phrase *fī sabīl Allāh*, in the path of God, jihad conveys a sense of struggle in the name of God – but this "struggle" has included such disparate incarnations as war and spiritual purification of the self.[12] Literal or figurative definitions of jihad alone cannot adequately portray its meaning, and even if we could render a simple definition, what we would define is an overly simplistic aspect of a complex concept. What counts as jihad is as challenging an issue as any other: it is historical, legal, and changing.

For nineteenth-century British imperial agents and South Asian Muslims alike, jihad was a religious legal concept as well as a potential outcome. Like any legal concept in Islam, it is addressed by trained scholars through relevant pronouncements (i.e., fatwas) that incorporate germane Qur'anic passages, *sunna* and *hadith* (examples and traditions of the Prophet Muhammad), and, in later texts, a discussion of previous legal rulings.[13] Classical Islamic law manuals and compendia often contain a section that deals with jihad. However, these sections were not standardized in any regard. We cannot categorically assert that classical jurists either approached the term uniformly or agreed upon its use, merit, and deployment. As historian Michael Bonner notes, these sections within legal corpora were sometimes referred to as *Book of Jihad*, other times *Book of Siyar* (law of war) or *Book of Jizya* (poll tax), even as their content was similar; sometimes, alternatively, legal scholars wrote freestanding books on jihad.[14] Legal scholars did not necessarily agree with one another, and when they disagreed they did so for numerous reasons: on principle, on interpretation, and on logical grounds, as well as along the so-called sectarian alignments (e.g., Shi'i, Sunni, and others) or classical legal schools (Ar., *madhāhib;* Ur., *mazāheb*) that were typically Sunni.

Simply put, Islamic legal scholars have debated jihad in terms of its uses, definitions, and deployments, and these jurisprudential conversations have been neither simple nor simplistic across epoch and region. As Bonner succinctly states, "jihad is a complex doctrine and set of practices."[15] Muslims have used jihad as part of state-building, in response to external threats and European colonial expansion and oppression, as a tool of destruction, and as a conceptual framework for self-betterment.[16] Each of these broad groupings, however, has entailed lengthy debates about apposite deployment of jihad and its appropriation.[17] Muslims have debated whether jihad prescribes violence, what sorts of acts count as jihad, and who may partake in it. David Cook, a scholar of Muslim martyrdom and apocalyptic literature, rightly highlights multiple uses of the so-called "greater" and "lesser" varieties, helpfully tracing definitional claims in which jihad was interpreted militantly, non-violently, and in ways that were "not exclusively violent."[18] Cook also demonstrates that jihad is predominately and primarily a militant issue, even as some historical and many Muslims today argue otherwise. Contemporaneously, conversations about definitions of jihad overemphasize a black-and-white conceptualization, where "war" is posited against "peace."[19]

Nineteenth-century Muslims, too, discussed jihad and the attendant possibilities and obligations signified by that "struggle." They debated whether struggle was violent, personal, or collective; they queried the nature of British rule and asked whether Muslims – in India and elsewhere – ought or were sanctioned to wage an armed struggle; they declared jihad's utility and then shied away from waging war entirely; and some still insisted that striving to perfect one's own soul was the "real" jihad. Historian Michael Bonner notes that the nineteenth century marked a shift in interpretations about jihad as "a body of juridical (and in some cases, apologetic) work emerged which defined the jihad as defensive warfare."[20] Bonner is quick to note that modernist Muslims' pronouncement that jihad is defensive war elides the ways in which classical texts discuss both offensive and defensive warfare, and that modern jurists would tend to be undermined in this point by classical jurists. Of course, interpretation and application rely on contexts, and nineteenth-century Muslims – living overwhelmingly in colonial and imperial regions – read classical texts through these lenses. In other words, while Europeans (as we saw in Hunter, Muir, and others) often viewed jihad as proof of violence and fanaticism, Muslims in the same period not only made defensive and apologetic responses to these charges, but also seriously considered the notion of jihad as part of resistance to imperial rule.[21]

The major issues of interpretation centered on India's *status* – namely, what sort of region India became under British rule and whether that rule impeded upon practicing Islam. The legal concepts of *dar-ul-islam* (a land of peace or Islam) or *dar-ul-aman* (a land of protection or peace) and *dar-ul-harb* (a land of war)[22] began to reign supreme in debates about the application of jihad beginning in the mid-eighteenth century and gained even more prominence in the early nineteenth century.[23] A region in which Islam had ascendancy was deemed by clerics *dar-ul-islam*, a notion that was tied classically to early Islamic history and expansion, but which retained legal importance well after the classical and medieval periods of Muslim political conquests. *Dar-ul-harb*, by contrast, referred to regions in which Islam had not yet spread or taken a position of primacy; in this way, *dar-ul-harb* marked territories that might merit just or holy wars.[24]

These terms effectively split the world in two, appearing to describe a rather stark dichotomy. In reality, though, most Muslim empires and, indeed, many jurists – especially Hanafi jurists[25] – resist such simplistic definitions.[26] To assume that *dar-ul-islam* and *dar-ul-harb* remained static from the earliest Islamic interpretations ignores legal developments in the intervening centuries. Similarly, overreliance on these concepts – as well as an insistence that they necessitate jihad – ignores other overarching legal principles.[27]

Historian David Motadel remarks that:

> Throughout the imperial age, European authorities were confronted with religious insurgency and Islamic anti-colonialism. Across Africa and Asia, religious leaders called for holy war against non-Muslim rule over the *dar-ul-islam*. At times, this call was combined with the appeal for emigration from the colonized territories, drawing on the concept of *hijra*.[28]

Many Muslim leaders deployed *dar-ul-islam* during their experience of imperialism. While it is folly to suggest that all experienced or reacted to imperialism in the same way, in general, *dar-ul-islam* became a mode through which to think about the conquest of Africa and Asia by Europeans. As Motadel notes, these Muslim leaders traded on the idea that their lands were properly *dar-ul-islam*, but under current rule by interloping non-Muslims, their land was threatened to turn or had already become *dar-ul-harb*, thereby interfering with practicing Islam. As Motadel also suggests, one solution to European imperialism was to fight – jihad – and the other was to flee – hijra (emigration). Both Hunter and Khan pick up on the debate about whether India was truly *dar-ul-islam* or *dar-ul-harb*, and both weigh in on whether these statuses then necessitated a religiously articulated fight or flight response.

Muslims reinterpreted and recast the notions of *dar-ul-islam* and *dar-ul-harb*, issues that gained urgency in the context of land-grabs and European expansion. Jihad, as a possible outcome of these designations, emerged as a concern across colonial contexts, certainly within the

British Empire but also for French, Russian, Dutch, and other European imperial powers. This is to say that British imperial officials expressed concern about anti-imperial movements led by Muslim religious leaders and based on Islamic doctrine; these concerns were not limited to South Asia, but instead applied across the multiple spaces in which Muslims lived under British control (including the Middle East, Africa, parts of the Caribbean, as well as South Asia). It is also to highlight a discursive similarity *among* European empires (primarily French, Russian, Dutch, and British), all of which experienced Muslim-led and religiously articulated insurgency.[29] Thus, there are two related issues here: first, the threat of anti-imperial movements, specifically those rooted in Islamic discourse; and second, a conceptualization of Islam and a Muslim identity as necessarily *sui generis*, or, put differently, a suspicion and fear of an intrinsic pan-Islamic identity.[30]

Pan-Islamism is a notion of unity that isolates Muslimness from culture and ethnicity – a notion that defies contemporary under-standings of how "religion," "culture," and "ethnicity" as categories operate, to be sure. However problematic such a conceptualization may seem, pan-Islamism is nevertheless a conceptualization of Muslims, at once authored and expressed by Muslims and used against them by others, which ideologically asserts a Muslim identity that *can* be divorced from all other identifiers. Most scholars cite the famed modernist Jamal al-Dīn al-Afghānī (d. 1897) for first articulating a specific Muslim unity with respect to – and as oppositional to – European colonial and imperial rule. Political scientist Margaret Kohn observes that, for Afghānī, "Islam is a necessary source of unity, identity, and mobilization against imperialism."[31] Other scholars note the relationship between pan-Islamism and the Ottoman Empire. Azmi Özcan, Ottoman historian, argues that the Ottomans used pan-Islamism as an important tool for state relations with European powers as well as internally to soothe ethnist and nationalist movements (e.g., Arab or Albanian) by uniting Muslims under one ideology.[32]

Non-Muslims, too, engaged in notions of pan-Islamism, often drawing upon deep-seated fears of Muslim legalism along with those of geopolitical movements. In the early twentieth century, American Archibald R. Colquhoun summarized the history, as he saw it, of pan-Islamism as well as its aims. First he expressed – as Hunter did – an understanding of Islam as rooted in law: "Islam is not only religion but law, and law is as essential to the religion as the religion to the law."[33] Then, Colquhoun insisted that pan-Islamism was a diffuse movement, unlikely to provide "revivication" of Islam, and that the "best exponents of Pan-Islam [...] desire to raise the general level of their co-religionists rather to place them in antagonism to their environments." But, he added, "the anti-foreign propaganda is the most tangible and most intelligible of the whole programme."[34] For Colquhoun, who positioned himself as a representative Western observer, pan-Islamism was a tactic to unify disparate Muslims globally, especially against foreign rule.

For Muslims like Afghānī or Ottoman state agents, this unification was imagined for differing purposes, but it was still ultimately related to the imposition of European expansion and control. Pan-Islamism relies on the premise that Muslims *can* and *ought* to be unified per their religious identification. For many imperialists, pan-Islamism recentered the idea of Muslims as threat: in this ideology, long-standing and historical differences among Muslims ceased to matter, leaving intact the notion that Islam was religion and law, and as such, binding to Muslims above all other authority. Pan-Islamism is related to jihad because each term recursively reinforces the other. Jihad is a legal category that British imperialists feared because it insinuated widespread and mandatory warfare of Muslims. Muslims, as we have seen above, were imagined as a unified collective, with all differences superseded by Islam's legalism and literalism. Pan-Islamism serves to prove both the idea of a *sui generis* Muslim identity as well as produce it anew. Circularity does not disprove these claims, but rather reinforces their logic and truth.

A *sui generis* Muslim identity – one that could and would stand in opposition to British imperial power – is all the more dangerous when joined by the religiously sanctioned, well-studied, and widely feared legal category of jihad. Like others, I locate the nineteenth century as the beginning of the discourse about jihad as a concern of empire and as a fixation of British rule in South Asia.[35] I suggest that these imperial concerns reference the Great Rebellion of 1857, and therefore demonstrate not only the relationship of jihad to revolt but the particular imbrication of conceptualizations of jihad and the Great Rebellion. In short, the definitions of jihad are secondary to the production by imperial actors of a situation in which jihad became primary both for particular imperial concerns and more generally (even Muslims in colonized spaces increasingly debated jihad). Jihad's "authentic" definition is − like claims of authenticity about religion broadly or Islam specifically − both unavailable and beside the point. However, how jihad is deployed − and it comes to overdetermine Muslim identification in colonial and imperial India − is of great consequence.

Making Muslims Jihadis

Muslims and Britons characterized and refuted characterization of the Great Rebellion as jihad. The process by which Muslims were *made* jihadis was complicated and messy, and involved Britons and Indian Muslims alike. While Muslim subjects of British rule defined their own textual, theological, and political deployment of jihad, their British rulers glossed the textual, theological, and political deployments of jihad. Though parallel, these definitional processes occurred in parallel were nonetheless related to one another; neither was an internal discourse for *only* Muslims or Britons. As both Muslims and Britons interpreted the Rebellion, differences between rebels, and fatwas declaring the Rebellion jihad, they collectively crafted a discourse in which Muslims were a unit, and that unit was jihadi. If the Great Rebellion was a jihad, then the Muslims participating in it were jihadis. The minoritization of Muslims informed this supposition: the ruling elite perceived Muslims as a unified collective and a distinctive problem.[36] A vast array of Muslim praxis and doxa came to be read through the lens of literalism, most often labeled Wahhabism by British observers. The minoritization of Muslims relied on simplistic conceptualizations that reduced the broad spectrum of Muslim practice, experience, and opinion to one identifiable unit.

The minoritization of Muslims in India is imbricated with their racialization. Religious markers delineated both ethnic and racialized boundaries in India.[37] After 1857, the diversity among Muslim-identified groups was formally gone, replaced by a narrow and rigid definition of Muslims as possessing "immutable, inheritable and quasi-biological behavioral attributes"[38] − namely, an inescapable penchant for violence and fanaticism, usually represented by Wahhabi literalism.

Hunter's work precisely illuminates this process of racialization, which links literalism to Wahhabism and authentic Islam, and finally to rebelliousness as a predicable, immutable trait. He pronounced Muslims inherently disloyal, and his claim centered on a read of Islam that imagined a standard set of obligations that each Muslim must uphold – and that each Muslim *would* uphold because of her very Muslimness. Of course, Hunter's primary concern was religiously sanctioned resistance against non-Muslim rule, and he cited Wahhabism as evidence of an immutable literalism amongst Muslims. As discussed in the previous chapter, he simultaneously lauded Wahhabi puritanism and railed against its risks to the British Empire in South Asia.

While Hunter used the term prodigiously and it was an operative category for Britons and Muslims in South Asia, it should be noted that the term "Wahhabi" and the movements it signifies have long been cited as problematic in the context of India.[39] As noted Islamic studies scholar Marcia Hermansen argues, Britons and Muslims used the categorical term rather differently. Britons used it to denote a pan-Islamic movement of varying levels of threat, and Muslims engaged it to denote particularity:

> The term [Wahhabi] was then later applied by both the British and the Indian Muslims in an oscillating series of moves to refer to groups with differing religious and political agendas. In the case of the successive British applications, the valence was negative due to a perceived threat of a Pan-Islamic political impulse to reject alien rule by armed resistance. Indian Muslims might acquiesce to, appropriate, use as a derogatory epithet, or resist the category.[40]

Even if used differently by Indian Muslims and Britons, and despite serious debate about the mercurial definition of "Wahhabi" itself, the category it represented became closely aligned with Muslims, a pan-Islamic identity, and the obligation of armed resistance.

"Wahhabi" thus became polemically applied to Muslims, especially, at the start of the Ahl-e Hadith movement in South Asia (as Syed Ahmad Khan both confirmed in his own usage and described historically in his *Review*[41]). As Hermansen notes, in the 1830s and 1840s, the term appears in official British dispatches.[42] "Wahhabi" was recognized by officials, identified with a particular movement and set of individuals, and was listed as a unique sect of Muslims in late nineteenth-century gazetteers.[43] Leading up to the Great Rebellion, the category of "Wahhabi" came to signify an especially literalist sect of Muslims who were committed to armed resistance (i.e., jihad).

In 1857 and afterward, the so-called Wahhabi movement in India came under even more heavy scrutiny. Wahhabism was directly implicated in the uprisings, and in the period following the Rebellion, the British launched a series of state-based trials against a number of individuals and leaders of the movement. Popularly known as the Wahhabi Trials, they "prosecuted those believed to be planning a new conspiracy against the British."[44] Hunter, for his part, conflated Wahhabis not only with a particular set of Muslims but with the bulk of Indian Muslims, whom he called "fanatic masses" in a number of places in *Indian Musalmans*.[45] Khan mentioned the trials as one factor in negative views of Muslims in India, in addition to the murder of Chief Justice Norman and, unsurprisingly perhaps, Hunter's book itself.[46] Khan also noted that Hunter's gloss on Wahhabis was simplistic, his views were superficial, and he drew imprecise conclusions.[47]

Whether British elites utilized the category of jihad accurately is irrelevant. The existence of the category itself and its varied but overwhelmingly incriminating uses by Britons – as well as Muslim authors' attempts to distance themselves and their communities from the category – illustrate the elisions among "Wahhabi," "Muslim," and violent rebel. Hunter made this connection explicitly, but other scholars, East India Company officers, and agents of the British Empire similarly contributed to the production of a category that had movement around the time of the Rebellion.[48]

As one poignant example, Sir Charles Edward Trevelyan (d. 1886), a British civil servant and officer in Bengal, penned a number of letters to *The Times* under the pseudonym "Indophilus." Some of these letters responded to "Philindus," pseudonym of famed philologist F. Max Müller (d. 1900), and others addressed various particularities in colonial India. Each of the collected letters appeared in *The Times* either in or after 1857, and nearly all address the problems of the Rebellion, British rule in India, and civic unrest in the subcontinent with specific attention to Islam and Muslims. Trevelyan was fairly critical of British actions in South Asia, citing variously the brutishness with which Britons acted as well as their inability to understand the locals – for racialized and minoritized reasons. He surmised that the Rebellion was a shock to Britons because "the self-relying, phlegmatic English do not understand the passionate, impulsive, mercurial natures of other people."[49]

Trevelyan/Indophilus's comments on the Great Rebellion and Muslims' roles in it are telling: printed in a highly noted and widely circulated newspaper, they demarcate a set of opinions both popular and representative. His first letter, titled "Retribution – Delhi," addressed the Muslims as a political issue. Speaking to a wide audience about a widely held perception, he noted, "the disposition at present is to put the Mahomedans under a ban."[50] Trevelyan continued, arguing that:

It is true that according to its principles as laid down in the Koran, Mahomedanism is a standing conspiracy against every government which is not Mahomedan, because the sword and the acquisition of temporal power are the predicted means of propagating this religion.[51]

Islam – Mahomedanism – is a standing conspiracy, requiring power and the sword. Although he did not use the terms holy war or jihad here, the inherent threat of religious war is on full display.

Interestingly, Trevelyan/Indophilus tempered these claims about Muslims, intoning, "But what people act fully up to the principles of their religion?"[52] He estimated that most people, including Christians,[53] do not actively live up to their religious obligations, and Muslims were, in this regard, no different. Yet, Trevelyan tacitly argued for a conceptualization of *proper* Muslim as jihadi insofar as legal requirements and the letter of the law were concerned. Should Muslims be either pious or obedient, they would be a militaristic risk, required to wage war. In other words, should Muslims be *real Muslims*, then the threat of Islam and of inherently Islamic traits would become manifest. Trevelyan repeated a post-Rebellion depiction and widely held truth: Islam is a vast conspiracy, and Muslims by extension are the conspirators.

In the same letter to the editor, Trevelyan offered another argument to address the popular suggestion that India's Muslims ought to be placed under a ban. He did not suggest that Muslims were falsely accused of disloyalty, nor did he counter the claims that Islam – as an identity-marker – espoused something beyond "the sword." Instead, he offered a logical, demographic argument. He suggested that Muslims in India must not be terribly religious given the size of the population and Britons' ability to hold Indian territory in the first place![54] Trevelyan additionally suggested that Muslims did not outnumber Hindus in the sepoy regiments, but because of disproportionate and inherent fanaticism did succumb to the "temptations" to express "hostility."[55] He labeled Muslim sepoys as distinctively violent and disproportionately mutinous. Trevelyan concluded, in a visually striking free-standing line, that "military execution will, of course, be done upon every mutineer taken in arms."[56]

In later letters, Trevelyan/Indophilus noted that Muslims may well have been "surprised" by the Rebellion, and as such ought not to be held specifically responsible, and yet he maintained that Muslims were exceptionally warlike and intrinsically moved by rebellion, hostility, and war. His responses perhaps articulate what was a moderate position: the Qur'an and Islam justify and require violent ends and a victorious Muslim population, but the Indian Muslims of specific concern to the British Empire had not demonstrated true piety and thus true Muslimness.

The elisions among Islam, anti-imperial ideologies, Wahhabism, and jihad reduced Muslims to, at best, dangerous subjects of the Queen and, at worst, rebels by definition. Khan attempted to dissuade audiences of this position in his *Review on Dr Hunter's Indian Musalmans* (1872), but he had previously presented similar arguments in *Causes of the Indian Rebellion* (Urdu 1858 and English translation 1873), and *Account of the Loyal Mahomedans of India* (1860). Both of these earlier works share a thread with his later reply to Hunter: in each text, Khan sets about demonstrating the "real" causes of revolt, which were, for him, rooted decidedly outside Islam. Furthermore, wherever Khan addressed the Rebellion, he highlighted Muslim allegiance to the Crown.

Sir Syed expressly stated that the purpose for *An Account of the Loyal Mahomedans of India* was to "publish a series of narratives" of "loyal acts" as a defense of Muslims after the Great Rebellion.[57] We ought not assume Sir Syed was on the offensive, attempting to portray Muslims in a good light simply to do so. Rather, he clearly indicated that he was writing *against* negative depictions in which Muslims were "freely represented as everything that is vile, treacherous, and contemptible."[58] In 1858 and 1860, Sir Syed already found himself writing against a socio-political narrative in which Muslims were demarcated as uniquely untrustworthy, and in some cases, distinctively culpable for the events of the Great Rebellion. He found himself writing against the minoritization and racialization of Muslims.

The language of culpability had some resonance with the actors involved in the uprising, the myths of greased cartridges and passed chapatis, and the officially deposed Mughal rulers. But many Britons and Muslims alike came to rest upon the concept of jihad not only to explain the Great Rebellion but also specifically to mark difference. For Hunter, jihad was an inescapable problem for all Indian Muslims, and solvable only by increasing British educational systems with a stated goal of undermining Islam.[59] Hunter maintained that the entire Qur'an assumed a victorious population, thereby creating a Muslim populace that would need political and social ascendancy in order to maintain its religious laws; he suggested that jihad was the only conclusion possible for Muslims, unless they were to be *less* faithful. In other words, Muslims were required to be jihadis, participants in and practitioners of holy war, until or unless they were *less* Muslim. Similarly, Trevelyan suggested that Indian Muslims had proven themselves to be lesser Muslims precisely because Britons had managed to gain and maintain control – with the hiccup of the Rebellion notwithstanding *and* simultaneously demonstrating – the ease with which Britain reigned. Khan attempted to disprove the legitimacy of calls for jihad by offering a condemnation of Wahhabism and citing fatwas that supported loyalty to British rule, but in doing so, he analogously rendered Indian Muslims as a cogent whole that stood as part of a larger Islamic unity. Khan responded to the discourse in its own terms, thereby replicating a sense of pan-Islamicism, racialized Islam, and a minoritized Indian Muslim population. These authors demonstrate the ways in which Indian Muslims came to be defined as one unified group, where jihad was seen as *the* distinguishing, inherent feature of Islam and Muslims.

Jihad in Imperial India and the Great Rebellion

South Asian Muslims utilized and declared jihad, and the complex issues surrounding jihad – namely, whether British rule in India met the legal requirements – spurred numerous and intense debates among the ulama. I attended to how the Great Rebellion first produced "the Muslims" as an identifiable group, and then how "the Muslims" were conceptualized as uniquely bent toward war (i.e., jihad) on the basis of literalism and legalism. The Rebellion – the most dangerous and shocking revolt for the British Empire – became both a warning of what *was yet to come* as well as a reminder of *what Indians*, Muslims in particular, *could do.*

Muslims emerge from the aftermath of Rebellion under suspicion of already being jihadis,[60] whether latent or active. However, this is not to argue that jihad is a concocted concept of the British deployed against Muslims, nor is it to suggest that Indian Muslims never advocated for the use of war – jihad or otherwise. Jihad is a real category that Muslims employed and deployed, not an idea British imperialists concocted in order to slander or control its Muslim subjects. Jihad was – and remains – condoned by some Muslims in the right circumstances. Below, I briefly examine South Asian calls for jihad in the nineteenth century,[61] the contexts in which they arose, and the ways in which they are read – or misread – by Britons and other Indian Muslims, as exemplified by Hunter and Khan.

While traditional histories of the Rebellion trace either elite Muslims' remarks on jihad[62] or estimate the role of lower-classed and Muslim laity among the rebels,[63] the combined picture is closest to accurate: Muslims of all walks of life across northern India helped define what jihad and religious war is in the context of the Great Rebellion. This includes the traditional Sunni ulama, modernist Muslims, Wahhabi or Ahl-e Hadis followers, and Muslim laity who partook in jihadi or *ghazi* (fighter, usually against non-Muslims) bands; all made claims affirming, condemning, or denying jihad during the outbreak and aftermath of the Great Rebellion. A wide swath of northern Indian Muslims participated in, contributed to, and contoured the discourse of jihad. Britons observing the Rebellion firsthand, as well as those who would comment later on the ramifications of 1857, picked up on this divergent discourse, sometimes highlighting the multiplicity of uses of jihad, but more often collapsing them into one definition for all Muslims. British understandings of rebellion-as-jihad and Muslims-as-jihadis followed the discursive collapse of religious diversity into a racialized essentialism. To sketch a discourse constitutive of Muslim and British voices, I focus below on proclamations and characters that were cited and well-known to both Muslim and British commentators.

Most narratives of Indian jihad begin in Balakot, a town noted historian Ayesha Jalal suggests was "in many ways the epicenter of jihad in South Asia."[64] Balakot is in contemporary North-West Frontier Province in Pakistan, and is the site where Syed Ahmed Barelvi and Shah

Ismail died in a battle against the Sikhs in 1831. This region remained a space of contentious interactions between locals and imperial agents, and across the nineteenth and twentieth centuries, Britons often noted deep tension in this area and expressed real concern for the Empire's tenuous hold over it. Balakot comes to represent the "epicenter of jihad in South Asia," and Shah Ismail and Barelvi come to represent paradigmatic Muslim warriors, for Muslims and Britons alike.

Tariq Hasan, an acclaimed Indian journalist and author, labels Barelvi's "legend and reality" crucial to understanding "the minds of the 21st century mujahideen (Islamic warriors)."[65] Beyond noting Barelvi's continuing imprint and legacy, Hasan notes that Barelvi's jihad was rooted in a compulsion to "rescue his co-religionists who he felt were being persecuted by Raja Ranjit Singh."[66] Barelvi's jihad is defensive, meant to protect Muslims from a non-Muslim ruler bent, in this reading, on limiting Islamic practice. Further, as noted Islamic studies scholar Iqtidar Alam Khan notes, Barelvi's "jihad was not aimed at establishing an Islamic state in the Punjab; it was, according to Saiyid Ahmad's own professions, solely focused on forcing the Sikh authorities to remove what were seen by the leaders of jihad as restrictions on the observance of Islamic ordinances."[67] This is, as above, a nineteenth-century development in the deployment of jihad – holy war as *defensive* and as a response to limits, perceived or real.

While the story of jihad in South Asia often begins with Balakot and Barelvi, these are not aberrations: they were working within an already extant tradition. Barelvi and Shah Ismail trace their discipleship in the intellectual lineage of Shah Wali Allah (d. 1763). Many derisively labeled this lineage Wahhabi, but as Sir Syed Ahmad Khan remarked in *Review on Dr Hunter's Indian Musalmans*, the movement preferred to be called Ahl-e Hadis, Followers of Hadith.[68] Barelvi was a disciple of Shah Abdul Aziz (d. 1823), himself the son and successor of Shah Wali Allah.[69] Shah Ismail, a scion of Shah Wali Allah's family, is regarded by many scholars as one of the best theoreticians of his era.[70] Barelvi and Shah Ismail's discipleship matters in this context because they drew upon and developed their predecessors' conceptualizations of jihad, many of which were rooted in the *dar-ul-islam* and *dar-ul-harb* dichotomization.

Shah Ismail's writings are crucial to the development of jihad (and its associated concepts) in South Asia. He was critical of monarchy, but he suggested that Muslim rulers of a delimited realm ought to be considered the *imam* – the religious head of state, in his gloss. He further conceptualized jihad in this framework. As Iqtidar Alam Khan summarizes, Shah Ismail called for jihad in terms of the ruler's violation of religious practice and the subsequent change of status to the region:

> A jihad would become binding on Muslims against a ruler only when he goes to the extreme of imposing restrictions on the observance of Islamic ordinances (*ahkam*), rendering the territory ruled by him a 'zone of war' (*dar-ul-harb*). Such a jihad would be led by a leader (*imam*) of the Islamic community located outside *dar-ul-harb*. There are, thus, two more preconditions for starting a jihad: (i) migration (*hijrat*) by the Muslims to a place outside the *dar-ul-harb*, and (ii) choice of a pious and capable person as the *imam* of the Islamic community.[71]

Shah Ismail's jihad relies upon territory under the rule of Muslims sliding from *dar-ul-islam* into *dar-ul-harb*. While he calls for Muslims to first flee the "zone of war" before appointing a leader (*imam*), he also makes the status of the region reliant on the ruler's treatment of Muslims.

But, as historian Ayesha Jalal is right to note, the jihad against Sikhs waged under the leadership of Barelvi and Shah Ismail is "the only real jihad ever fought in the subcontinent" – and "it ended in dismal failure."[72] Both Barelvi and his predecessor Shah Abdul Aziz had complicated relationships with jihad and the British. In 1804, Shah Abdul Aziz issued a fatwa describing areas under British control as *dar-ul-harb*, but he did not issue a fatwa calling for jihad (in these regions or elsewhere).[73] The fatwa declared that there is no proper Muslim ruler (*Imam al-Muslimim*), and that there is no check on the rule or power of Christian officers. The fatwa conceded that "certain Islamic rituals" like *jummah* and Eid prayers, "*azan* [call to prayer] and cow-slaughter" have been left untouched, but it also argued that Britons place no value on these rituals – Abdul Aziz reasoned that the demolition of mosques demonstrates "lordship" and total authority.[74] Abdul Aziz's 1804 fatwa declared British India *dar-ul-harb*, but he did not go as far as to declare jihad against the British. It is clear that his fatwa had deep influence over Muslim intellectuals because his disciples and others return to it in 1857 in order to determine whether to declare jihad during the Rebellion. Further, Abdul Aziz's fatwa served – for Muslims and Britons – as the first "determined expression of Muslim attitude towards the establishment of British rule in India," as noted historian Taufiq Ahmed Nizami writes.[75]

Abdul Aziz's proclamation continued to reverberate in 1857 but so did his example: Muslims during the Rebellion were left to decide whether to act upon the *dar-ul-harb* classification or to follow Abdul Aziz's example and leave jihad a stone unturned. Britons, for their part, were left to debate and attempt to predict whether the threat of jihad would remain a threat or become reality. Like his predecessor, Barelvi never declared jihad against the British, and "even accepted assistance and hospitality from persons in their service."[76] Abdul Aziz, Shah Ismail, and Barelvi, as noted examples of the Wahhabi movement in South Asia, each articulated and demonstrated through their actions a nuanced and multifaceted relationship with jihad, *dar-ul-islam*, and *dar-ul-harb*.

The experience and ramifications of continued colonial rule marked South Asia's nineteenth century. The concepts of *dar-ul-islam* and *dar-ul-harb* became, at once, inherent parts of legal terminologies about jihad and newly meaningful in light of a loss of political, legal, and individual sovereignties. British imperial practices in India framed the discourse about jihad, especially during the latter half of the century. In 1857, various Muslim populations claimed and disowned jihad. The ulama could not and did not agree on whether to declare a jihad.[77]

Yet religious elites – despite their obvious significance to both Muslim interpretation and British knowledge – were not the only Muslims claiming ownership of jihad. Popularly, some of the rebels were known as jihadis or ghazis; bands of jihadis "mainly consisted of armed volunteers from the Muslim population of the towns, and only occasionally were Muslim sepoys opting out from the revolting platoons."[78] Many Wahhabi leaders were ambivalent about declaring jihad largely because many rebels were uninterested in or ignorant about *properly* establishing a holy war – that is to say, electing a pious Muslim to serve as the imam and waging jihad with the express goal, as articulated by Shah Abdul Aziz and Shah Ismail, of reestablishing an authentic *dar-ul-islam*.[79] Other elites, especially modernists like Syed Ahmad Khan, had also written about whether jihad was to be declared during the Great Rebellion; while Khan was not classically trained, his opinions carried weight among intellectual circles, Indian and British alike.

A series of fatwas argued that as long as Muslims were able to practice Islamic rituals without interference as protected people (*mustamīn*) then India was an abode of peace. This includes Syed Ahmad Khan, as we have seen.[80] It also includes both Abdool Luteef Khan, the founder of the Mahomedan Literary Society of Calcutta, and Maulvi Karamat Ali – a follower of Barelvi – who issued the aforementioned Calcutta decision that declared jihad against the British unlawful.[81] Syed Ameer Ali (d. 1928), a student of Karamat Ali, similarly denounced the legality of jihad. While these examples questioned the validity of a jihad against the British, other Muslim intellectuals questioned the role of jihad and war altogether. Outstandingly, this group includes the founder of the Ahmadi movement in Punjab Mizra Ghulam Ahmad (d. 1908), who rejected armed jihad as archaic and whose contemporary followers, the Ahmadiyya Muslim community, continue to interpret jihad non-violently as a core principle.[82] Historian Ayesha Jalal includes Maulana Sayyid Nazir Husain Dehalvi (d. 1902), an influential member of the Ahl-e Hadis, among those challenging the necessary connection between jihad and violence, suggesting that his political quietism within an atmosphere of loyalty to the Raj disrupts neat conceptualizations of even those groups known for robust support of armed jihad.[83]

However, not all Indian Muslims challenged either the lawfulness or the premise of jihad, and some explicitly called for jihad during the Rebellion of 1857. Among the main characters associated with kicking off the revolution, both Maulvi Ahmadullah Shah Faizabadi (d. 1858) and Fazl-i-Haqq Khairabadi (d. 1861) espoused jihad. Briton Colonel Malleson, author of the important *Indian Mutiny of 1857*, described Ahmadullah as follows:

> The Maulaví was a very remarkable man. His name was Ahmad-ullah, and his native place was Faizábád in Oudh. In person he was tall, lean, and muscular, with large deep-set eyes, beetle brows, a high aquiline nose, and lantern jaws. Sir Thomas Seaton, who enjoyed, during the suppression of the revolt, the best means of judging him, described him 'as a man of great abilities, of

undaunted courage, of stern determination, and by far the best solider among the rebels.'[84]

Malleson credited – or rather blamed – "the Maulaví" for devising the chapati conspiracy,[85] which in Malleson's view not only spread rebellion but also indicated the depths to which Indians (and perhaps especially Indian Muslims like Ahmadullah) would go to revolt. Britons like Malleson and Sir Thomas Seaton saw Ahmadullah as a prototypical Muslim rebel.

Ahmadullah was certainly both political and savvy, as well as religiously inspired, but he was ultimately unconcerned with theological detail. Tipu Sultan and Barelvi inspired him and he traveled to England; as part of his return journey, he performed hajj and began a spiritual journey. He met a Sufi saint, Mehrab Khan Qalandar, who told him to wage jihad.[86] In early 1857, Ahmadullah did just that: he declared jihad against the British, who obstructed the rights of Muslims, and pronounced that anyone who died in this war would be "venerated as a martyr" (*shahīd*) but anyone who refused to fight "would be execrated as an infidel and a heretic."[87] Ahmadullah's ideas were popularly known, and as historian Faruqui Anjum Taban notes, his words appeared in Urdu newspapers like *Tilism* at the time leading up to and during the Great Rebellion.[88] Unlike many in the ulama, however, Ahmadullah did not sort the fine details of jihad, but rather used it as a tool through which to inspire and incite political upheaval. His jihad, in other words, is theologically suspect, even as its ideology is squarely rooted in a nineteenth-century anti-imperialist framework.

Fazl-i-Haqq Khairabadi is another of the oft-cited major agitators and jihadis of the 1857 Rebellion. While few debate Ahmadullah's role in political upheaval, Fazl-i-Haqq remains a controversial figure. He died imprisoned in the Andaman Islands' penal colony for (allegedly) signing a fatwa on jihad. Yet many point to his family's well-established collaboration with the British, casting doubt on his jihadi credentials. Similarly, others note that in 1855 Fazl-i-Haqq opposed calling for a jihad against Hindus and argued that fighting against established authority – even non-Muslim authority – was prohibited by Islamic law.[89] Fazl-i-Haqq's jihadi status is at once corroborated by his imprisonment for that crime and spurious in light of a dearth of evidence that he committed the crime in the first place.[90] His example demonstrates both the lasting imagination of jihad, and its uses during the Rebellion: scholars still debate his exact role, but his legacy remains that of a Muslim leader of Rebellion *specifically* vis-à-vis religious frameworks (i.e., jihad).[91]

Additionally, two of the great thinkers of the revivalist Deobandi school, Maulana Muhammad Qasim Nanautawi (d. 1879) and Maulana Rashid Ahmad Gangohi (d. 1905), took up arms against the British, wrote about jihad, and served short sentences in jail. However, as many scholars are quick to point out, not all the Deobandis supported jihad, as later rifts between and among Deobandis, Barelvis, and Ahl-e Hadis intellectuals help elucidate.[92]

These elite Muslims may have shaped the events of 1857 as well as the Rebellion's historiography, but this does not necessarily indicate a lack of popular support for the Rebellion — or for the use of jihad with respect to it.[93] As historian Faruqui Anjum Taban notes, popular Urdu weekly newspapers demonstrate growing unrest in the mid-1850s; he argues that these newspapers highlight "widespread resentment among the people of Awadh" beginning as early as 1856, which was not limited to sepoy regimens, but rather was also "widespread among the civil population."[94] Like other scholars, Taban further suggests that the East India Company's annexation of Awadh led to a decline in the income of the (formerly) ruling Muslim elite, but he links this economic shortfall to decline in the Muslim elites' support for religious institutions through charitable donations — forcing the religious elites to leave the city in search of livelihood.[95] *Tilism*, an Urdu newspaper based in Lucknow, reported that the city had once been a shining example of Muslim piety but in the mid-1850s the centers of Muslim religious life — mosques, *madrasas* (religious schools), and *imambaras* (congregations of Shi'i Muslims) — were deserted.[96] Taban's careful work with Urdu newspapers helps elucidate popular, autochthonous, and predominately Muslim[97] conceptualizations of disillusionment and unrest.

While political and religious elites debated the appropriate course of action, two other groups of Indians actively participated in the Rebellion on the ground — and thus, in its construction. Sepoy regimens *chose* to participate in the revolts. As Eric Stokes points out, sepoys conceptually represented the "peasant armed."[98] For the sepoy, this meant a dual role: they were trained soldiers within formal colonial military structures and yet still remained part of rural contexts of families, castes, mother tongues, and religions. Margrit Pernau consistently points to the ambivalence of the peasant armed as contributing to the ongoing challenge of characterizing the Rebellion in any one particular set of terms, be those political, religious, or economic.[99] Pernau calls attentions to sources that suggest that sepoys often abandoned their regimens when they had "collected enough loot."[100] While jihad may not preclude material gain, leaving battle because of material gain troubles the strict interpretation of Muslim sepoys as jihadis. In other words, if jihadis were primarily motivated by *religion*, then it is inconsistent to find them abandoning the religious cause for economic triumph.

Neither all sepoys nor all rebels were Muslim. Fatwas calling for or denying the legality of jihad were most often written for a Muslim community, but lesser-known fatwas were addressed to both Muslims and Hindus. And while these fatwas were broadly concerned with religious sentiment, many Muslims and Hindus alike remained unhampered by "niceties of Islamic law and theology."[101] Jalal notes that:

Fatwas were often obtained by force, forged, or attributed to people without their knowledge, thereby provoking opposition from Sunni and Shia ulema, who issued rulings of their own. The contradictory fatwas on jihad illustrate how religiously informed cultural identities were articulated in the early struggles against colonialism.[102]

The legitimacy of the official legal backing for jihad is contested and contingent. Fatwas that were plagiarized, obtained under duress, or addressed to non-Muslims were not accepted by Islamic orthodoxy of various denominations. Yet, if Muslims followed these fatwas, then regardless of their legitimacy, it would be fallacious to suggest they were not real.

Hunter and Khan illuminate major facets of this discourse in their textual exchange. Ultimately, nineteenth-century arguments about jihad constitute a debate about authenticity. Jihad may have been declared and India proclaimed *dar-ul-harb* by serious and authentically credentialed Muslim elites; these categories were similarly disregarded, proved wrong, and ignored by other similarly serious and credentialed Muslim elites. Elite Muslims, sepoys, and the bands of ghazis acted upon fatwas declaring jihad – and didn't. In other words, whether jihad was real or realized during the Rebellion has as much to do with debates about authentic, proper, or legitimate Islam – a set of definitions at which the contemporary scholar of religion often balks. It is not for the scholar to determine whether declarations of jihad "count" as such, nor whether those who followed those declarations did so under purely religious or theological banners. What is clear in all this ambiguity is that the location of jihad as a key identification of rebels and Muslims maintains its place in the historiography. This very debate about the authentic jihad during the Rebellion demonstrates jihad's priority; its legitimacy ceases to matter in light of the circular relationship crafted in the wake of 1857 between rebel and jihad, jihad and Islam, Muslim and jihadi.

Conclusions

I have used Hunter and Khan as a window through which to view the discursive shifts about Muslims after the Rebellion. Hunter's work exemplifies a gloss of the Rebellion that renders it a natural conclusion given its participants. He rendered the Rebellion itself as a jihad, and one that Britons would be smart to note, since defense against such revolts was paramount to maintenance of control of South Asia. Sir Syed, in an attempt to denature what Hunter rendered natural, refuted Hunter's claim that Muslims were Wahhabis, but in doing so obliquely bolstered a gloss of Muslims as unified in their aims, means, and methods. In other words, both authors made a pan-Islamic identity out of the events of the Great Rebellion – both authors replicated and redefined a Muslim identity that was pan-Islamic, racialized, and minoritized. For Hunter, this identity rested upon the broadest imagination of pan-Islamic identity, one that properly had roots in Arabia; for Khan, this identity assumed an inherent Indianness, though he also imagined Muslims as a distinctive and identifiable whole.

For both authors, Indian Muslims maintain a unique identity, one that is immutable and transferrable by birth – that is, a *racialized* identity.[103] Hunter used race like many of his contemporaries, who denoted ethnicities and religions as distinctive races.[104] However, Hunter's participation in discourses of race are less important than his deployment and support of racialized categories: the Muslims Hunter renders are Muslims foreign to the British Empire, unique in their current land (South Asia), but related essentially to all other Muslims. Khan, too, imagines Muslims as distinctive in South Asia and part of a global whole. For both authors, these embedded claims indicate a distinctive Muslim identity that goes beyond religious text or creed. Both authors denoted religious and legal responses to colonial rule as evidence of an *essential* Muslim identity, despite ample contemporaneous evidence that "Muslim" as a primary identifier was uncommon beyond the pale of those part of the elite, ruling class to which Khan belonged.[105] Both authors therefore *made*, even as they attempted (albeit in differing ways and with radically different aims) to *unmake* certain Muslim categories, which then were more deeply inscribed as real, unreal, or primary.

In the post-Rebellion context, jihad and Wahhabism carried deeper relevance than their literal translations. Jihad and Wahhabism served as markers of "true" Islam for Hunter and other Britons. Sir Syed, among other Muslims, was left to justify Islam against these "truths." As Ayesha Jalal frankly notes, "few concepts have been subjected to more consistent distortion than the Arabic word jihad,"[106] and nineteenth-century Indian texts bear this out. South Asian Muslims both declared and exploited jihad for political and religious reasons, though these were rarely mutually exclusive. The complex issues surrounding jihad – namely, whether British rule in India met the legal requirements of *dar-ul-islam* – spurred numerous and intense debates among the ulama, modernist Muslims, and British observers, as well as inspiring various sets of actions by Muslims from differing classes, regions, and denominational alignments.

Preceding the Rebellion, a number of Muslims led and participated in anti-imperial movements inspired by – or couched in – religious language. Shah Abdul Aziz, Syed Ahmed Barelvi, and Shah Ismail represent the best-known Indian Muslims who shaped how jihad was interpreted, deployed, and navigated in the nineteenth century. Abul Aziz's fatwa declared India *dar-ul-harb*, but he never went as far as to declare jihad. Barelvi and Shah Ismail died in battle against the Sikhs in what some – including Sir Syed – have called the only legitimate jihad.[107] However, modernists like Khan disputed whether Barelvi and Shah Ismail were using religious law legitimately; Khan sardonically remarked that Barelvi may have been a leader of jihadis, but he was not a preacher.[108] During and after the Rebellion, Muslim sepoys were marked as jihadis, but many often fled their regiments once they had amassed enough loot to help their families. Muslims living in the North-West Frontier Province were assumed to be warlike and anti-British, and Sir Syed attempted to explain this as part of their (racialized) natures as opposed to Hunter's sense that Islam's notion of jihad made these "tribes" more warlike.[109] Hunter, among others, prioritized various historical events, legal interpretations, and an assumed pan-Islamic appeal of the textualist minority movement. This reduced the multiplicity and nuance in Muslims' varying interpretive frameworks, especially the movements labeled "Wahhabi," to the singular and simplified "Muslim." "Muslim" in turn came to signify "jihadi."

Elites, ulama, modernists, Wahhabis, sepoys, and North-West Frontier Province "tribals" are wildly different; these groups did not equally or evenly participate in the Rebellion, nor did they agree – between or among them – that the Rebellion was jihad. Yet interpretations of the Great Rebellion produced and produce them as "the Muslims," and "the Muslims" were uniquely bent toward war (jihad) on the basis of literalism and legalism. Muslims emerged from the Great Rebellion minoritized and racialized, a group with immutable traits, stripped of power and access. Muslims after the Great Rebellion were – and perhaps remain – always already a distinctive threat.

CONCLUSION

RELIGION, REBELS, AND JIHAD: LEGACIES AND ONGOING IMPACT

The Great Rebellion holds a place in Indian historiography and popular imagination that has far outlasted the battles and massacres of 1857–8. Its immediate effects were myriad, in legal, political, militaristic, and social domain. It was invoked as the independence movement gathered momentum, and it continues to be remembered on its major anniversaries as part of a teleology in which India (and Pakistan and Bangladesh) began their independence from Britain in May 1857, some 90 years before achieving it.[1] Even more broadly, the Great Rebellion is undoubtedly woven into the fabric of the popular conceptualization of South Asia. Its events, themes, and persona have been portrayed in countless Indian books, film, television, and other popular media,[2] and it has a foothold in English-language popular culture as well.[3] The Rebellion's effects – and the often brutally enforced imperialism that followed – reverberate on the contemporary nation states of India, Bangladesh, and Pakistan, as they continue to struggle with colonial and imperial legacies. These include, of course, issues of language, education, infrastructure, and imperial laws still on the books.[4] The Rebellion is often described as the "watershed moment" in British rule of India, and as cliché as this phrase has become, it nevertheless accurately communicates a complex history: it altered the flow of power in the Subcontinent, and it heralded an era of imperialism that saw major social, economic, and political upheaval – in addition to well-documented imperial violence committed against Indians.[5]

The Great Rebellion actively looms in Indian conceptualizations of history and national identity. In May 2007, India celebrated the 150th anniversary of the Great Rebellion – or, rather, as it was memorialized at the time, the India's First War of Independence. In his reflection on the 150th commemoration of the Great Rebellion, renowned historian and theorist Dipesh Chakrabarty explored the politics of remembering acts of revolt. He suggested that commemorations display a tension between celebrating a date in the life of the nation and that date's representation of a "perpetual incitement to future rebellion."[6] He argues that the process of simultaneously remembering and forgetting – a dearth of sources explicating affective responses of average folks makes remembering impossible – renders 1857 as only a memorialized and memorized signifier.[7] In other words, its impact lies in the acts of celebration and eulogization; it is important because of the ways it is imagined and reinscribed.

In May 2015, for example, the northern Indian state of Haryana's government announced that it would establish a memorial to the "martyrs of 1857 mutiny at Ambala Cantonment." A *bhūmi pūjā*, or groundbreaking ceremony, was performed as government officials laid the foundation stone on May 11, one of the mid-May dates remembered as the start of the Rebellion. *The Hindu* reported that after the ceremony, Haryana's Health, Sports and Youth Affairs Minister Anil Vij said that establishing this memorial to the martyrs was "historic," and "future generations would always remember the present government for this important step."[8] The government of Haryana built a memorial to the martyrs of the Great Rebellion that died in its state, timed its foundation to the calendric occurrence of the first revolts, and offered a (largely Hindu) ceremonial groundbreaking. Moreover, as Minister Vij suggested, the memorialization of the Great Rebellion aimed to serve a dual purpose: it would commemorate those lost in the revolts, to be sure, but it would additionally commit the contemporary government to the popular memory, as well. This government would be remembered for properly remembering – memorializing – the Great Rebellion.

Of note, as well, is the way in which the Haryana memorial symbolically claimed its space in broadly Hindu symbolism and ritual. A *bhūmi pūjā* is a ceremony that ritually blesses the ground or earth (*bhūmi*), and it has a classical Sanskritic source in the *Vāstu śāstra*, a Hindu system of architecture. It is important to note the ways in which the government cast those who died in the earliest part of the revolt as martyrs for India, and the ceremony to establish that memorial in religious terminologies, marking the martyrs and those remembering them as Hindu. Religion here is deployed in fascinating ways: it marks the physical memorial; it marks those memorialized (the martyrs); it marks the cause (the Rebellion); and it marks the current political states (Haryana and India). Religion – the religion of Hindus – is constructed in this example as the religion of the rebels, of the Rebellion, and of current and future Haryana citizenry. Muslims are notably absent.

One of the enduring products of the Great Rebellion is the production of religions in South Asia. Eminent historian Nile Green notes the "grand narrative of intrinsic Muslim fanaticism" that played "such a prominent role in colonial politics from 1857 to the present day."[9] "The Muslims" were produced – minoritized, racialized – as a direct consequence of the Rebellion. And it is this identification and ability to identify "the Muslims" that simultaneously produces "the Hindus," their religious counterpart and opposite in this classificatory system. Hindu nationalism, the articulation of India as necessarily Hindu, has many discursive roots and routes of transmission, one of which is the Great Rebellion.[10] The Great Rebellion served to homogenize and define the two primary and imperially controlled religious groups of India. The Rebellion mobilized "the Muslims" as a category, and in turn, "the Hindus" as well. In Haryana, the state government recently memorialized the Great Rebellion in exclusively Hindu vernaculars. This is possible precisely because "the Muslims," a British imperial category – as foreign, violent, incapable of being subjects of non-Muslim rulers – lingers in this memorialization, regardless of who deployed it.

The classification of religions – especially Islam and Hinduism – came to be a hallmark of the British Empire. Despite statistical data and often personal experience, on the whole, Britons were convinced of the "essentially religious character of Indians and the mutual exclusivity between Hindu and Muslim communities."[11] The imperial project in India instantiated a classificatory system in which religion was the operative category; the import of this category – the stress on the differences between and among Indians on the basis of religion – is most evident during and after the Great Rebellion. The definition and classification of Indians on the basis of religion reflects British imperial tactics of control as well as the racialization of the population. Religion, in this classificatory system, is not merely a set of beliefs, texts, practices, or ideologies; instead, one's religion is a transmittable, inheritable set of characteristics. Defining religion in India was therefore about both the definition of populations and the demarcation of racialized identifiers. Muslims were *not Hindus*, in part on the basis of beliefs and practices, but ultimately on the imperial delineation of inborn characteristics that necessarily and intrinsically demarcated and separated these groups intrinsically.

Sir William Wilson Hunter and Sir Syed Ahmad Khan's intertextual debate represents a window into the processes of minoritization and racialization. On their own, their writings look like relics of elite, literate nineteenth-century north India. But this debate offers meaningful insight into the essentialization of Islam and Muslims in India – a discursive process that involved literate elites, agents of empire, lawmakers, and political actors. The effects of an essentialized, racialized Muslim population cannot be overstated. These are the discursive norms that prefigure and influence later movements based upon these categories: Hindi–Urdu classification;[12] independence movements;[13] the Muslim League;[14] Partition and Independence;[15] religious nationalism in India;[16] and ongoing debates about Muslim citizenship in India.[17]

These legacies also include the ongoing nexus of debates about what it means to be an Indian in the post-colonial moment: issues of religious categorization continue to influence politics, citizenship, and identification. Religion in India remains a racialized identification, and Muslims in India in particular (though not alone) find themselves minoritized, racialized, and often still represented as a monolith. Observing that Indian Muslims are "doubly marginalized," sociologist Maidul Islam asks whether Muslims can be seen as both a religious minority and an economic one.[18] Issues we saw in fatwas and debates about whether British India was treating Muslims correctly – like cow slaughter – still dominate Indian newspapers' headlines and op-eds.[19] As we think through the narrative Hunter and Khan helped to co-constitutively shape, it is vital to imagine not just the nineteenth-century realities these texts tried to honestly portray, but how they continue to influence contemporary imaginations, depictions, and estimations.

This is not to argue that Hunter, having written the answer to his titular question — *Are Muslims bound in conscience to rebel against the Queen?* — wrote the next hundred years of Indian history as well. He did not singlehandedly create an image of Muslims as a unitary whole, neither did he invent the elision between jihad and Rebellion, nor did he concoct Muslims as inherently rebellious. He drew upon extant notions — some based upon long-standing European depictions (and stereotypes) of Islam, and others based upon newer political and theological movements' tracts, like Wahhabism. However, his interpretations of and elisions among categories of Islam, Wahhabism, Indian Muslims, and jihad were widely circulated, cited, and reprinted. His arguments can and ought to be seen as both demonstrating and manufacturing the discourse that produced "the Muslims" as jihadis and the Rebellion as jihad.

In *Review on Dr Hunter's Indian Musalmans*, Khan took Hunter's premises as his starting point. He even wrote that Muslims, aware of unjust characterizations about themselves, "deemed it necessary to issue the *futwas* alluded to by Hunter" (i.e., the Calcutta decision).[20] Sir Syed, while clearly arguing a divergent perspective, can and ought to be seen, along with Hunter, as both demonstrating and creating the discourse that reified and replicated images of "the Muslims" as a unified, particular, and racialized group. Although Khan countered Hunter by presenting Muslims as religiously diverse, and not by definition violent and rebellious, Khan nevertheless reinforced and reproduced Hunter's basic assumption, that Muslims were a demographic and identifiably community:

> Like begets likes; and if cold acquiescence is all that Mahomedans receive at the hands of the ruling race, Dr Hunter must not be surprised at the cold acquiescence of the Mahomedan community.[21]

Muslims here are posited against the ruling race, Britons, as a collective. They are identified not by practice, but rather as a definable and recognizable category.

The memory and memorialization of the Great Rebellion ties Islam to revolt, paints Muslims as rebels, and marks Muslims as jihadis. It is a rhetorical and discursive shift, and Muslims like Sir Syed demonstrate its reach: a loyalist, a knighted Indian, and a well-known modernist *still* had to defend himself and his community against the dominant norm, by repeatedly denouncing jihad, the Rebellion as a jihad, and those Muslims who preached jihad. *Causes of the Indian Revolt* is an argument against the static background noise as much as it is a refutation of the direct statement of Hunter's *Indian Musalmans.* Sir Syed is often described as an apologist, and while I do not necessarily disagree with this label, I do not find it a reason to dismiss him out of hand. That he is an apologist illustrates, rather than negates, the prevailing characterization and categorization of Muslims as rebellious, seditious jihadis. The defensive stance in his writings demonstrates his positionality vis-à-vis imaginations of Muslims as necessarily *not* what he was – as decidedly *disloyal* compared to his loyalty, *extremist* compared to his moderateness, *jihadi* in light of his pacifism.

By insisting that Hunter's and Khan's writings and intertextual exchange paradigmatically represent how Muslims came to be minoritized and racialized, I have not proposed that they have singlehandedly invented conceptualizations of Muslims as violent, seditious, or rebellious, nor have I suggested that their texts have invented the very real legal concept of jihad, or its related legal criteria (i.e., *dar-ul-islam, dar-ul-harb*). Rather, I have demonstrated that these representations are exemplars – neat and robust illustrations of how descriptions and concerns about Indian Muslims shifted from the early nineteenth century to the period during and after the 1857 Rebellion.

I also have not suggested that Islam is a race, but instead that Islam was racialized in this historical moment. This is an important difference for a variety of reasons, including primarily that Islam is a set of beliefs, practices, and ideologies influenced by textual, ritual, regional, and linguistic particularities that are, and have been, in flux; Muslims represent the globe's multiplicity, and it is counter to my point to insist that various Muslim communities constitute a unitary Islam. Instead, echoing other scholars, I have asserted that Islam and its practitioners were – and continue to be – racialized. The vast diversity of Islamic practice, textual interpretation, and legal preferences come to mean very little in a system of racialization where Muslims are understood to possess *natural* and *inherent* qualities. Race is a social construct, and Indian Muslims in the wake of Rebellion were constructed to be part of a particular – and particularly violent and conspiratorial – race.

This book demonstrates through an examination of widely circulated texts how the 1857 Rebellion shaped the classification of religion, rebels, and jihad. Before the Great Rebellion, religion was a primary category of concern for Britons ruling India in India and from London, with the religions of Hindus and Muslims of particular import. Islam was a greater concern than Hinduism, but before the Rebellion, it was portrayed merely as that – a concern – and not typically as a direct or even immanent threat. This drastically changed after 1857. After the Rebellion, there was an intellectual and imperial impetus to sort out its causes, to punish the perpetrators, and prevent future rebellion by identifying its conspirators. Rebels were portrayed as Muslims, and so Muslims disproportionately felt the burden of this label, politically and practically. A major rationale for Muslims-as-rebel and Rebellion-as-religion was jihad; in turn, jihad came to symbolize all of Islam and Muslims.

I have used a particular exchange between two foremost Anglo-Indian intellectuals in order to render clearly the shift in how Muslims were represented, conceived of, and ultimately produced after the Great Rebellion. It is unreasonable to condense the Great Rebellion to political or military history, as both its causes and effects were and are so commonly described in terms of religion. The Rebellion has been constructed, discursively, as a set of acts couched in or caused by religion, namely Islam, and specifically as a consequence of doctrines of jihad. The watershed moment in Indian history continues to cast its shadow contemporarily, and despite its centrality in histories and historiographies, we have yet to scratch the surface of the ways that the Rebellion enabled a categorical, racialized, and minoritized definition of Muslims that still lingers.

The exchange between Hunter and Khan stands to demonstrate how "the Muslims" were produced in the wake of the Great Rebellion. The ways in which this exemplifies the construction of category, its deployment, and its reification is not limited to India, however. This exchange is a microcosm of how Britons during British imperialism created religion and religions; Britons exported these classificatory systems to their other imperial territories across the globe, as well as to other European (and American) imperial systems and agents. The Great Rebellion was, of course, a very real and very terrible set of events, but the way it came to be remembered, theorized, and (officially) recorded demonstrates that the process of defining religion was pervasive and inordinately powerful. Britons used minoritization and racialization to create "the Muslims" as necessarily jihadi, as incapable of living under non-Muslim rule, as a (foreign) threat to India, and as a threat within *all* British imperial lands. While others have contended that the process of defining religion in India demands the attention of any scholar of religion, if nothing else, *Indian Muslim Minorities and the 1857 Rebellion* has brought to light the specific ways in which racialization and minoritization of Muslims after 1857 informs the construction of religion-as-category.

EPILOGUE

1857 FROM TODAY'S VERMONT

CHUCK TODD: So, do you believe Islam is consistent with the Constitution?

DR. BEN CARSON: No, I don't, I do not.[1]

ANDERSON COOPER: Do you think Islam is at war with the west?

DONALD TRUMP: Islam hates us. There is something – there is something there that is a tremendous hatred there. There's a tremendous hatred. We have to get to the bottom of it. There's an unbelievable hatred of us.[2]

If you are a Muslim and you love America and freedom and you hate terror, stay here and help us win and make the future together. We want you.
— Former President Bill Clinton, July 26, 2016[3]

American political hopefuls and major players, as in the examples above, demonstrate the ways in which Muslims come to be portrayed in terms of their (in)ability to be trusted to follow secular, state law. The 2016 American presidential election has depicted another context in which Muslims and Islam are debated, and that is whether pundits have been outwardly dismissive of the possibility of Muslims to live as citizens – dismissive, that is, of Islam's compatibility with the American

Constitution – or whether they have offered qualified acceptance of Muslim citizenship – that is, an assumption of Muslim inclusion *if and only if* she is demonstrably anti-terror.

The view from the state of Vermont – where I have done the bulk of the writing of this book – of the American contemporary political moment strikes me as one of the tangible ways in which the legacies of the Great Rebellion still linger. The 2016 presidential campaign bore the mark of post-Rebellion discourse. The contemporary United States is neither imperial India nor Britain, and of course, it has its own contextual space for anti-Muslim, Islamophobic ideologies and conceptualizations. Yet, a lasting and evident aspect of contemporary discourse about Muslims directly evokes assumptions that became solidified, popularized, and primary as a result of the Great Rebellion of 1857. As we see above, Muslims are still imagined as suspect and disloyal in terms of *law* – specifically their imagined inability to be citizens in light of Islamic law.

Dr. Ben Carson, a neurosurgeon and early contender for the Republican party's presidential nomination, talked on a few occasions about Muslims and their compatibility with the US, American values, and the US Constitution. In an interview with NBC's "Meet the Press," a weekend political and the longest running show on American television, Carson discussed Islam and Muslims. "Meet the Press" anchor Chuck Todd asked Dr. Carson if a president's faith should matter, and he replied: "If it's inconsistent with the values and principles of America, then of course it should matter." Todd followed up, and asked: "So, do you believe Islam is consistent with the Constitution?" Carson replied, without hesitation: "No, I don't, I do not." He added: "I would not advocate that we put a Muslim in charge of this nation. I absolutely would not agree with that."[4]

One day after the interview, Ben Carson took to his public Facebook page to clarify his comments. He wrote:

> Know this, I meant exactly what I said. I could never support a candidate for President of the United States that was Muslim and had not renounced the central tenant of Islam: Sharia Law.[5]

He added: "Under Islamic Law, homosexuals – men and women alike – must be killed. Women must be subservient. And people following other religions must be killed."[6]

Carson's sentiments are his own — they would not stand up to legal scrutiny, given that the Constitution specifically bars the establishment of any one religion as well as safeguards the free exercise of religion and prohibits a religious test to take or hold office.[7] But it is worth noting that Ben Carson offered his original, televised opinion as a Republican primary candidate for the presidency as well as a co-author of a then-forthcoming book on the Constitution, titled *A More Perfect Union: What We the People Can Do to Reclaim Our Constitutional Liberties*.[8] As he "doubled down"[9] on his claim that a Muslim could not be president, he did so in the same vein: as a presidential hopeful, a frontrunner for the Republican party's nomination, a doctor, a leader — in short, an authority. He claimed that because of (his gloss of) their religion and specifically their religious laws, Muslims were neither suited to the highest office in the United States nor was their religion, at its core, compatible with the Constitution.

Carson, of course, is not alone. Donald Trump, America's 45th President as of January 2017, similarly portrayed Islam as *textually* negative and *legally* exhorting Muslims to violence. In the interview with CNN's Anderson Cooper cited above, Trump echoed depictions of Muslims that are racialized in terms of textuality and literalism: he suggested that families can radicalize each other and that the families of terrorists should be involved, in part, in the plans to go after terrorists.[10] Put differently, Trump imagined Islam as contagious, conspiratorial, and corrosive. While Carson and Trump have necessarily garnered attention as part of the presidential campaign, they reflect — as did our nineteenth-century interlocutors — a popular discourse.

It is easy, perhaps, to dismiss the Republican hopeful Carson and later Republican nominee (and eventual President) Trump — often assumed hawkish and courting particular strains of Christian voters who have historically been suspicious of non-Christians, immigrants, and other "Others." It is even easier, I imagine, to dismiss the rhetoric of Trump as an outlier, whose presidential campaign was marked — frighteningly, I will bluntly add — by the support of white supremacist and nationalist organizations, including but not limited to current and former high-profile members of the Klu Klux Klan and neo-Nazi organizations.[11] But while Trump and, though to a lesser degree, Carson represent hardline rhetoric that fundamentally refuses to engage with Muslim citizenship or Islam as "compatible," Democratic presidential candidate

Hillary Rodham Clinton and her campaign similarly trafficked in conceptualizations of Muslims and Islam as necessarily suspect.

As quoted above, in his speech supporting her nomination, former President Bill Clinton addressed Muslims in the audience by stating: "We want you." But he qualified these remarks – no doubt direct reponses to the Republican National Convention's many speeches vilifying terrorism and Islam[12] – with problematic language: "If you are a Muslim and you love America and freedom and hate terror, stay here and help us win and make a future together."[13] Bill Clinton's statement qualifies not only to which Muslims he spoke but also which Muslims can be reasonably viewed as desirable: Muslims who love America and freedom and hate terror. Further, Clinton underscored a very real stereotype of American Muslims by inviting qualified Muslims to "stay here." The Muslims Clinton addresses are immigrants – presumably ones who could "leave" or "go home," and not refugees, second or third generation descendants of immigrants, and certainly neither African American Muslims who might trace their lineage to the transatlantic slave trade[14] nor white converts.[15] In other words, Bill Clinton posits an American Muslim who must necessarily prove her loyalty via a (demonstrable, one assumes) hatred of terror while he simultaneously assumes that she is necessarily foreign to America.

Democratic candidate for President Hillary Clinton, in the last weeks of her campaign, released an advertisement some deemed her most emotional and effective.[16] It featured Khizr Khan, a Muslim American and father of United States Army Captain Humayun Khan, a solider killed while serving during the Iraq War in 2004. Khizr Khan had been a speaker at the Democratic National Convention, as well, and was accompanied by his wife, Ghazala Khan; her silence during his speech at the Convention garnered attention, with pundits and politicians – most notably Donald Trump himself – claiming she was not allowed to speak because of her religion.[17] In the 60-second television ad, an emotional Khizr Khan recounts his son's service to the United States Army while the camera pans across Captain Khan's medals, awards, and diplomas; the elder Khan is shown holding and gently touching the triangularly-folded American flag presented to the families of deceased soldiers. At the end and climax of the advertisement, Khan says, with tears in his eyes: "I want to ask Mr. Trump: Would my son have a place in your America?"[18]

Captain Khan, a Bronze Medal and Purple Heart recipient, made "the ultimate sacrifice" for America. Khizr Khan, highlighting his unspeakable sorrow, tearfully asks if there would be space for his son, the hero, the solider in Trump's America. The ad hinges, of course, on Trump's anti-Muslim and anti-immigrant rhetoric. Yet it also reveals something about Clinton's conception of Muslims, too. Specifically, through this ad we see the casting of an ideal Muslim – one similar to the assumed Muslim audience of Bill Clinton's speech: a loyal Muslim, a hater of terrorism, who has demonstrated his loyalty and dedication to America (and antipathy to that which America hates) by making the ultimate sacrifice. In other words, Clinton, like Trump and Carson, participates in the estimation of Muslims as suspect and suspicious, perhaps incompatible with America precisely because her campaign uses an ideal type to ask Trump whether or not there would be room for Muslims – and, vitally, Muslims *like Captain Khan,* willing to fight and serve and die for American values.

Beyond the presidential campaign and beyond specific references regarding the ability of Muslims to be American citizens, another way to think about how the 1857 Rebellion's legacy continues to reverberate is through anti-shari'a laws. By way of further poignant example are the numerous states that have sought or seek to ban shari'a law in their jurisdictions, and while superior courts rule on the constitutionality of such bans, other states have sought or seek to ban "foreign law."[19]

Between 2010 and 2012, lawmakers in at least 32 states introduced bills to restrict the circumstances in which state courts can consider foreign or religious laws in their decisions.[20]

Jihad in the post-Rebellion context was held up as a requirement Muslims could not escape *because* of Islam's demands of legalism and literalism; it was used as a mechanism to cast doubt upon the collective ability of Muslims to be subjects of the British Empire, and it was further used as evidence of their distinctive, immutable character and intrinsic penchant for violence. Shari'a, here, holds a similar discursive space: it is used as evidence that Muslims, always already loyal to an external and incompatible legal system, cannot be proper citizens of the United States. Moreover, the threat of Islamic law is so great that the American legal and political system must preemptively challenge it – or risk losing the fundamentals of American democracy altogether.[21]

America in the twenty-first century is a rather different place than nineteenth-century South Asia. And yet the abovementioned pronouncements are eerily similar to those that appeared in the wake of the 1857 Rebellion. Then, Britons and Muslims argued about whether and under what circumstances Muslims could be subjects of the Queen, or more specifically, be trusted, loyal, and law-abiding subjects of the Empire. Hunter, Muir, Carey, and all the aforementioned others claimed that Muslims had legal obligations beyond and beside those to the British Empire. This is what marked Muslims as a threat after the Rebellion, and this is what marks Muslims as a threat in contemporary America. The discursive shift inaugurated by the Great Rebellion lingers in our contemporary characterizations of Muslims, often alongside other historically located stereotypes and images. And so, as I continue to witness the minoritized, racialized tropes of the 1857 Rebellion play out in contemporary politics, I cannot help but evoke William Faulkner's over-cited line: "The past is never dead. It's not even past."[22]

NOTES

Introduction

1. Malcolm Lewin, Esq., ed., *Causes of the Indian Revolt, by a Hindu Bengali* (London: Edward Stanford, 6, Charing Cross, [October] 1857), 12.
2. E.g., Partha Chatterjee, "For an Indian History of Peasant Struggle," *Social Scientist* Vol. 16, no. 11 (November, 1988), 3–17.
3. E.g., Richard King, *Orientalism and Religion: Postcolonial Theory, India and 'The Mystic East'* (London: Routledge, 1999).
4. Many have discussed, defined, and redefined "minoritization." A particularly concise and productive definition appears in Wisdom Tettey, and Korbla P. Puplampu, *The African Diaspora in Canada: Negotiating Identity & Belonging* (Calgary: University of Calgary Press, 2005), 94.
5. E.g., *The Law Relating to India, and the East-India Company; with Notes and an Appendix*. 2nd ed. (London: W. H. Allen, 1841); Ebrahim Moosa, "Colonialism and Islamic Law." *Islam and Modernity Key issues and debates*, ed. Muhammad Khalid Masud, Armando Salvatore and Martin van Bruinessen (Edinburgh: Edinburgh University Press, 2009), 158–81; Alan Guenther, "A Colonial Court Defines a Muslim," in *Islam in South Asia in Practice*, ed. Barbara D. Metcalf (Princeton: Princeton University Press, 2009), 293–304.
6. E.g., Sanjay Sharma, "The 1837–38 Famine in U.P.: Some Dimensions of Popular Action," *Indian Economic and Social History Review* 30, no. 3 (1993), 337–72; Rachel Lara Sturman, *The Government of Social Life in Colonial India: Liberalism, Religious Law, and Women's Rights* (New York: Cambridge University Press, 2012); David Lelyveld, "Colonial Knowledge and the Fate of Hindustani," *Comparative Studies in Society and History* 35.4 (1993), 665–82.
7. E.g., Peter Robb, "South Asia and the Concept of Race," in *The Concept of Race in South Asia*, ed. Peter Robb, SOAS Studies on South Asia: Understandings and Perspectives series (New Delhi: Oxford University Press, 1995), 1.

8. Sylvester A. Johnson, *African American Religions, 1500–2000: Colonialism, Democracy, and Freedom* (New York: Cambridge University Press, 2015), 383, 398–400.

9. E.g., Pierre Bourdieu and John B. Thompson, *Language and Symbolic Power* (Cambridge, MA: Harvard University Press, 1991); Ranajit Guha, "The Prose of Counter-Insurgency," in *Selected Subaltern Studies*, Ranajit Guha and Gayatri Chakravorty Spivak, eds (New York: Oxford University Press, 1988), 45–86; Laurent Dubreuil and David Fieni, *Empire of Language: Toward a Critique of (Post)colonial Expression* (Ithaca, NY: Cornell University Press, 2013).

Chapter 1   The Company, Religion, and Islam

1. W. W. Hunter, *Imperial Gazetteer: Vol. 2. Bengal to Cutwa* (London: Trubner and Co., 1881), 18.

2. Sir Sayyid Ahmed Khan, *An Account of the Loyal Mahomedans of India* (Meerut: J. A. Gibbons, at Motussilite Press, 1860), Part I: 4.

3. E.g., Humphrey Prideaux, *The True Nature of Imposture Fully Display'd in the Life of Mahomet*, 1697.

4. E.g., Vicente Cantarino, "Dante and Islam: History and Analysis of a Controversy (1965)," *Dante Studies, with the Annual Report of the Dante Society*, no. 125, *Dante and Islam* (2007), 37–55.

5. E.g., Frederick Quinn, *The Sum of All Heresies: The Image of Islam in Western Thought* (Oxford; New York: Oxford University Press, 2008); Sophia Rose Arjana, *Muslims in the Western Imagination* (New York: Oxford University Press, 2015).

6. Peter Gottschalk and Gabriel Greenberg, "Common Heritage, Uncommon Fear: Islamophobia in the United States and British India, 1687–1947," in ed. Carl W. Ernst, *Islamophobia in America: Anatomy of Intolerance* (New York: Palgrave Macmillan, 2013), 30.

7. Ibid.

8. Chartered by Elizabeth I (d. 1603) in 1600, the East India Company increasingly sent Britons to India, for purposes of colonizing, civilizing, and, especially early on in its history, trading in South Asia. In the late eighteenth century, the Company expanded influence and power alongside the declination of centralized Mughal control; by the nineteenth century, the impact and role of the Company became the subject of scrutiny, as the possibility for wealth and a more explicit expansion of the British Empire increased. All along, however, agents of the East India Company produced various forms of writing about all manner of issues, including religion and religious subgroups. East India Company officers participated in legitimately sponsored and privately supported data collection and production; these often influential works came to inform scholastic endeavors, Parliamentary acts, and official writs. As an example, see: Penelope Carson, *The East India Company and*

Religion, 1698–1858 (Woodbridge, Suffolk and Rochester, NY: Boydell Press, 2012).

9. No author, "Preface," in George Chapman, LLD, *Tracts of East India Affairs viz., Collegium Bengalense, a Latin Poem with an English trans., and a dissertation on the best means of Civilizing the Subjects of the British Empire in India, and of Diffusing the Light of Christian Religion throughout the Eastern World*, 2nd ed. (Edinburgh: John Moir, Royal Bank Close, 1805), n.p., dated October 1804.

10. Chapman, *Tracts of East India Affairs*, 11.

11. Ibid., 16–17. Emphasis in original.

12. *The Parliamentary Register: Or, an impartial report on the debates that have occurred in the two Houses of Parliament, in the course of the first session of the Fifth Parliament of the United Kingdom of Great Britain and Ireland*, Vol. III (London: Printed for John Stockdale, Piccadilly, 1813), 246.

13. Ibid., 247.

14. Ibid., 104–5, 245.

15. Philip J. Stern, *The Company-State: Corporate Sovereignty and the Early Modern Foundations of the British Empire in India* (New York: Oxford University Press, 2012), 19–20.

16. The practical effects of the Charter Act were manifold, and included the increased presence of Britons in South Asia; an increased imperial presence, especially with regard to judiciary concerns; formal permission for British, Christian missionaries to work in South Asia; and funds reserved for the education of Indians. See, as examples: *The Law Relating to India, and the East-India Company; with Notes and an Appendix*, 2nd ed. (London: W. H. Allen, 1841); Anthony Webster, "The Strategies and Limits of Gentlemanly Capitalism: The London East India Agency Houses, Provincial Commercial Interests, and the Evolution of British Economic Policy in South and South East Asia 1800–50," *Economic History Review* 59, no. 4 (2006), 743–64; and Nancy Gardner Cassels, *Social Legislation of the East India Company: Public Justice versus Public Instruction* (New Delhi; Thousand Oaks, CA: Sage Publications, 2010).

17. *Abstract of the Minutes of Evidence Taken in the Honourable House of Commons before a Committee of the Whole House to Consider the Affairs of the East India Company*, by the editor of the East India Debates (London: Black, Perry, and Co., 1813), 54.

18. Ibid., 58.

19. Ibid., 59.

20. E.g., Ibid., 80, 83, 125, 127.

21. *Minutes of Evidence Taken Before the Select Committee of the Honourable House of Commons, appointed for the purpose of taking the examination of such Witnesses as shall be ordered by the House to attend the Committee of the Whole House, on the Affairs of the East-India Company, and to report the MINUTES of such Evidence from time to time* (London: by order of the Court of Directors for the information of the Proprietors, Cox and Son, 1813), 430.

22. Ibid.

23. Salahuddin Malik, *1857 War of Independence or Clash of Civilizations?: British Public Reactions* (Karachi: Oxford University Press, 2008), 13.

24. Ibid., 34.

25. E.g., Avril A. Powell, *Muslims and Missionaries in Pre-mutiny India*, London Studies on South Asia, no. 7 (Richmond, Surrey: Curzon Press, 1993); Dana Lee, Robert, ed. *Converting Colonialism: Visions and Realities in Mission History, 1706–1914*, Studies in the History of Christian Missions (Grand Rapids, MI: William B. Eerdmans, 2008).

26. E.g., Peter van der Veer, *Imperial Encounters: Religion and Modernity in India and Britain* (Princeton, NJ: Princeton University Press, 2001), 15–29.

27. *Minutes of Evidence Taken Before the Select Committee of the Honourable House of Commons*, 522, 539.

28. *The Parliamentary Register: Or, an impartial report on the debates that have occurred in the two Houses of Parliament, in the course of the first session of the Fifth Parliament of the United Kingdom of Great Britain and Ireland*, Vol. II (London: Printed for John Stockdale, Piccadilly, 1813), 177.

29. Ibid., 183.

30. Ian Copland, "Christianity as an Arm of Empire: The Ambiguous Case of India under the Company, C. 1813–1858," *The Historical Journal* 49, no. 4 (December 2006), 1030.

31. Carson, *The East India Company and Religion, 1698–1858*, 153–4.

32. Ibid., 155.

33. Ibid., 158–162.

34. E.g., Syed Ahmed Khan, *The Causes of the Indian Revolt, in Urdoo, in 1858, and translated into English by his two European friends* (Benares: Benares Medical Hall Press, 1873), 17–25.

35. While shari'a has made it into contemporary parlance as "Islamic law," it does not neatly line up with state-based conceptions of law, an immobile cannon, nor one unique *thing*. Scholar Marion Katz writes that shari'a is law "in the sense that it encompasses the realm of judicially enforceable rules and the conduct of the state, even while extending to realms of ritual practice and private ethics exceeding the purview of modern Western 'law,'" in "Pragmatic Rule and Personal Sanctification in Islamic Legal Theory," in Austin Sarat, Lawrence Douglas and Martha Merrill Umphrey, *Law and the Sacred* (Stanford: Stanford University Press, 2007), 91. Late historian of Islam Shahab Ahmed problematized the reduction of Islam to law, offering both a gloss on Euro-American attempts to parse "religion" from "culture," as well as the variety of Islamic terms involved in Islamic law beyond shari'a, including *fiqh* (jurisprudence), *adab* (etiquette), and *kalam* (theology) in *What is Islam? The Importance of Being Islamic* (Princeton, NJ: Princeton University Press, 2015), 167–77. Other scholars of Islam and Islamic jurisprudence have further stressed the idealized nature of shari'a: it is a goal of an Islamic community, in addition (sometimes) to an active state- or religious set of laws. Carl W. Ernst specifically terms "the complex of Islamic law as an ideal, usually known as

shari'a," in *Following Muhammad: Rethinking Islam in the Contemporary World* (Chapel Hill: University of North Carolina Press, 2003), 104.

36. *Minutes of Evidence taken before the Select Committee of The House of Lords, appointed to enquire into the Present State of the Affairs of The East-India Company, and into the Trade between Great Britain, the East-Indies, and China, and to Report to the House* (London: Parbury, Allen, and Co., 1830), 93.

37. Ibid.

38. Appendix to Report from the Select Committee XII: Crimes & Misdemeanors in *Affairs of the East India Company, 16 August 1832* (London: printed by the Honourable Court of Directors, J L Cox and Son, 1833), 564.

39. Most relevant is famed philologist F. Max Müller. See especially: *Introduction to the Science of Religion* (London, 1873), "India – What Can It Teach Us? (1883)," in *Historical Thinking in South Asia: A Handbook of Sources from Colonial Times to the Present*, edited by Michael Gottlob (New Delhi: Oxford University Press, 2003), 104–7; *Lectures on the science of language, delivered at the Royal Institution of Great Britain in April, May & June 1861* (Delhi: Munshi Ram Manohar Lal, 1965). See also: Tomoko Masuzawa, *The Invention of World Religions: Or, How European Universalism was Preserved in the Language of Pluralism* (Chicago: University of Chicago Press, 2005); Tomoko Masuzawa, "Our Master's Voice: F. Max Müller after A Hundred Years of Solitude," *Method & Theory in the Study of Religion* 15, no. 4 (2003) 305–28.

40. Jonathan Z. Smith, "Religion, Religions, Religious," in Mark C. Taylor, ed., *Critical Terms for Religious Studies* (Chicago: University of Chicago Press, 1998), 269–84.

41. E.g., David Chidester, *Empire of Religion: Imperialism and Comparative Religion* (Chicago: University of Chicago Press, 2014), 17, 31.

42. While some of these sources maintain that "religion" and "politics" are separate realms, many scholars of religion trouble this dichotomy. As examples: Jason Bivins, *Religion of Fear: The Politics of Horror in Conservative Evangelicalism* (Oxford: Oxford University Press, 2008); Peter van der Veer, *Religious Nationalism: Hindus and Muslims in India* (Berkeley, CA: University of California Press, 1994); Richard M. Eaton, "The Political and Religious Authority of the Shrine of Baba Farid," in Richard M. Eaton, ed., *India's Islamic Traditions, 711– 1750* (New Delhi: Oxford University Press, 2003), 263–84.

43. E.g., Chidester, *Empire of Religion*, 308–9.

44. E.g., *Abstract of the Minutes of Evidence Taken in the Honourable House of Commons before a Committee of the Whole House to Consider the Affairs of the East India Company*, by the editor of the East India Debates (London: Black, Perry, and Co., 1813), 9–10, 22, 34.

45. Lewin, ed., *Causes of the Indian Revolt*, 12.

46. E.g., Sir Alfred Lyall, *Race and Religion: An Address, May 5, 1902*, Reprinted from *The Fortnightly Review*, December 1902 (London: Social and Political Education League, ND), 11–12.

168

47. John L. Esposito, *The Islamic Threat: Myth or Reality?* (New York: Oxford University Press, 1992), 45.

48. If we can indeed define what "religion" is, was, or might still be. E.g., Russell T. McCutcheon, *Manufacturing Religion The Discourse on Sui Generis Religion and the Politics of Nostalgia* (New York: Oxford University Press, 1997).

49. Peter Gottschalk, *Religion, Science, and Empire: Classifying Hinduism and Islam in British India* (New York: Oxford University Press, 2013), 5.

50. I am indebted to Kathleen Foody and Megan Goodwin, who in conversations about classification and categorization made an excellent and illustrative point: turkeys are not mammals, for example, unless power structures redefine them as such. The seemingly obvious *mis*categorization of a turkey as a mammal relies on having accepted the very premise of taxonomy itself: after centuries of debate and discussion, *birds* have come to dominate and distinguish the category that boasts "feathers." All classifications are rooted in power and are socially constructed, even for the turkey. Cf. Gottschalk's "platypus syndrome" analogy, *Religion, Science, and Empire*, 198.

51. As examples: Sitakant Mahapatra, "The Mutiny and the Sociology of Literary Imagination," *Indian Literature* 53, no. 1 (249) (January/February 2009), 172; Tapti Roy, "Visions of the Rebels: A Study of 1857 in Bundelkhand," *Modern Asian Studies* 27, no. 1, Special Issue: How Social, Political and Cultural Information Is Collected, Defined, Used and Analyzed (February, 1993), 205; James W. Hoover, "Indian Mutiny," in *International Encyclopedia of Military History*, ed. James C. Bradford (New York: Routledge, 2006), 643.

52. Peter Harrington, *Plassey, 1757: Clive of India's Finest Hour* (Westport, CT: Praeger, 2005).

53. E.g., John Campbell, *Memoirs of the Revolution in Bengal, Anno. Dom. 1757. By Which Meer Jaffeir Was Raised to the Government of That Province, Together with Those of Bahar and Orixa* (London: Printed for A. Millar, 1760).

54. Ranajit Guha, "A Conquest Foretold," *Social Text* 54 (Spring 1998), 85.

55. Ibid., 86.

56. E.g., David Baker, "Colonial Beginnings and the Indian Response: The Revolt of 1857–58 in Madhya Pradesh," *Modern Asian Studies* 25, no. 3 (July 1991), 511–12.

57. Kamaluddin Ahmed, *Plassey to Proclamation: A Study of Indian Muslim Resistance to British Colonial Expansion in India* (Kolkata: Mudrakar, 2010).

58. Ranajit Guha, *Elementary Aspects of Peasant Insurgency in Colonial India* (Delhi: Oxford, 1983).

59. Biswamoy Pati, "Introduction: the Nature of 1857," in *The 1857 Rebellion*, ed. Biswamoy Pati (New Delhi: Oxford University Press, 2007), xvii.

60. Ibid. Cf. Subhas Bhattacharya, "The Indigo Revolt of Bengal," *Social Scientist* 5, no. 12 (July 1977), 13–23.

61. Ian Copland, *The British Raj and the Indian Princes: Paramountcy in Western India, 1857–1930* (Bombay: Orient Longman, 1982), 1.

62. E.g., Majumdar, *The Sepoy Mutiny and the Revolt of 1857* (Calcutta: Firma K. L. Mukhopadhyay, 1957 (reprint 1963)).

63. Francesca H. Wilson, *Rambles in Northern India. With Incidents and Descriptions of Many Scenes of the Mutiny, Including Agra, Delhi, Lucknow, Cawnpore, Allahabad, Etc. With Twelve Large Photographic Views.* (London: Sampson Low, Marston, Low, and Searle, 1876). Cf. Majumdar, *The Sepoy Mutiny and the Revolt of 1857*, 192–225.

64. Many have written on women, gender, and the Rebellion. As examples: Alison Blunt, "Embodying war: British women and domestic defilement in the Indian 'Mutiny' 1857–8," *Journal Of Historical Geography* 26, no. 3 (July 2000), 403–28; Penelope Tuson, "Mutiny narratives and the imperial feminine: European Women's Accounts of the Rebellion in India in 1857," *Women's Studies International Forum* 21, no. 3 (1998), 291–303.

65. E.g., C. A. Bayly, *Empire and Information: Intelligence Gathering and Social Communication in India, 1780–1870* (Cambridge: Cambridge University Press, 1996), 315–37.

66. Andrea Major and Crispin Bates, "Introduction: Fractured Narratives and Marginal Experiences," in *Mutiny at the Margins: New Perspectives on the Indian Uprising of 1857, vol. 2: Britain and the Indian Uprising*, eds. Andrea Major and Crispin Bates (London: Sage Publications, 2013), xvi.

67. Sarmistha De, "Marginal Whites and the Great Uprising: A Case Study of the Bengal Presidency," in *Mutiny at the Margins: New Perspectives on the Indian Uprising of 1857, vol. 2: Britain and the Indian Uprising*, eds. Andrea Major and Crispin Bates (London: Sage Publications, 2013), 166–7.

68. Arshad Islam, "The Backlash in Delhi: British Treatment of the Mughal Royal Family following the Indian 'Sepoy Mutiny' of 1857," *Journal Of Muslim Minority Affairs* 31, no. 2 (June 2011), 197–215.

69. Meredith Townsend, *The Annals of Indian Administration, Volume III* (Serampore: J. C. Murray, 1859), 129. Cf. Clare Anderson, *The Indian Uprising of 1857–8 Prisons, Prisoners, and Rebellion* (London: Anthem Press, 2007), 132.

70. Andrea Major and Crispin Bates, "Introduction," xvi–xvii.

71. E.g., Colonel G. B., C. S. I. Malleson, *The Indian Mutiny of 1857* (London: Seeley and Co., Limited, 1891), vii–ix.

72. E.g., T. R. Holmes, *A History of the Indian Mutiny, 4th ed.* (London: W. H. Allen, 1904), 98.

73. Ibid., 34–5.

74. E.g., Sir George Forrest, *A History of the Indian Mutiny: Reviewed And Illustrated From Original Documents, vol. 1* (Edinburgh: W. Blackwood, 1904), 5; Syed Ahmed Khan, *The Causes of the Indian Revolt, in Urdoo, in 1858, and translated into English by his two European friends* (Benares: Benares Medical Hall Press, 1873), 0.4 (2).

75. Malleson, *The Indian Mutiny of 1857*, 38.

76. Majumdar, *The Sepoy Mutiny and the Revolt of 1857*, 76.

77. Malleson, *The Indian Mutiny of 1857*, viii.

78. Malleson, *The Indian Mutiny of 1857*, 19.
79. Ibid., 20.
80. Ibid., 33.
81. E.g., Syed Ahmed Khan, *The Causes of the Indian Revolt, in Urdoo, in 1858, and translated into English by his two European friends* (Benares: Benares Medical Hall Press, 1873), 0.4 (2); Majumdar, *The Sepoy Mutiny and the Revolt of 1857*, 375; Faisal Devji, "The Mutiny to Come," *New Literary History* 40, no. 2, India and the West (Spring 2009), 412–14; Benjamin Disraeli in Salahuddin Malik, *1857 War of Independence or Clash of Civilizations?*, 64; Major and Bates, "Introduction," in *Mutiny at the Margins*, xvii.
82. Surendra Nath Sen, *Eighteen Fifty-Seven* (Delhi: Publications Division, Ministry of Information & Broadcasting, Govt. of India, 1957), 398–401. NB: Passing chapatis was a common practice, and functioned similarly to "chain letters;" however, while a number of commentators note an increase in the appearance of chapatis near the beginning of the Great Rebellion, given the system's clandestine nature, perhaps, hard evidence that the one necessarily indicates the other is lacking.
83. Peter Burke, "The 'Discovery' of Popular Culture," in *People's History and Socialist Theory*, ed. Raphael Samuel (London: Routledge & Kegan Paul, 1981), 218.
84. Malleson, *The Indian Mutiny of 1857*, 19.
85. John William Kaye, *A History of the Sepoy War in India, 1857–58* (London: W. H. Allen, 1880), 519.
86. W. H. Carey, *The Mahomedan Rebellion; Its Premonitory Symptoms, the Outbreak and Suppression; with an Appendix* (Roorkee: The Directory Press, 1857).
87. Malik, *1857 War of Independence or Clash of Civilizations?*, 113.
88. Carey, *The Mahomedan Rebellion*, 70–2.
89. W. H. Carey, *The Mahomedan Rebellion; Its Premonitory Symptoms, the Outbreak and Suppression; with an Appendix* (Lahore: Sang-e-Meel Publications, 2007 (reprint Roorkee: The Directory Press, 1857)), 9.
90. Ibid.
91. Ibid., 12.
92. Ibid., 10–12.
93. Ibid., 12.
94. Senzil Nawid, "The State, the Clergy, and British Imperial Policy in Afghanistan during the 19th and Early 20th Centuries," *International Journal of Middle East Studies* 29, no. 4 (November 1997), 581–2.
95. Shah of Persia in Carey, *The Mahomedan Rebellion*, 11.
96. Ibid., 12–13.
97. Ibid., e.g., 70–2, 83, 85–7.
98. Malik, *1857 War of Independence or Clash of Civilizations?*, 114–17.
99. Ibid., 115.
100. *The Examiner*, 1 August 1857. For similar opinions, Cf. Malleson, *The Indian Mutiny of 1857*, 43; Sir Alfred Lyall, *Race and Religion: An Address, May 5,*

1902, Reprinted from *The Fortnightly Review*, December 1902 (London: Social and Political Education League, ND), 3, 11–14.

101. Malleson, *The Indian Mutiny of 1857*, viii–ix.
102. Maulvi Ahmadulla of Faizabad is discussed more fully in chapter 4.
103. Ibid., e.g., 33.
104. R. C. Majumdar efficiently contends that there is both a lack of reliable evidence to demonstrate this and Malleson himself provided evidence that is incongruous with his own conclusions. See: Majumdar, *The Sepoy Mutiny and the Revolt of 1857*, 339.
105. Malleson, *The Indian Mutiny of 1857*, 17.
106. Ibid.
107. Ibid., 18–19, 27, 356.
108. Ibid., 114.
109. This is the thrust of her varied and celebrated career. See, as pertinent examples: Romila Thapar, "Imagined Religious Communities? Ancient History and the Modern Search for a Hindu Identity," *Modern Asian Studies* 23, no. 2 (1989), 209–31; "Was there Historical Writing in early India?" in *Knowing India: Colonial and Modern Constructions of the Past*, ed. Cynthia Talbot (New Delhi: Yoda Press, 2011), 281–307.
110. Ibid., 170.
111. E.g., S. M. Azizuddin Husain, "1857 as Reflected in Persian and Urdu Documents," in *Mutiny at the Margins: Volume VI: Perception, Narration and Reinvention: The Pedagogy and Historiography of the Indian Uprising* (New Delhi: Sage Publications, 2014), 171.
112. Arshad Islam, "The Backlash in Delhi: British Treatment of the Mughal Royal Family following the Indian 'Sepoy Mutiny' of 1857," 197.
113. E.g., W. Carey, *The Mahomedan Rebellion*, 1–4.
114. Carey, *The Mahomedan Rebellion*, 249.
115. Malleson, *The Indian Mutiny of 1857*, 307.
116. Islam, "The Backlash in Delhi: British Treatment of the Mughal Royal Family following the Indian 'Sepoy Mutiny' of 1857," 199. Cf. Hasan Nizami, "Delhi ki Jankani" (Delhi: Near to Death), in *1857 Majmuah Khawaja Hasan Nizami*, ed. Muhammad Ikram Chaghtai, "A Collection of Essays by Khawaja Hasan Nizami," (Lahore: Sang-e-Mel Publications, 2007), 496–7, 524.
117. E.g., Chidester, *Empire of Religion*, 26–8, 46–7, 48.
118. E.g., Jenny Berglund, "Princely Companion or Object of Offense? The Dog's Ambiguous Status in Islam," *Society & Animals* 22, no. 6 (December 15, 2014), 545–59.
119. Bernard S. Cohn, *An Anthropologist among the Historians and Other Essays*, with an introduction by Ranajit Guha (Delhi: Oxford University Press, 1987), 646.
120. G. C. Narang and Leslie Abel, "Ghalib and the Rebellion of 1857," *Mahfil* 5, no. 4, GHALIB ISSUE (1968–9), 46.

121. E.g., ibid., 45, 51–3. Cf. Masood Ashraf Raja, "The Indian Rebellion of 1857 and Mirza Ghalib's Narrative of Survival," *Prose Studies* 31, no. 1 (2009), 40–54.

122. Ibid., 52. Cf. Mirza Asadullah Khan Ghalib, and Imtiyāz ʿAlī Khā ʿArshī, *Makātīb-i Ghālib* (Rāmpūr: Rāmpūr Isṭaṭ Lāʾibrerī, 1949), 1, 8.

123. Masood Ashraf Raja, "The Indian Rebellion of 1857 and Mirza Ghalib's Narrative of Survival," 40.

124. Ghalib in G. C. Narang and Leslie Abel, "Ghalib and the Rebellion of 1857," 53.

125. Mushirul Hasan, "The Legacies of 1857 among the Muslim Intelligentsia of North India," in Crispin Bates, ed., *Mutiny at the Margins: New Perspectives on the Indian Uprising of 1857 Vol. V: Muslim, Dalit and Subaltern Narratives* (New Delhi: Sage Publications, 2014), 108.

126. Avril A. Powell, "Questionable Loyalties: Muslim Government Servants and Rebellion," in Crispin Bates, ed., *Mutiny at the Margins: New Perspectives on the Indian Uprising of 1857 Vol. V: Muslim, Dalit and Subaltern Narratives* (New Delhi: Sage Publications, 2014), 84.

127. Ibid., 88.

128. E.g., Alan Guenther, "A Colonial Court Defines a Muslim," in *Islam in South Asia in Practice*, ed. Barbara D. Metcalf (Princeton: Princeton University Press, 2009), 293–304.

129. Husain, "1857 as Reflected in Persian and Urdu Documents," 184.

130. G. C. Narang and Leslie Abel, "Ghalib and the Rebellion of 1857," 47–51.

131. Husain, "1857 as Reflected in Persian and Urdu Documents," 178.

132. *Minutes of Evidence Taken Before the Select Committee of the Honourable House of Commons*, 278–81.

133. Ibid., e.g., 403–4, 408–9, 430.

134. Malcolm Lewin, Esq., ed., *Causes of the Indian Revolt, by a Hindu Bengali* (London: Edward Stanford, 6, Charing Cross (October) 1857), 12.

135. During this period, a number of British scholars or agents of the Company reported "authentic" accounts of "natives," only later to be determined to have been written by British authors in the guise of Hindus or Muslims. Famously, Sir Alfred Lyall confessed to this type of writing. While I am not accusing Lewin of the same, the edited treatise he presents closely follows the style and assumptions of Lyall's; it is merely worth noting that connection, the broader context of the valuation of "authentic" reports, and a desire by some Britons to critique British actions *by way of* native voices. See: Parveen Shaukat Ali, *Pillars of British Imperialism: A Case Study of the Political Ideas of Sir Alfred Lyall, 1873–1903* (Lahore: Aziz Publishers, 1976), 34.

136. Chidester, *Empire of Religion*, 1; Gottschalk, *Religion, Science, and Empire*, 7–9.

137. E.g., *Minutes of Evidence Taken Before the Select Committee of the Honourable House of Commons, appointed for the purpose of taking the examination of such Witnesses as shall be ordered by the House to attend the Committee of the Whole House, on the Affairs of the East-India Company, and to report the MINUTES of such Evidence*

from time to time (London: by order of the Court of Directors for the information of the Proprietors, Cox and Son, 1813), 420–39.

138. Ibid., 522.

139. E.g., *Abstract of the Minutes of Evidence Taken in the Honourable House of Commons before a Committee of the Whole House to Consider the Affairs of the East India Company*, by the editor of the East India Debates (London: Black, Perry, and Co., 1813), 9–11, 34.

140. E.g., Malleson, *The Indian Mutiny of 1857*, 15–16.

141. Bhagwan Josh, "V. D. Sarwarkar's *The Indian War of Independence:* The First Nationalist Reconstruction of the Revolt of 1857," in Crispin Bates, ed., *Mutiny at the Margins: New Perspectives on the Indian Uprising of 1857 Vol. VI: Perception, Narration, and Reinvention: the Pedagogy and Historiography of the Indian Uprising* (New Delhi: Sage Publications, 2014), 34–5.

Chapter 2   Suspect Subjects: Hunter and the Making of a Muslim Minority

1. P. Hardy, *The Muslims of British India* (Cambridge, UK: Cambridge University Press, 1972), 62.

2. As but one example on the castes of Muslims, see: Imtiaz Ahmad, ed., *Caste and Social Stratification among the Muslims* (Delhi: Manohar Book Service, 1973).

3. The Mughal Empire was an empire ruled by Muslims. I am careful not to insist that the Mughal Empire was "Muslim rule," since this implies a contemporary notion of Islamic law governing all subjects. The Mughal emperors had varying and complex relationships to networks of Muslim authorities, including the 'ulama and Sufi, especially Chishti, elite. Cf. Jamal Malik, *Islam in South Asia: A Short History* (Leiden: Brill, 2008), especially "Part II: Between Islamic and Islamicate," pp. 85–213.

4. Many have discussed, defined, and redefined "minoritization." A particularly concise and productive definition appears in Wisdom Tettey, and Korbla P. Puplampu, *The African Diaspora in Canada: Negotiating Identity & Belonging* (Calgary: University of Calgary Press, 2005), 94.

5. E.g., Partha Chatterjee, *Nationalist Thought and the Colonial World: A Derivative Discourse?* (London: Zed, 1986).

6. E.g., David Chidester, *Empire of Religion*, 45.

7. S. C. Mittal, *India Distorted: A Study of British Historians on India* (New Delhi: M. D. Publications, 1996), 170.

8. Alex Padamsee, *Representations of Indian Muslims in British Colonial Discourse* (New York: Palgrave Macmillan, 2005), 151.

9. Peter Gottschalk and Gabriel Greenberg, "Common Heritage, Uncommon Fear: Islamophobia in the United States and British India, 1687–1947," in ed. Carl W. Ernst, *Islamophobia in America: Anatomy of Intolerance* (New York: Palgrave Macmillan, 2013), 32.

10. E.g., W. A. Wilson, "The Situation in India," in *Islam and Missions: Being Papers Read at the Second missionary Conference on Behalf of the Mohammedan World at Lucknow, January 28–29, 1911* (New York, London: Fleming H. Revell, 1911). Permalink: http://hdl.handle.net/2027/uc2.ark:/13960/t6542ms59. Accessed April 10, 2017.

11. I use scare quotes to mark Hunter's use, and so retain his spelling of Wahabi, instead of Wahhabi.

12. Hardy, *The Muslims of British India*, 62.

13. Thomas R. Metcalf, *The Aftermath of Revolt: India 1857–1870* (Princeton, NJ: Princeton University Press, 1965), 298.

14. William Muir, and T. H. Weir. *The Life of Moḥammad from Original Sources* (London: Smith, 1878).

15. William Muir, *The Caliphate; Its Rise, Decline, and Fall, from Original Sources*, 2nd ed., Rev.; with Maps (London: Religious Tract Society, 1892).

16. Hardy, *The Muslims of British India*, 62.

17. William Muir, *Records of the Intelligence Department of the North-West Provinces of India during the Mutiny of 1857*, vol. 1 (Edinburgh, 1902), 46.

18. William Muir, *Records of the Intelligence Department of the North-West Provinces of India during the Mutiny of 1857*, vol. 2 (Edinburgh, 1902), 258.

19. Avril A. Powell, *Scottish Orientalists and India: The Muir Brothers, Religion, Education and Empire* (Woodbridge, UK: Boydell Press, 2010), 256.

20. Muhammad Bahadur Shah Zafar (r. 1837–57, d. 1862), also known popularly as Bahadur Shah II, was the last Mughal emperor, though his reign was more or less titular; the East India Company had long since assumed primary control of South Asia, had imprisoned his father Akbar II, and had even given the emperor a pension. He was an Urdu poet, and while a majority of his works was destroyed in the Rebellion, a large collection exists and is titled *Kullīyyat-i-Ẓafar.* See: Muhammad Bahadur Shah. *Kulliyāt-i Ẓafar.* Dihlī: Mashvarah buk ḍipo, 1966.

21. Charles Raikes, *Notes on the Revolt in the North Western Provinces of India* (London: Longman, Brown, Green, Longmans & Roberts, 1858), 159.

22. John Lawrence in P. Hardy, *Muslims of British India*, 63.

23. Sir George Campbell, *Memoirs of my Indian Career*, vol. II (London and New York: Macmillan and Co., 1893) 398–9.

24. Hardy, *Muslims of British India*, 68.

25. As discussed more fully in the previous chapter, these changes include: the East India Company abolishment, the Queen's assumption of full sovereignty over India, and India not only becoming constitutionally part of the Empire, but also beginning its transformation in a British imagination from far-most imperial frontier to jewel in the English crown. On this last point, see especially: Bernard S. Cohn, *Colonialism and its Forms of Knowledge: The British in India* (Princeton, NJ: Princeton University Press, 1996), 118–19.

26. Eric Stokes, "Traditional Elites in the Great Rebellion of 1857," in *The 1857 Rebellion*, ed. Biswamoy Pati (New Delhi: Oxford University Press, 2007),

185; reprinted from Eric Stokes, *The Peasant and the Raj: Studies in Agrarian Society and Peasant Rebellion in Colonial India* (Cambridge: Cambridge University Press, 1978).

27. I use "small-p protestant" following Winifred Sullivan's astute observations. See: Winnifred Fallers Sullivan, *The Impossibility of Religious Freedom* (Princeton, NJ: Princeton University Press, 2007).

28. Mufti, *Enlightenment in the Colony: the Jewish Question and the Crisis of Postcolonial Culture* (Princeton, NJ: Princeton University Press, 2007), 2.

29. Ibid., 94.

30. Ibid., 1.

31. Ibid., 93.

32. Ibid., 111.

33. Metcalf, *The Aftermath of Revolt*, 301–4.

34. Mufti, *Enlightenment in the Colony*, 112, 140–53.

35. Anne Norton masterfully takes on the theoretical labeling of Muslims as a problem. See: Anne Norton, *On the Muslim Question*, Public Square (Princeton, NJ: Princeton University Press, 2013).

36. Christopher Hitchens, *The Illusion of Permanence: British Imperialism in India* (Princeton, NJ: Princeton University Press, 1967), 80–2; Peter van der Veer, *Imperial Encounters: Religion and Modernity in Britain and India* (Princeton, NJ: Princeton University Press, 2001), 13.

37. William Wilson Hunter, *The Indian Musalmans: Are They Bound in Conscience to Rebel against the Queen?* (London: Trübner and Co., 1872).

38. Francis Robinson, *Islam and Muslim History in South Asia* (New Delhi: Oxford University Press, 2001), 37–8.

39. Aaron Lazare, *On Apology* (New York: Oxford University Press, 2004), 99. See also: Bruce Mccall, "The perfect non-apology apology," *New York Times*, 22 April 2001: WK, General OneFile, web, 23 December 2014, Document URL: http://go.galegroup.com.ezproxy.uvm.edu/ps/i.do?id=GALE%7CA73542871&v=2.1&u=vol_b92b&it=r&p=ITOF&sw=w&asid=981b6e02804883288df015fde3768f81. Accessed December 23, 2014.

40. Hunter, *Indian Musalmans*, 141.

41. Ibid.

42. Aryanism and theories of Aryan people and languages are complex and tangential concepts here. It is worthy of note that W. W. Hunter's dissertation was on non-Aryan languages and literatures, titled: *A Comparative Dictionary of the Languages of India and High Asia, with a Dissertation Based on the Hodgson Lists, Official Records, and Mss.* (London: Trübner, 1868). Available digitally: http://ebooks.library.ualberta.ca/local/comparativedicti00huntuoft. Accessed April 10, 2017.

43. E.g., *Minutes of Evidence taken before the Select Committee of The House of Lords, appointed to enquire into the Present State of the Affairs of The East-India Company, and into the Trade between Great Britain, the East-Indies, and China, and to Report to the House* (London: Parbury, Allen, and Co., 1830).

44. E.g., *Correspondence relating to the Establishment of an Oriental College in London: Reprinted from the "Times," with Notes and Additions* (Edinburgh and London: Williams and Norgate, 1858).

45. Thomas Metcalf, *Ideologies of the Raj* (Cambridge: Cambridge University Press, 1994), 199.

46. Hunter, *Indian Musalmans*, 10.

47. Gayatri Chakrabarty Spivak, "Can the Subaltern Speak?" in *Marxism and the Interpretation of Culture*, Cary Nelson and Lawrence Grossberg, eds (Urbana: University of Illinois Press, 1988), 271–313.

48. Hunter, *Indian Musalmans*, 58.

49. Ibid., 71.

50. Harlan O. Pearson, *Islamic Reform and Revival in Nineteenth-century India: the Tarīqah-i-Muhmammadīyah* (New Delhi: Yoda Press, 2008), 33, 44–5.

51. E.g., Samira Haj, *Reconfiguring Islamic Tradition: Reform, Rationality, and Modernity* (Cultural Memory in the Present) (Stanford, CA: Stanford University Press, 2009).

52. Ibid., 84–6. Cf. Muin-ud-din Ahmad Khan, *Selections from Bengal Government Records on Wahhabi Trials (1863–1870)* (Dacca: Asiatic Society of Pakistan, 1961); Muhammad Abdul Bari, "A Comparative Study of the Early Wahhābi Doctrines and Contemporary Reform Movements in Indian Islām," Dissertation: D. Phil. University of Oxford, 1954.

53. Ibid., 11.

54. Hunter, *Indian Musalmans*, 10.

55. There is, of course, nothing "natural" about legalism, nor any real evidence that Muslims are distinctively legalistic; this is a part of the nineteenth-century debates about race, ethnicity, and religion, where so-called Semitic religions (Judaism, Islam) produce racially unique actors (Jews, Muslims) who have particular characteristics, like legalism. See, as one example: Masuzawa, "Chapter 6 – Islam: a Semitic religion," in *The Invention of World Religions*, 179–206.

56. Hunter, *Indian Musalmans*, 10.

57. Ibid., 10–11.

58. Ibid., 43.

59. Ibid., 11.

60. Ibid., 15–16, 22–6, 36, 38, 39, 41–6, 86, 97, 105, 147, 151.

61. Ibid., 24.

62. Ibid.

63. Ibid.

64. Alex Padamsee, *Representations of Indian Muslims in British Colonial Discourse*, 168–9.

65. It is unclear precisely what Hunter means by "army." In some cases, he moves between lamenting the problem of formal armies while simultaneously expressing scorn about the disorganized, chaotic nature of rebels; this is especially the case where he mentions the frontiers, a source of fear for him and concern for the Empire.

66. Hunter, *Indian Musalmans*, 15.
67. Ibid., 43.
68. As one might expect, as imperial forces and subjects moved into new areas, these areas were called Frontier Settlements; thus, his use of that name does not necessarily pinpoint his exact location. Based on the incidents described, and as stated, his career in the Bengal settlement, it is likely this is the region in question.
69. Hunter, *Indian Musalmans*, 44.
70. Ibid., 48.
71. Ibid., 50–1.
72. This dyad is still operative in contemporary depictions of Muslims. See especially: Mahmood Mamdani, *Good Muslim, Bad Muslim: America, the Cold War, and the Roots of Terror* (New York: Pantheon Books, 2004).
73. Hunter, *Indian Musalmans*, 15.
74. Charles Allen, "The Hidden Roots of Wahhabism in British India," *World Policy Journal* 22, no. 2 (Summer 2005), 87–8.
75. Pearson, *Islamic Reform and Revival in Nineteenth-century India*, 39.
76. Hunter, *Indian Musalmans*, 73.
77. Ibid., 66.
78. Ibid., 70–1. Cf. "Jama Tafasír," *Calcutta Review* (Delhi: 1857), 391–3.
79. Hunter, *Indian Musalmans*, 78–9.
80. Ibid., 115.
81. Of course, Muslims do not believe that the Qur'an is comprised of Muhammad's precepts, as Hunter states, but rather is the direct word of God, as heard (or recited) by Muhammad. Hunter's technical understanding – or lack thereof – is inconsequential for our purposes.
82. Hunter, n.p. Recall his prefatory statement to the 1872 reprint of *Indian Musalmans*: the government sanctioned his work, and he wrote it with use of the government's archives, but it is merely "demi-official" in nature.
83. Hunter, *Indian Musalmans*, 1.
84. Ibid., 109.
85. Ibid., 110.
86. Ibid., 122.
87. Ibid. Hunter inserts *dar-ul-islam* as the second footnote on this page, rather than in the text, as I have.
88. Ibid.
89. Ibid., 124.
90. Ibid.
91. Ibid. My emphasis.
92. Peter Gottschalk and Gabriel Greenberg, "Common Heritage, Uncommon Fear: Islamophobia in the United States and British India, 1687–1947," in ed. Carl W. Ernst, *Islamophobia in America: Anatomy of Intolerance* (New York: Palgrave Macmillan, 2013), 35.
93. Hunter, *Indian Musalmans*, 125.

94. Ibid. Emphasis in original.
95. Ibid., 133.
96. Some transliterate Abdool Luteef following more contemporary conventions as Abdul Latif.
97. *Abstract of the Proceedings of the Mahomedan Literary Society of Calcutta at a Meeting held at the Residence of Moulvie Abdool Luteef Khan Bahadoor on Wednesday, the 23rd of November, 1870* (Calcutta: Erasmus Jones, Cambrian Press, 1871), n.p.
98. E.g., Lester Hutchinson, *The Empire of the Nabobs: A Short History of British India* (London: Allen and Unwin, 1937); Ivor Lewis, *Sahibs, Nabobs, and Boxwallahs, a Dictionary of the Words of Anglo-India* (Bombay: Oxford University Press, 1991).
99. Ibid., n.p.
100. Ibid., n.p.
101. I purposefully mention both peace and Islam, because it is clear that these possible translations are at play, and the interplay between "Islam" and "peace" are not lost on Muslim commentators, but unbelievable for Hunter and British observers.
102. Ibid., 1.
103. Ibid., 4–5.
104. Hunter, *Indian Musalmans*, 125.
105. Ibid.
106. Ibid., 126.
107. Ibid.
108. E.g., Peter Gottschalk, *Religion, Science, and Empire: Classifying Hinduism and Islam in British India* (New York: Oxford University Press, 2013); Tomoko Masuzawa, *The Invention of World Religions: Or, How European Universalism was Preserved in the Language of Pluralism* (Chicago: University of Chicago Press, 1995).
109. E.g., Carl W. Ernst, *Following Muhammad* (Chapel Hill: University of North Carolina Press, 2003), 3, 57–61; Bruce B. Lawrence, "The Eastward Journey of Muslim Kingship: Islam in South and Southeast Asia," in *The Oxford History of Islam*, ed. John L. Esposito (New York: Oxford University Press, 1999), 395–434.
110. Hunter, *Indian Musalmans*, 126.
111. *Abstract of the Proceedings of the Mahomedan Literary Society of Calcutta at a Meeting held at the Residence of Moulvie Abdool Luteef Khan Bahadoor on Wednesday, the 23rd of November, 1870* (Calcutta: Erasmus Jones, Cambrian Press, 1871), n.p.
112. Hunter, *Indian Musalmans*, 126.
113. Ibid., 128.
114. Ibid.
115. Ibid.
116. Ibid.
117. Ibid., 131. FN 1: *Bilád-ul-Islám.*

118. Ibid., FN 2: *Farz-àin*.
119. Ibid., 131.
120. E.g., Mary A. Procida, *Married to the Empire: Gender, Politics and Imperialism in India, 1883–1947*, Studies in Imperialism (Manchester, UK: Manchester University Press, 2014).
121. Ibid., e.g., 126.
122. Ibid., 132. Emphasis in original.
123. Ibid., 133.
124. Ibid., 76.
125. *Jama Tafasír*, printed at Delhi 1867, 391. Cf. Hunter 70–1.
126. Ibid., 137–8.
127. Ibid., 139.
128. Ibid., 140.
129. Ibid.
130. Ibid., n. p.
131. Hunter, *Indian Musalmans*, 196.
132. Ibid., 213.
133. Ibid., 214.
134. Ibid., 142.
135. State-based and secular educations have long been tools of governance and dominance, across various imperial regimes and practices (albeit in differing and particular ways). See: Bernard Cohn, *Colonialism and its forms of Knowledge*, 45, 47–53.
136. P. Hardy, *The Muslims of British India* (Cambridge, UK: Cambridge University Press, 1972), 62.

Chapter 3   "God save me from my friends!": Syed Ahmad Khan's *Review on Dr Hunter*

1. Syed Ahmed Khan, B. D. R., C. S. I., *Review on Dr Hunter's Indian Musalmans: Are they Bound in Conscience to Rebel Against the Queen? The Original English Corrected by a Friend* (Benares: Printed at the Medical Hall Press, 1872), 6.
2. Ilyse R. Morgenstein Fuerst, "Sir Sayyid Aḥmad Khān," in *Biographical Dictionary of Islamic Civilisation and Culture*, ed. Mustafa Shah (London: I.B.Tauris, forthcoming).
3. E.g., Sayyid Ahmed Khan, "Lecture on Islam," in *Modernist Islam: A Sourcebook, 1840–1900*, ed. Charles Kurzman (New York: Oxford University Press, 2002), 291–313. Cf. Ali Qadir, "Between secularism/s: Islam and the institutionalization of modern higher education in mid-nineteenth century British India," *British Journal Of Religious Education* 35, no. 2 (March 2013), 125–139.
4. As mentioned above, I use small-p protestant following Winifred Sullivan. She argues that protestant ideals are coded within Western conversations of

civilization, even if those conversations do not specifically reference Christianity. See: *The Impossibility of Religious Freedom*, 7–8.

5. E.g., J. S. Bandukwala, "Indian Muslims: Past, Present and Future," *Economic and Political Weekly* 41, no. 14 (2006), 1341–4.

6. Faisal Devji, "Apologetic Modernity," *Modern Intellectual History* 4, no. 1 (April 2007), 64.

7. Syed Ahmed Khan, principal Sudder Ameen of Mordabad, *An Essay on the Causes of Indian Revolt* (Agra: printed by J. A. Gibbons, Mofussilite Press, 1859). See also: *Cause of the Indian Revolt: Three Essays*, ed. Salim al-Din Quraishi (Lahore: Sang-e Meel Publications, 1997).

8. Syed Ahmed Khan, *The Causes of the Indian Revolt, in Urdoo, in 1858, and translated into English by his two European friends* (Benares: Benares Medical Hall Press, 1873).

9. The closeness in dates and reprinting in English may signal a timely interest in these works, a need for dissenting critique of a normative depiction of Muslims as suspicious, a British champion of Sir Syed, or a combination of these factors. The closeness in publication in English certainly indicates, however, an English-speaking audience for these texts.

10. This is reminiscent of the debates preceding the Charter Act of 1813, where numerous Britons warned against missionary involvement for reasons quite similar to the ones Sir Syed expressed some 45 years later. See chapter 1 for a fuller discussion.

11. Sullivan, *The Impossibility of Religious Freedom*, 7–8. Because Khan does not specify denomination, I use "christianity" to highlight his broad-based conceptualization of the factors at play. Within the colonial, imperial, and civilizing missions at play within Khan's historical moment, small-c christianity better captures these overlapping ideological trends as he experienced them than Sullivan's small-p protestantism.

12. Syed Ahmed Khan, *The Causes of the Indian Revolt, in Urdoo, in 1858, and translated into English by his two European friends* (Benares: Benares Medical Hall Press, 1873), 3.

13. Ibid., 5.

14. Ibid., 5, 6.

15. Ibid., 7.

16. Ibid., 10.

17. Ibid., 15–16.

18. Sanjay Sharma, "The 1837–38 Famine in U.P.: Some Dimensions of Popular Action," *Indian Economic and Social History Review* 30, no. 3 (1993), 341. Cf. C. A. Bayly, *Rulers, Townsmen and Bazaars: North Indian Society in the Age of British Expansion 1770–1870* (Cambridge: Cambridge University Press, 1983), 263–302.

19. Khan, *Causes of the Indian Revolt*, 17.

20. Ibid.

21. Ibid., 19.

22. Ibid., 19–20. NB: Politics of language, its formalization, and its ties to ethnicity, caste, and religion is a compilation of hotly debated topics with ties to imperial programs of colonization. See, as examples: Kavita Saraswathi Datla, *The Language of Secular Islam: Urdu Nationalism and Colonial India* (Honolulu: University of Hawai'i Press, 2013); N. Krishnaswamy and Archana S. Burde, *The Politics of Indians' English: Linguistic Colonialism and the Expanding English Empire* (Delhi: Oxford University Press, 1998); Bernard Spolsky, ed., *The Cambridge Handbook of Language Policy* (Cambridge: Cambridge University Press, 2012).

23. Khan, *Causes of the Indian Revolt*, 22.

24. Ibid., 25. Each of these subjects is fodder for a fuller discussion that touches on a wide variety of issues in imperial history in South Asia. See, as examples: Dana Lee Robert, ed. *Converting Colonialism: Visions and Realities in Mission History, 1706–1914*, Studies in the History of Christian Missions (Grand Rapids, MI: William B. Eerdmans, 2008); Avril A. Powell, *Muslims and Missionaries in Pre-mutiny India*, London Studies on South Asia 7 (Richmond, Surrey: Curzon Press, 1993); Rachel Lara Sturman, *The Government of Social Life in Colonial India: Liberalism, Religious Law, and Women's Rights*, Cambridge Studies in Indian History and Society 21 (New York: Cambridge University Press, 2012).

25. For a fuller discussion of Act XXI and its effects, see: Rachel Sturman, "Property and Attachments: Defining Autonomy and the Claims of Family in Nineteenth-Century Western India," *Comparative Studies in Society and History* 47, no. 3 (2005), 611–37.

26. Khan, *Causes of the Indian Revolt*, 24.

27. Gauri Viswanathan, *Outside the Fold: Conversion, Modernity, and Belief* (Princeton, NJ: Princeton University Press, 1998), 88.

28. Khan, *Causes of the Indian Revolt*, 17–18. Emphasis mine.

29. Ibid., 25.

30. Ibid., 18.

31. Missionaries were formally allowed access under the Charter Act of 1813, but with various regulations. For an excellent compilation of conflicting definitions, histories, and implications of missionary allowances and exclusion, see: Robert Eric Frykenberg and Alaine M. Low, eds. *Christians and Missionaries in India: Cross-Cultural Communication Since 1500, with Special Reference to Caste, Conversion, and Colonialism* (Grand Rapids, MI: W. B. Eerdmans Pub, 2003).

32. Khan, *Causes of the Indian Revolt*, 18.

33. *Minutes of Evidence Taken Before the Select Committee of the Honourable House of Commons, appointed for the purpose of taking the examination of such Witnesses as shall be ordered by the House to attend the Committee of the Whole House, on the Affairs of the East-India Company, and to report the MINUTES of such Evidence from time to time* (London: by order of the Court of Directors for the information of the Proprietors, Cox and Son, 1813), 283–7. NB: The 1813 Charter Act hearings were more fully discussed in chapter 1.

34. Syed Ahmed Khan, *Causes of the Indian Revolt*, 23–6.

35. Ibid., 33.
36. Ibid., 36.
37. It is worth noting that in at least one Urdu reprint, citations and an appendix including selected full primary source texts are also present. See: Sayyid Ahmad Khan, and Salim al-Din Quraishi, *The Causes of the Indian Revolt* (Patna: Khuda Bakhsh Oriental Public Library, 1995).
38. E. Edmonds in Ibid., 55.
39. His Honourable Lieutenant Governor of Bengal in Ibid., 61.
40. Syed Ahmed Khan, principal Sudder Ameen of Mordabad, *An Essay on the Causes of Indian Revolt* (Agra: printed by J. A. Gibbons, Mofussilite Press, 1859), 6.
41. Ibid., 7–8.
42. The Rebellion as jihad, along with debates about the legitimacy of fatwas, is discussed in the next chapter.
43. Syed Ahmed Khan, principal Sudder Ameen of Mordabad, *An Essay on the Causes of Indian Revolt* (Agra: printed by J. A. Gibbons, Mofussilite Press, 1859), 7–8.
44. Khan, *Causes of the Indian Revolt*, 17, 18–19, 26.
45. Lieut.-Colonel. G. F. I. Graham, B. S. C., *The Life and Work of Syed Ahmed Khan* (London: William Blackwood and Sons, 1885), 33.
46. Ibid., 19, 31, 32.
47. Syed Ahmed Khan, B. D. R., C. S. I., *Review on Dr Hunter's* Indian Musalmans: Are they Bound in Conscience to Rebel Against the Queen? *The Original English Corrected by a Friend* (Benares: Printed at the Medical Hall Press, 1872).
48. Ibid., 3–5.
49. Ibid.
50. Ibid.
51. Ibid., 6.
52. Hunter, *Indian Musalmans*, n.p.
53. Despite Hunter's claims of neutrality and "demi-official" positionality, recall that Hunter was commissioned to write *Indian Musalmans* by the Viceroy Lord Mayo; even though it was typically a termed position, it was the highest-ranking administrative position in British India and answered directly to the sovereign.
54. Khan, *Review*, 6.
55. Ibid., 7.
56. Ibid.
57. Ibid.
58. Ibid., 30–1.
59. Ibid., 21, 32–3.
60. Ibid., 37.
61. Ibid., 42.
62. Sir Sayyid Ahmed Khan, *An Account of the Loyal Mahomedans of India* (Meerut: J. A. Gibbons, at Motussilite Press, 1860), 10–11, 19, 38.

63. Sean Oliver-Dee, *Muslim Minorities and Citizenship: Authority, Communities and Islamic Law* (London: I.B.Tauris, 2012), 81.

64. Khan, *Review*, 42.

65. Hunter, *Indian Musalmans*, 140.

66. Khan, *Review*, 44.

67. Ibid. NB: The legal issues of a country's status are more fully discussed in Chapter 1. The relationship between a country's status and jihad are discussed more fully in Chapter 4.

68. Ibid. Cf. Hunter, *Indian Musalmans*, 141.

69. Ibid., 44–5.

70. Qur'an 5:85, trans. George Sale, in Khan, *Review*, 45. NB: Most standard translations of the Qur'an indicate that this verse is 5:82, not 5:85. Cf. Marmaduke William Pickthall, *The Meaning of the Glorious Qur'an: Text and Explanatory Translation* (New York: Muslim World League, 1977). I have maintained the translation in the *Review* because of what it represents, not what it says particularly; i.e., its use symbolically and authoritatively is more important than its content.

71. Khan, *Review*, 45.

72. This is a well-rehearsed set of arguments, with proponents and detractors from all sides of many political spectra. Short pieces that feature purposeful considerations of "greater *jihad*," i.e., the struggle against ones' inner desires and demons, as the "real *jihad*," include but are not limited to: Onder Bakircioglu, "A Socio-Legal Analysis of the Concept of Jihad," *The International and Comparative Law Quarterly* 59, no. 2 (2010), 413–40; Paul L. Heck, "'Jihad' Revisited," *The Journal of Religious Ethics* 32, no. 1 (2004), 95–128; Mahmood Ahmad Ghazi, "The Law of War and Concept of Jihad in Islam," *Policy Perspectives* 5, no. 1 (2008), 69–86; Noor Mohammad, "The Doctrine of Jihad: An Introduction," *Journal of Law and Religion* 3, no. 2 (1985), 381–97; Mark Sedgwick, "Jihad, Modernity, and Sectarianism," *Nova Religio: The Journal of Alternative and Emergent Religions* 11, no. 2 (2007), 6–27.

73. Khan, *Review*, 47.

74. Hunter, *Indian Musalmans*, 145, FN 1. Cf. Khan, *Review*, 45.

75. Khan, *Review*, 47.

76. Ibid.

77. Ibid.

78. Ibid., 51.

79. Ibid., 49.

80. Ibid., 50.

81. See, as examples: Aziz Ahmad, "The Role of Ulema in Indo-Muslim History," *Studia Islamica* 31 (1970), 1–13; Ishtiaq Husain Qureshi, *Ulema in Politics; A Study Relating to the Political Activities of the Ulema in the South-Asian Subcontinent from 1556 to 1947* (Karachi: Ma'aref, 1972); Asghar Ali Engineer, "Muslims and Education," *Economic and Political Weekly* 36, no. 34 (2001), 3221–2.

82. Ibid., 22–3. Cf. Hunter, *Indian Musalmans*, 10.

83. Khan, *Review*, 23.

84. Ibid., 23.

85. Ibid.

86. Ibid., 23–4.

87. R. C. Majumdar, *The Sepoy Mutiny and the Revolt of 1857* (Calcutta: Firma K. L. Mukhopadhyay, 1963), 69–76, 99–107.

88. E.g., ibid., 18, 25.

89. Khan, *Review*, 20.

90. Ibid., 26.

91. Ibid., 27.

92. E.g., Major Fosberry, "On Some of the Mountain Tribes of the N. W. Frontier of India," *The Journal of the Ethnological Society of London (1869–1870)* 1, no. 2 (1869), 182–93.

93. Khan, *Review*, 19.

94. Ibid., 25.

95. Ibid., 35.

96. Ibid., 55–7.

97. Ibid., 62. NB: I assume Hunter relied here on the Islamic eschatological concept of *mahdi*, a prophesized redeemer whose appearance foreshadows the Day of Judgment (*yawm al-qiyamah*). Generally speaking, Shi'i Muslims have more fully developed this concept theologically, and understand the *mahdi* to have already been born; Sunni Muslims, on the other hand, typically state that *mahdi* is Muhammad's successor who is yet to come. Of relevance are modern Sunni interpretations often that imagine the *mahdi* will come in the form of a political reformer – a person perhaps not unlike Syed Ahmed Barelvi. See: David Cook, *Contemporary Muslim Apocalyptic Literature, 1st ed.* (Syracuse, NY: Syracuse University Press, 2005). It is unclear, however, both from Hunter's singular use of the term *mahdi* (63) as well as an atypical dearth of citations how he decided that Syed Ahmed's role was that of "great Imam" that would "precede the final coming of Christ."

98. Hunter, *Indian Musalmans*, 64.

99. Ibid., 73.

100. Ibid., 76, 78–9.

101. Khan, *Review*, 39.

102. Ibid., 70–5. These included: (1) the leadership and appearance of Syed Ahmed (1823–30), in which there was a legal *jihad* against Sikhs and Sikh armies; (2) a brief period, 1830–1, which Hunter called the "reconquest of Peshawar" and in which Syed Ahmed died; (3) the span of 1831–47 in which Wahhabis Inayat Ali and Waliyat Ali garnered great influence; (4) the passing of both Inayat and Waliyat Ali in 1847; and (5) the "present period," which Hunter called the period of "Wahabi insurrection."

103. Hunter, *Indian Musalmans*, 131.

104. Khan, *Review*, 8.

105. Ibid., 11–12.
106. E.g., Aamir Mufti, *Enlightenment in the Colony*, 8–9, 41–69.
107. The Proclamation, issued on November 1, 1858, formally announced the end of the East India Company's rule in India, and declared they would thereafter govern India by proxy in the name of the British monarch. It made public and official the Government of India Act of 1858, and the Queen's right to appoint a Principal Secretary of State. See: Stanley Wolpert, *A New History of India*, 3rd ed. (New York: Oxford University Press, 1989), 239–40.
108. *Proclamation of the Queen to the Princes, Chiefs & People of India {giving Notice of the Transfer of the Affairs of the East India Company to the Government, and Declaring a General Amnesty for Political Offences Committed During the Mutiny}. 1 November 1858. Translated into the Native Languages of British India. {with a Map of India Showing the Various Tracts Where the Several Languages Are Spoken.}*. Calcutta, 1858. British Library Shelfmark: 14999.e.1.
109. C. S. Adcock, *The Limits of Tolerance: Indian Secularism and the Politics of Religious Freedom* (New York: Oxford University Press, 2014), 33.
110. Khan, *Review*, 14.
111. Ibid. NB: Khan dates this jihad to 1824, but most usually date it to 1826. See, for example: Mu'īn-Ud-Dīn Aḥmad Khān, "Sayyid Aḥmad Shahīd's Campaign Against the Sikhs," *Islamic Studies* 7, no. 4 (1968), 317–38.
112. Khan, *Review*, 16.
113. Hunter, *Indian Musalmans*, 126.
114. Ibid., 9.
115. Ibid.
116. Ibid., 11.
117. I have retained Syed Ahmad Khan's spellings, but we would more readily encounter this term in transliteration as *ahl al-hadith*.
118. Khan, *Review*, 12.
119. Hunter, *Indian Musalmans*, 78–80.
120. Khan, *Review of Hunter*, 17.
121. Ibid.
122. Ibid., 18.
123. Hunter, *Indian Musalmans*, 125–6, 131.
124. Ibid., 44.
125. Ibid., 19–20.
126. Ibid.
127. Hunter, *Indian Musalmans*, 213–14.
128. Khan, *Review*, 52.
129. Ibid.
130. Ibid., 53.
131. Ibid., 53.
132. Hunter, *Indian Musalmans*, n.p. (preface), 141, 196.
133. Khan, *Review*, 6.
134. Ibid., 53.

135. E.g., Nicholas B. Dirks, *The Scandal of Empire: India and the Creation of Britain* (Cambridge, MA: Belknap Press of Harvard University Press, 2006), 26–8; Ranajit Guha, *Dominance without Hegemony: History and Power in Colonial India* (Cambridge, MA: Harvard University Press, 1997), 60–94; 156–75.

136. E.g., Walter D. Mignolo, *Local Histories/Global Designs: Coloniality, Subaltern Knowledges, and Border Thinking*, Princeton Studies in Culture/power/history (Princeton, NJ: Princeton University Press, 2000); Walter D. Mignolo, "The Global South and World Dis/Order," *Journal of Anthropological Research* 67, no. 2 (Summer 2011), 165–88; Nicholas B. Dirks, "Castes of Mind," *Representations* 37, Special Issue: Imperial Fantasies and Postcolonial Histories (Winter 1992), 56–78.

137. Franz Fanon, Jean-Paul Sartre, and Constance Farrington, *The Wretched of the Earth* (New York: Grove Press, Inc., 1965).

138. Graham, *The Life and Work of Syed Ahmed Khan*, 231.

139. W. A. Wilson, "The Situation in India," in *Islam and Missions*, 146, 147–9. Cf. Gottschalk and Greenberg, "Common Heritage, Uncommon Fear," in *Islamophobia in America*, 32.

140. Bashir Ahmed Dar, *Religious Thought of Syed Ahmed Khan* (Lahore: Jadeed Urdu Press, 1957), 14–15.

141. Padamsee, *Representations of Indian Muslims*, 155–7.

142. Khan, *Review*, 40.

143. Padamsee, *Representations of Indian Muslims*, 156.

144. Khan, *Review*, 6.

145. E.g., Faisal Devji, "Apologetic Modernity," *Modern Intellectual History* 4, no. 1 (April 2007), 61–76.

Chapter 4   Rebellion as Jihad, Jihad as Religion

1. Ayesha Jalal, *Partisans of Allah: Jihad in South Asia* (Cambridge, MA: Harvard University Press, 2008), 3.

2. Hunter uses "Puritan" to describe Muslims in a number of places. He describes Sunni Muslims as "the Puritans of Islam" in *Indian Musalmans*, 58. Elsewhere, he states that "abhorrence of the Infidel" is the "essence of Muhammadan Puritanism," *Imperial Gazetteer*: Vol. 2. Bengal to Cutwa (London: Trubner and Co., 1881), 18. Where he refers to Muslims as Puritans – or as I have rendered it grammatically, puritanical – he indicates an austerity and an extremism in religion. Some continue to replicate this usage. See, as examples: Giovanni Bonacina, *The Wahhabis Seen through European Eyes (1772–1830): Deists and Puritans of Islam*, History of Oriental Studies, Volume 1 (Leiden; Boston: Brill, 2015); Barry Vann, *Puritan Islam: The Geoexpansion of the Muslim World* (Amherst, NY: Prometheus Books, 2011).

3. Khan, *Review on Dr Hunter*, 10–11.

4. I reference here with Benedict Anderson's influential notion of imagined communities as part and parcel of developing the nation. See: *Imagined Communities: Reflections on the Origin and Spread of Nationalism* (London: Verso, 1983).

5. Zaheer Baber, "'Race', Religion and Riots: The 'racialization' of Communal Identity and Conflict in India," *Sociology* 38, no. 4 (2004), 703.

6. E.g., J. Rex, "The Concept of Race in Sociological Theory," in Sami Zubaida, ed., *Race and Racialism* (London: Tavistock, 1970), 39; Robert Miles, *Racism* (London: Routledge, 1991), 75.

7. Baber, "'Race', Religion and Riots," 712.

8. While Mughal authority did not *de jure* cease until 1857, Mughal leadership had *de facto* ceded its authority well before this date; many standard historiographies locate Mughal decline in the mid-eighteenth century. See: John F. Richards, *The Mughal Empire* (Cambridge: Cambridge University Press, 1993), 253–81.

9. Jalal, *Partisans of Allah*, 3.

10. Shahab Ahmed, *What is Islam? The Importance of Being Islamic* (Princeton, NJ: Princeton University Press, 2015), 318.

11. Jihad is both unavoidable in contemporary media and little defined in mass usage. Journalistic and entertainment media alike deal with the topics of religious violence and terrorism, especially as it relates to the actions of Muslims. These actions are often labeled jihad by Euro-American media, sometimes before the perpetrators (and their motives) are known, or before such a claim is made or verified by Muslim perpetrators. These violent or terroristic acts are also often claimed as jihad by various Muslim extremist organizations as often as they are denounced as irreligious and anti-Islamic (and therefore, one assumes, *not authentically* jihad) by myriad other Muslims. All of which suggests that the uses of jihad by Muslims and non-Muslims alike remain complicated and contentiously defined.

12. Violent jihad is sometimes described as an "outer" or a "lesser" struggle, contrasted with "inner" or "greater" jihad, the struggle of the individual to conquer her religiously inappropriate urges, desires, and thoughts. As we can see from the framing of "lesser" and "greater," some have argued that the true meaning of jihad is, in fact, a non-violent attempt at bettering oneself. Shahab Ahmed notes that the idea that jihad is primarily a spiritual struggle is based upon a famous "non-canonical Hadith." Ahmed, *What is Islam?*, 318. Canonical or not, this is a well-established idea that has been written about widely. As an example that works particularly well, see: Abdulaziz Sachedina, "The Development of Jihad in Islamic Revelation and History," in *Cross, Crescent, and Sword: The Justification and Limitation of War in Western and Islamic Traditions*, ed. J. T. Johnson and J. Kelsay (Westport: Greenwood Press, 1990), 35–50.

13. Topical overviews about jihad seem to proliferate rapidly. For a concise but comprehensive overview of the topic, see: Sohail H. Hashmi, "Jihad,"

Encyclopedia of Islam and the Muslim World, Vol. 1., ed. Richard C. Martin (New York: Macmillan Reference USA, 2004); 377–9.

14. Michael David Bonner, *Jihad in Islamic History: Doctrines and Practice* (Princeton, NJ: Princeton University Press, 2006), 3. Cf. Reuven Firestone, *Jihād: The Origin of Holy War in Islam* (New York: Oxford University Press, 1999), 13–18.

15. Bonner, *Jihad in Islamic History*, 174.

16. Asma Afsaruddin nimbly traces the theological roots and eschatological uses of jihad in her recent work: *Striving in the Path of God: Jihād and Martyrdom in Islamic Thought* (New York: Oxford University Press, 2013).

17. Faisal Devji, *Landscapes of the Jihad: Militancy, Morality, Modernity* (Ithaca, NY: Cornell University Press, 2005), 33.

18. David Cook, *Understanding Jihad* (Berkeley: University of California Press, 2005), 34–5.

19. What had historically been a heavily debated and, at once, a specific set of Islamic legal questions as well as a broad categorical frame of analysis has become all the more fraught in a post-September 11, 2001 and global War on Terror context. There is a lot at stake for various constituencies in defining "jihad," especially after 9/11/01. While 9/11/01 marks the date of terrorist attacks in the United States (at the Pentagon in Washington, D.C. and World Trade Towers in New York City), it is also a date that many cite as the start of the US-led but internationally supported global War on Terror. Other European and/or Western nations have experienced terrorist attacks (the Madrid train bombings of March 2004; the underground bombings in London on 7/7/05; the 2015 gunman attacks in Paris, first at Charlie Hebdo and later at the Bataclan theater), but the 9/11 attacks mark a global shift in military responses to Islamic terrorism. Many – including Muslims – elide Islamic terrorism with jihad. For opposing views on whether Muslims terrorists necessarily participate in global jihad, see: Charles B. Strozier, "The Global War on Terror, Sliced Four Ways," *World Policy Journal* 24, no. 4 (2007/2008), 90–8; and Parvez Ahmed, "Terror in the Name of Islam – Unholy War, Not Jihad," *Case Western Reserve Journal Of International Law* 39, no. 3 (September 2007), 759–88.

20. Bonner, *Jihad in Islamic History*, 160.

21. Ibid. Cf. Margrit Pernau, *Ashraf into Middle Classes: Muslims in Nineteenth-Century Delhi* (New Delhi: Oxford University Press, 2013), 203–4.

22. *Dar* literally means "abode," and many scholars render *dar-ul-islam* and *dar-ul-harb* as abode of peace and war, respectively. *Dar-ul-aman* appears less frequently. In the imperial context, the issues of conquest, expansion, and control of *land* are primarily important to these debates, and so I prefer land, country, or region for *"dar."*

23. E.g., Taufiq Ahmad Nizami, *Muslim Political Thought and Activity in India During the First Half of the Nineteenth Century*, with a foreword by Mohammad Habib (Aligarh, India: Singh for T. M. Publications Aligarh, 1969), 3–4, 23–5.

24. Just war tends to be a term used in Western contexts, and has a rich history of philosophical reasoning and militaristic deployment. I use both just and holy war, here, to gesture toward the complexity of jihad traditions as well as attempt to capture the ways in which legal, political, and religious debates about jihad have been framed. For a concise comparison of just and holy war, see: Khalid Yahya Blankinship, "Parity of Muslim and Western Concepts of Just War," *Muslim World* 101, no. 3 (July 2011), 412–26. For a longer explication of jihad as just war, see John Kelsay, *Arguing the Just War in Islam* (Cambridge, MA: Harvard University Press, 2007).

25. The Hanafi *madhhab*, or school of legal thought, is one of the four primary Sunni *madhāhib*. It is also the foremost *madhhab* in South Asia, though not the singular legal school represented.

26. Muhammad Mushtaq Ahmad, "The Notions of Dār Al-ḥarb and Dār Al-islām in Islamic Jurisprudence with Special Reference to the Ḥanafī School," *Islamic Studies* 47, no. 1 (2008), 6.

27. Ibid., 8–10.

28. David Motadel, "Islam and the European Empires," *The Historical Journal* 55 (2012), 841.

29. It is beyond the scope of this project to outline all of the resistances to European imperialism in Africa, Asia, the Middle East, and the (so-called) New World in which Muslims were active participants or specifically called for jihad. As examples of Muslim resistance to colonial or imperial rule outside South Asia, see: Edward E. Curtis, "Islamic Jihad or Just Revolt? African Muslims in Latin America and the Caribbean," in *The Call of Bilal: Islam in the African Diaspora*. Islamic Civilization & Muslim Networks (Chapel Hill, NC: University of North Carolina Press, 2014), 111–34; B. G. Martin, "Muslim Politics and Resistance to Colonial Rule: Shaykh Uways B. Muhammad Al-Barāwī and the Qādirīya Brotherhood in East Africa," *The Journal of African History* 10 (1969), 471–86; Mallam M. Bashir Abubakar, "Muslim Responses to British Colonialism in Northern Nigeria as Expressed in Fulfulde Poems," *Islamic Africa* 4, no. 1 (2013), 1–14; Douglas Northrop, "Subaltern Dialogues: Subversion and Resistance in Soviet Uzbek Family Law," *Slavic Review* 60, no. 1 (2001), 115–39; Spencer D. Segalla, *The Moroccan Soul: French Education, Colonial Ethnology, and Muslim Resistance, 1912–1956*, France Overseas (Lincoln: University of Nebraska Press, 2009); Syed Muhd Aljunied, Khairudin, *Radicals: Resistance and Protest in Colonial Malaya* (DeKalb, IL: Northern Illinois University Press, 2015).

30. Elsewhere, Motadel notes that the idea of a *sui generis* Muslim community and pan-Islamic political and religious ideologies was not feared or viewed as suspect by European powers, but instead thought of and used as a political tool. For example, in his short essay "Jihad 1914," Motadel states that at the start of World War I, Ottoman leaders pushed for pan-Islamism, and drew on fatwas about jihad to draw support within and beyond their imperial borders; but, he notes that *Germans* "pushed for the jihad declaration," because they

hoped Muslims, who predominately lived within British, French, or Russian empires, would revolt. Germans deployed jihad, therefore, as a tactic by which to make Muslims (perhaps unwitting) allies against a common enemy. David Motadel, "Jihad 1914," *History Today* 64, no. 9 (September 2014), 41–2. Motadel also points out similar deployments of the notion of pan-Islamism and jihad by Nazi Germany leading up to and during World War II in his recent monograph, *Islam and Nazi Germany's War* (Cambridge, MA: The Belknap Press of Harvard University Press, 2014).

31. Margaret Kohn, "Afghānī on Empire, Islam, and Civilization," *Political Theory* 37, no. 3 (2009), 399.

32. Azmi Özcan, *Pan-Islamism: Indian Muslims, the Ottomans, and Britain (1877–1924)* (Leiden: E. J. Brill, 1997).

33. Archibald R. Colquhoun, "Pan-Islam," *The North American Review* 182.595 (1906), 906.

34. Ibid., 915.

35. E.g., Tariq Hasan, *Colonialism and the Call to Jihad in British India* (New Delhi: Sage Publications, 2015).

36. Wisdom Tettey and Korbla P. Puplampu, *The African Diaspora in Canada: Negotiating Identity & Belonging* (Calgary: University of Calgary Press, 2005), 94.

37. Baber, "'Race', Religion and Riots," 703.

38. Ibid., 712.

39. Marcia Hermansen, "Wahhabis, Fakirs and Others: Reciprocal Classifications and the Transformation of Intellectual Categories," in ed. Jamal Malik, *Perspectives of Mutual Encounters in South Asian History 1760–1860* (Leiden: Brill, 2000), 30.

40. Ibid., 31.

41. Khan, *Review*, 11–12.

42. Hermansen, "Wahhabis, Fakirs, and Others," 32. Cf. British Library, India Office Records, P/Sec/IND/22 July 17 1839.

43. E.g., Khan Bahadur Fazlullah Lutfallah Faridi, *Gazetteer of the Bombay Presidency*, Vol ix pt. 2, Bombay, 1899, pp. 12–13.

44. Hermansen, "Wahhabis, Fakirs, and Others," 32. Cf. Ahmad, "Chapter VIII: State Trials of Wahhabi Leaders, 1863–5," in *The Wahhabi Movement in India*, 200–34.

45. Hunter, *Indian Musalmans*, e.g., 43–4, 94–5, 106.

46. Khan, *Review*, 5. Chief Justice Norman (d. September 1871) was a magistrate in the Calcutta High Court, and was stabbed on his way home from chambers. His murder became a sensational story in many parts of the British Empire, and many presses and journals ran stories, sometimes with salacious details, about the murder and, later, the murder trial. As representative examples, see: "The Assassination of Chief Justice Norman," *The Sydney Morning Herald* (NSW: 1842–1954), October 28, 1871: 5. Accessed September 9, 2015. http://nla.gov.au/nla.news-article13247208. Cf. *The Law Magazine and Law*

Review, Or, Quarterly Journal of Jurisprudence, March to August 1871 (London: Butterworths, 1871).

47. Khan, *Review*, 8–9.

48. As examples: W. H. Carey, *The Mahomedan Rebellion; Its Premonitory Symptoms, the Outbreak and Suppression; with an Appendix* (Roorkee: The Directory Press, 1857); John William Kaye, *A History of the Sepoy War in India, 1857–58* (London: W. H. Allen, 1880); William Muir and T. H. Weir, *The Life of Mohammad from Original Sources* (London: Smith, 1878); William Muir, *Records of the Intelligence Department of the North-West Provinces of India during the Mutiny of 1857*, vols 1 and 2 (Edinburgh: 1902); William Muir, "The Mahommedan Controversy," *Calcutta Review*, IV (December 1845); William Muir, "Biographies of Mohammed for India," *Calcutta Review* 17, no. 34 (1852).

49. *The Letters of Indophilus to "The Times" With additional notes* (London: Longman, Brown, Green, Longmans and Roberts, *N.D.*), 36.

50. Ibid., 6.

51. Ibid.

52. Ibid.

53. Ibid.

54. Ibid., 6–7.

55. Ibid., 7, 8.

56. Ibid., 8.

57. Khan, *An Account of the Loyal Mahomedans of India*, Part I: 7.

58. Ibid., 4.

59. Hunter, *Indian Musalmans*, 214. As quoted above: "Without interfering in any way with their religion, and in the very process of enabling them to learn religious duties, we should render that religion perhaps less sincere, but certainly less fanatical. The rising generation of Muhammadans would tread the steps that have conducted the Hindus, not long ago the most bigoted nation on earth, into their present state of easy tolerance. Such a tolerance impress a less earnest belief than their fathers had; but it has freed them, as it would liberate the Musalmans, from the cruelties which they inflicted, the crimes which they perpetrated, and the miseries which they endured, in the name of mistaken religion."

60. One who participates in jihad is a *mujāhid* (pl., *mujahidīn*). Contemporary terrorism scholars and foreign policy makers and scholars use "*jihadi*" or "*jihadi*s." I choose to use jihadi precisely to mark its definition in relation to Western use, power, and interpretation; jihadi, as an Anglicized term, better captures the ways in which jihad, as a complex legal subject, comes to be redefined and reinterpreted *in light of* geopolitical realities of the nineteenth century and beyond.

61. I focus here on the time immediately relevant to our topic. However, precolonial as well as early colonial/late Mughal debates about jihad both existed and, given the ways in which Islamic law at least in part relies upon

legal precedent, influenced the later debates. However, my purpose is not to elucidate the complexities of jihad in all of South Asian Islamic history and writing, but rather to explore the formation of debates about jihad leading up to, during, and following the 1857 Rebellion. Ayesha Jalal has written the history of jihad in South Asia masterfully: *Partisans of Allah: Jihad in South Asia* (Cambridge, MA: Harvard University Press, 2008).

62. E.g., Salim al-Din Quraishi, ed. and comp., *Cry for Freedom: Proclamations of Muslim Revolutionaries of 1857* (Lahore: Sang-e-Meel, 1997).

63. E.g., Eric Stokes, *The Peasant and the Raj: Studies in Agrarian Society and Peasant Rebellion in Colonial India* (Cambridge: Cambridge University Press, 1978).

64. Jalal, *Partisans of Allah*, 1.

65. Tariq Hasan, *Colonialism and the Call to Jihad in British India* (New Delhi: Sage Publications), 27.

66. Ibid., 28.

67. Iqtidar Alam Khan, "The Wahabis in the 1857 Revolt: A Brief Reappraisal of Their Role," *Social Scientist* 41, no. 5/6 (2013), 17.

68. Khan, *Review on Dr Hunter*, 11–12.

69. I am moving briskly through this movement's history and connections. The classic study of Indian Wahhabis/Ahl-e Hadis is: Qeyamuddin Ahmad, *The Wahabi Movement in India* (Cambridge University Press, Calcutta, 1966).

70. Iqtidar Alam Khan, "The Wahabis in the 1857 Revolt," 16.

71. Ibid. Cf. Shah Ismail, *Mansab-i imamat*, passages translated by M. Mujeeb in *The Indian Muslims* (New Delhi: Munshiram Manoharlal, 1985), 463.

72. Jalal, *Partisans for Allah*, 1.

73. Ibid., 124.

74. Abdul Aziz quoted in Taufiq Ahmad Nizami, *Muslim Political Thought and Activity in India During the First Half of the Nineteenth Century*, 23–4. Cf. *Fatawa-i-Azizi*, Urdu trans. (Kanpur: n.d.).

75. Nizami, *Muslim Political Thought and Activity in India During the First Half of the Nineteenth Century*, 25.

76. Khan, "The Wahhabis and the 1857 Revolt," 16.

77. Jalal, *Partisans for Allah*, 114. Cf. Hasan, *Colonialism and the Call to Jihad in British India*, 42–4; Pernau, *Ashraf into Middle Classes*, 229.

78. Khan, "The Wahhabis and the 1857 Revolt," 18.

79. Ibid., 19. Cf. Jalal, *Partisans of Allah*, 115–16.

80. Khan, *Review*, 16, 23. See chapter 3 for a fuller discussion.

81. *Abstract of the Proceedings of the Mahomedan Literary Society of Calcutta at a Meeting held at the Residence of Moulvie Abdool Luteef Khan Bahadoor on Wednesday, the 23rd of November, 1870* (Calcutta: Erasmus Jones, Cambrian Press, 1871), 1. See Chapter 3 for a fuller discussion.

82. E.g., John H. Hanson, "Jihad and the Ahmadiyya Muslim Community: Nonviolent Efforts to Promote Islam in the Contemporary World," *Nova Religio: The Journal of Alternative and Emergent Religions* 11, no. 2 (2007), 77–93.

83. Jalal, *Partisans for Allah*, 116.

84. Colonel G. B. Malleson, C. S. I., *The Indian Mutiny of 1857* (London: Seeley and Co., Limited, 1891), 17.

85. As a reminder, the so-called chapati conspiracy refers to the passing of chapati breads to signal the beginning of the revolts in northern India. See chapter 1 for a fuller discussion.

86. Saiyid Zaheer Husain Jafri, "The Profile of a Saintly Rebel: Maulvi Ahmadullah Shah," *Social Scientist* 26, no. 1/4 (1998), 40.

87. Salim al-Din Quraishi, ed. and comp., *Cry for Freedom: Proclamations of Muslim Revolutionaries of 1857* (Lahore: Sang-e-Meel, 1997), viii.

88. Faruqui Anjum Taban, "The Coming of the Revolt in Awadh: The Evidence of Urdu Newspapers," in *Facets of the Great Revolt: 1857*, Shireen Moosvi, ed. (New Delhi: Tulika Books, 2008), 12.

89. Mushirul Haq, *Shah Abdul Aziz: His Life and Times* (Lahore: Institute of Islamic Culture, 1995), 59. Cf. Jalal, *Partisans of Allah*, 122.

90. Jalal, *Partisans of Allah*, 122.

91. Fazl-i-Haqq wrote an account of the Great Rebellion from the penal colony. In it, Fazl-i-Haqq both praised and critiqued other leaders, including Ahmadullah. While the text, as we might expect, is written in rather coded language, it does not state support for jihad, even by allusion. For a brief commentary and translation, see: S. Moinul Haqq, "The Story of the War of Independence by Allamah Fadl-i Haqq of Kharyabad," *Journal of the Pakistan Historical Society* 5, no. 1 (1957), 23–57.

92. R. A. Geaves, "India 1857: A Mutiny or a War of Independence? The Muslim Perspective," *Islamic Studies* 35, no. 1 (1996), 42. On Deoband, see Barbara Metcalf's definitive work, *Islamic Revival in British India: Deoband, 1860–1900* (Princeton, N. J: Princeton University Press, 1982).

93. See: Salim al-Din Quraishi, *Cry for Freedom: Proclamations of Muslim Revolutionaries of 1857* (Lahore: Sang-e-Meel Publications, 1997).

94. Taban, "The Coming of the Revolt in Awadh: The Evidence of Urdu Newspapers," 11–12.

95. Ibid., 13.

96. Ibid., 14.

97. Urdu and thus Urdu literacy were never *solely* limited to north Indian Muslims. However, Urdu's use in the nineteenth century was increasingly a marker of an Indian Muslim identity. See: Christopher King, *One Language, Two Scripts: The Hindi Movement in Nineteenth Century North India* (New Delhi: Oxford University Press, 1994). On Syed Ahmad Khan's role in the Urdu movement: Abdul R. Khan, *The All India Muslim Educational Conference: Its Contribution to the Cultural Development of Indian Muslims, 1886–1947* (Karachi: Oxford University Press, 2001), especially chapter 6: "Promotion of Urdu Language and Literature (1900–1945)."

98. Eric Stokes, *The Peasant Armed: The Indian Revolt of 1857*, ed. C. A. Bayly (Oxford: Clarendon Press, 1986).

99. E.g., Pernau, *Ashraf to Middle Class*, 223.

100. Jivan Lal quoted in Pernau, 223. Cf. Jīvana Lāla, and Dara<u>kh</u>shān Tājvar, *Sargu<u>z</u>asht-i Dihlī: Inqilāb 1857 Kī Kahānī Jīvan Lāl Kī Zabānī* (Rāmpūr: Rāmpūr Razā Lā'ibrerī, 2007).
101. Jalal, *Partisans of Allah*, 124.
102. Ibid.
103. As but one example, Sir Syed wrote about the discontent programs for orphans caused in the wake of the devastating 1837 droughts, and suggested that these orphans – reared "in principles of Christian faith" – were being secretly converted from their natural religions. Khan, *Causes of the Indian Revolt*, 17.
104. E.g., Hunter, *Indian Musalmans*, 11.
105. Farzana Shaikh, *Community and Consensus in Islam: Muslim Representation in Colonial India, 1860–1947*, Cambridge South Asian Studies 42 (New York: Cambridge University Press, 1989), 79.
106. Jalal, *Partisans of Allah*, 1.
107. Ibid. Cf. Nizami, *Muslim Political Thought and Activity in India during the first half of the Nineteenth Century*, 4. Khan mentions this as well: *Review on Dr Hunter*, 11, 14–16.
108. Khan, *Review*, 14.
109. Ibid., 19. Hunter, *Indian Musalmans*, 29.

Conclusion   Religion, Rebels, and Jihad: Legacies and Ongoing Impact

1. E.g., In honor of India's Independence Day, *Hindustan Times* ran a piece outlining the road to independence that began in August 1947 but traced origins to 1857. Saudamini Jain, "At the stroke of the midnight hour: The story of India's independence," August 11, 2015. http://www.hindustantimes.com/india/at-the-stroke-of-the-midnight-hour-the-story-of-india-s-independence/story-m6Lp74lEyp3WWJWeUTFnPM.html. Accessed March 29, 2016.
2. As examples: Farrukh Dhondy, et al. *Mangal Pandey the rising* (Mumbai: Yash Raj Films, 2005); Shashi Kapoor, Shyam Benegal, Shabana Azmi, Jennifer Kendal, Nafisa Ali, and Ruskin Bond, *Junoon* (Secaucus, NJ: Eros International (distributor, 2000)); Ruskin Bond, *A Flight of Pigeons* (Bombay: IBH Pub. Co., 1980); *1857 Kranti*, 104 episodes, dir. Sanjay Khan (Numero Uno International Limited, 2002); Javed Siddiqui, *1857: Ek Safarnama*, 2008. See also: Badri Narayan, "Popular Culture and 1857: A Memory Against Forgetting," *Social Scientist* 26, no. 1/4 (1998), 86–94.
3. As examples: J. G. Farrell, *The Siege of Krishnapur* (New York: Carroll & Graf, 1985 (orig. 1973; Booker Prize winner)); Mary Margaret Kaye, *Shadow of the Moon* (New York: St. Martin's Press, 1979); John Masters, *Nightrunners of Bengal, a Novel* (New York: Viking, 1951). See also: Albert D. Pionke, *Plots of Opportunity: Representing Conspiracy in Victorian England* (Columbus: Ohio State University Press, 2004).

4. The Indian Constitution retains a number of laws from the colonial/imperial period; recently, for example, Chapter XVI, Section 377 of the Indian Penal Code has gained attention. Dating to 1860, it criminalizes sexual acts "against the order of humanity," largely interpreted as homosexual sex. In 2013, four years after repealing this Section, the Indian Supreme Court reinstated it. In February 2016, *Reuters* reported that: "Supreme Court on Tuesday said it will review a decision over whether to uphold a colonial-era law that criminalizes gay sex in a victory for homosexual rights campaigners at a time when the nation is navigating a path between tradition and modernity." "Supreme Court will review law criminalizing homosexuality," *Reuters*, republished in *Times of India*, February 2, 2016. http://timesofindia.indiatim es.com/india/Supreme-Court-will-review-law-criminalizing-homosexuality/ articleshow/50823515.cms. Accessed March 9, 2016.

5. As examples: Robert McLain, *Gender and Violence in British India: The Road to Amritsar, 1914–1919* (New York: Palgrave Macmillan, 2014); Elizabeth Kolsky, *Colonial Justice in British India*, Cambridge Studies in Indian History and Society 17 (Cambridge; New York: Cambridge UP, 2010).

6. Dipesh Chakrabarty, "Remembering 1857: An Introductory Note," *Economic and Political Weekly* 42, no. 19 (May 12–18, 2007), 1692.

7. Ibid., 1693.

8. "Memorial to be set up in memory of 1857 mutiny martyrs," *The Hindu*, May 11, 2015. http://www.thehindu.com/news/national/other-states/memorial-to-be-set-up-in-memory-of-1857-mutiny-martyrs/article7191386.ece. Accessed March 29, 2016.

9. Nile Green, *Islam and the Army in Colonial India: Sepoy Religion in the Service of Empire* (New York: Cambridge University Press, 2009), 67.

10. E.g., Vinayak D. Savarkar and G. M. Joshi, *The Indian War of Independence, 1857* (Bombay: Phoenix Publications, 1947 [1909]).

11. Gottschalk, *Religion, Science, and Empire*, 1.

12. E.g., Christopher King, *One Language, Two Scripts: The Hindi Movement in Nineteenth Century North India* (New Delhi: Oxford University Press, 1994).

13. E.g., Balshastri Hardas, *Armed Struggle for Freedom: Ninety Years War of Indian Independence, 1857 to Subhash* (Poona: KAL Prakashan, 1958).

14. E.g., Syed Sharifuddin Pirzada ed., *Foundations of Pakistan: All-India Muslim League Documents, 1906–1947.* (Karachi: National Pub. House, 1969); Ayesha Jalal, *The Sole Spokesman: Jinnah, the Muslim League, and the Demand for Pakistan*, Cambridge South Asian Studies 31 (Cambridge; New York: Cambridge University Press, 1985).

15. E.g., David Page, *Prelude to Partition: The Indian Muslims and the Imperial System of Control, 1920–1932* (Delhi: Oxford University Press, 1982).

16. E.g., Peter Van Der Veer, *Religious Nationalism: Hindus and Muslims in India* (Berkeley: University of California Press, 1994).

17. Gyanendra Pandey, *Hindus and Others: The Question of Identity in India Today* (New Delhi: Viking, 1993); Ornit Shani, "Conceptions of Citizenship in India

and the 'Muslim Question,'" *Modern Asian Studies* 44, no. 1 (2010), 145–73; James Traub, "Is Modi's India Safe for Muslims?" *Foreign Policy*, June 26, 2015. http://foreignpolicy.com/2015/06/26/narendra-modi-india-safe-for-muslims-hindu-nationalism-bjp-rss/. Accessed August 15, 2015.

18. Maidul Islam, "Rethinking the Muslim Question in Post-colonial India," *Social Scientist* 40, no. 7/8 (2012), 64.

19. E.g., "The states where cow slaughter is legal in India," *Indian Express*, October 8, 2015. http://indianexpress.com/article/explained/explained-no-beef-nation/. Accessed March 9, 2016.

20. Khan, *Review*, 23.

21. Ibid., 45.

Epilogue   1857 from Today's Vermont

1. Ed Demaria, "Ben Carson Does Not Believe a Muslim Should Be President," via "Meet the Press," *NBC News*. http://www.nbcnews.com/meet-the-press/ben-carson-does-not-believe-muslim-should-be-president-n430431. Accessed April 5, 2016.

2. Donald Trump interview with Anderson Cooper. Anderson Cooper 360, March 9, 2016. CNN. Full transcript: http://www.cnn.com/TRANSCRIPTS/1603/09/acd.01.html. Accessed April 5, 2016.

3. President Bill Clinton, Democratic National Convention Speech for Hillary Clinton's Democratic Party Nomination, July 26, 2016. Full transcript: http://www.politico.com/story/2016/07/full-text-bill-clinton-dnc-speech-226269#ixzz4OlQ2fQaD. Accessed November 1, 2016.

4. Ed Demaria, "Ben Carson Does Not Believe a Muslim Should Be President," via "Meet the Press," *NBC News*. http://www.nbcnews.com/meet-the-press/ben-carson-does-not-believe-muslim-should-be-president-n430431. Accessed April 5, 2016.

5. Dr. Ben Carson's public Facebook page, post dated September 21, 2015. https://www.facebook.com/realbencarson/posts/532081783624959. Accessed April 5, 2016.

6. Ibid.

7. The first amendment to the Constitution begins: "Congress shall make no law respecting an establishment of religion, or prohibiting the free exercise thereof." Further, Article VI of the Constitution states: "No religious Test shall ever be required as a Qualification to any Office or public Trust under the United States." See: http://www.archives.gov/exhibits/charters/constitution_transcript.html. Accessed April 5, 2016.

8. Dr. Ben Carson and Candy Carson, *A More Perfect Union: What We the People Can Do to Reclaim Our Constitutional Liberties* (New York: Sentinel, an imprint of Penguin Random House LLC, 2015).

9. Juliagrace Brufke, "Ben Carson Doubles Down On Muslim In The White House Comments," *The Daily Caller*, September 22, 2015. http://dailycaller.

com/2015/09/22/ben-carson-doubles-down-on-muslim-in-the-white-house-comments/. Accessed April 5, 2016.

10. Donald Trump interview with Anderson Cooper. Anderson Cooper 360, March 9, 2016. CNN. Full transcript: http://www.cnn.com/TRANSCRIPTS/1603/09/acd.01.html. Accessed April 5, 2016.

11. As examples, see: NBC News, "KKK leader disavows violent past, declares Trump 'best' for president," May 9, 2016. http://www.nbc12.com/story/31846257/kkk-leader-disavows-violent-past-declares-trump-best-for-president. Accessed November 1, 2016; J. M. Berger, "How White Nationalists Learned to Love Donald Trump," Politico.com, October 25, 2016. http://www.politico.com/magazine/story/2016/10/donald-trump-2016-white-nationalists-alt-right-214388. Accessed November 1, 2016; and Mike Lofgren, "Trump, Putin, and the Alt-Right International," *The Atlantic* online, October 31, 2016. http://www.theatlantic.com/international/archive/2016/10/trump-putin-alt-right-comintern/506015/. Accessed November 1, 2016.

12. E.g., Jeremy Diamond, "Muslim Trump supporter's message amid 'no Islam' shout," CNN.com, July 20, 2016. http://www.cnn.com/2016/07/20/politics/american-muslim-for-trump-no-islam-response/. Accessed October 30, 2016 and "Watch: Rudy Giuliani addresses 'Islamic extremist terrorism' in Republican National Convention speech," *LATimes.com* (video recording). July 18, 2016. http://www.latimes.com/politics/87898481-132.html. Accessed November 1, 2016.

13. President Bill Clinton, 2016 Democratic National Convention Speech, http://www.politico.com/story/2016/07/full-text-bill-clinton-dnc-speech-226269#ixzz4OlQ2fQaD. Accessed November 1, 2016.

14. Edward E. Curtis IV, *Muslims in America: A Short History* (New York: Oxford University Press, 2009), 4.

15. E.g., Pew Research Center, "Muslim Americans," subsection "Islamic Affiliation and Converts of Islam," August 30, 2011. http://www.people-press.org/2011/08/30/section-2-religious-beliefs-and-practices/#fn-20034306-2. Accessed January 3, 2017. NB: While I point out white converts to Islam, the Pew Report only indicates conversion statistics, with no reference to race: "Among American Muslims, 20% are converts to Islam, saying they have not always been Muslim." For a comparative project on race and conversion, see: Juliette Galonnier, "The Racialization of Muslims in France and the United States: Some Insights from White Converts to Islam," *Social Compass* 62, no. 4 (2015), 570–83.

16. E.g., Chris Cillizza, "This Khizr Khan Ad for Hillary Clinton is Incredibly Powerful," *The Washington Post*, October 21, 2016. https://www.washingtonpost.com/news/the-fix/wp/2016/10/21/this-khizr-khan-ad-for-hillary-clinton-is-incredibly-powerful/. Accessed November 1, 2016.

17. Ghazala Khan, "Trump criticized my silence. He knows nothing about true sacrifice," *The Washington Post*, op-ed, July 31, 2016. https://www.washingtonpost.com/opinions/ghazala-khan-donald-trump-criticized-my-silence-he-knows-nothing-about-true-sacrifice/2016/07/31/c46e52ec-571c-

11e6-831d-0324760ca856_story.html?utm_term=.1c8eda7ab47a. Accessed October 30, 2016.

18. "Captain Khan," Hillary Clinton campaign, October 21, 2016. https://www.youtube.com/watch?v=WCqFCCgU1xk. Accessed November 1, 2016.

19. E.g., "Bans on Sharia and International Law," American Civil Liberties Union, https://www.aclu.org/bans-sharia-and-international-law. Accessed April 5, 2016.

20. "State Legislation Restricting Use of Foreign or Religious Law," Pew Research Center, April 8, 2013. http://features.pewforum.org/sharia-law-map/. Accessed April 6, 2016.

21. E.g., "Shariah in American Courts: The Expanding Incursion of Islamic Law in the U.S. Legal System," January 5, 2015. http://www.centerforsecuritypolicy.org/2015/01/05/shariah-in-american-courts-the-expanding-incursion-of-islamic-law-in-the-u-s-legal-system/. Accessed April 5, 2016.

22. William Faulkner, *Requiem for a Nun*, Act I, Scene 3 (New York: Random House, 1951).

BIBLIOGRAPHY

Original Sources

Abstract of the Minutes of Evidence Taken in the Honourable House of Commons before a Committee of the Whole House to Consider the Affairs of the East India Company, by the editor of the East India Debates. London: Black, Perry, and Co., 1813.

Abstract of the Proceedings of the Mahomedan Literary Society of Calcutta at a Meeting held at the Residence of Moulvie Abdool Luteef Khan Bahadoor on Wednesday, the 23rd of November, 1870. Calcutta: Erasmus Jones, Cambrian Press, 1871.

Affairs of the East India Company, 16 August 1832. London: printed by the Honourable Court of Directors, J. L. Cox and Son, 1833.

Ahmad Khan, Muin-ud-din. *Selections from Bengal Government Records on Wahhabi Trials (1863–1870).* Dacca: Asiatic Society of Pakistan, 1961.

Appendix to Report from the Select Committee XII: Crimes & Misdemeanors in Affairs of the East India Company, 16 August 1832. London: printed by the Honourable Court of Directors, J.L. Cox and Son, 1833.

"The Assassination of Chief Justice Norman." *The Sydney Morning Herald* (NSW: 1842–1954) 28 October 1871: 5. Accessed September 9, 2015. http://nla.gov.au/nla.news-article13247208.

British Library, India Office Records, P/Sec/IND/22, July 17, 1839.

Campbell, Sir George. *Memoirs of my Indian Career*, vol. II. London and New York: Macmillan and Co., 1893.

Campbell, John. *Memoirs of the Revolution in Bengal, Anno. Dom. 1757. By Which Meer Jaffeir Was Raised to the Government of That Province, Together with Those of Bahar and Orixa.* London: Printed for A. Millar, 1760. http://find.galegroup.com/ecco/infom ark.do?contentSet=ECCOArticles&docType=ECCOArticles&bookId=0536 700200&type=getFullCitation&tabID=T001&prodId=ECCO&docLevel= TEXT_GRAPHICS&version=1.0&source=library. Accessed April 10, 2017.

"Captain Khan." Hillary Clinton campaign video, October 21, 2016. Accessed November 17, https://www.youtube.com/watch?v=WCqFCCgU1xk.

Carey, W. H. *The Mahomedan Rebellion; Its Premonitory Symptoms, the Outbreak and Suppression; with an Appendix.* Roorkee: The Directory Press, 1857.

————. *The Mahomedan Rebellion; Its Premonitory Symptoms, the Outbreak and Suppression; with an Appendix.* Roorkee: The Directory Press, 1857. Reprint, Lahore: Sang-e-Meel Publications, 2007.

Carson, Ben. Facebook post dated September 21, 2015. https://www.facebook.com/realbencarson/posts/532081783624959. Accessed April 5, 2016.

Carson, Ben and Candy Carson. *A More Perfect Union: What We the People Can Do to Reclaim Our Constitutional Liberties.* New York: Sentinel, an imprint of Penguin Random House LLC, 2015.

Chapman, George, LLD. *Tracts of East India Affairs viz., Collegium Bengalense, a Latin Poem with an English trans., and a dissertation on the best means of Civilizing the Subjects of the British Empire in India, and of Diffusing the Light of Christian Religion throughout the Eastern World.* 2nd ed. (Includes preface by unnamed author.) Edinburgh: John Moir, Royal Bank Close, 1805.

Clinton, President Bill. "2016 Democratic National Convention Speech," transcript. Accessed November 1, 2016. http://www.politico.com/story/2016/07/full-text-bill-clinton-dnc-speech-226269#ixzz4OlQ2fQaD.

Colquhoun, Archibald R. "Pan-Islam." *The North American Review* 182, no. 595 (1906): 906–18.

Correspondence relating to the Establishment of an Oriental College in London. Reprinted from the "Times," with notes and additions. Edinburgh and London: Williams and Norgate, 1858.

Duff, Alexander. *The Indian Rebellion: Its Causes And Results.* London: James Nisbet, 1858.

The Examiner. August 1, 1857.

Faridi, Khan Bahadur Fazlullah Lutfallah. *Gazetteer of the Bombay Presidency,* Vol ix pt. 2, Bombay, 1899.

Fatāwa-i-Azizi, Urdu trans. Kanpur: n.d.

Faulkner, William. *Requiem for a Nun,* Act I, Scene 3. New York: Random House, 1951.

Forrest, Sir George. *A History of the Indian Mutiny: Reviewed And Illustrated From Original Documents, vol. 1.* Edinburgh: W. Blackwood, 1904.

Fosberry, Major. "On Some of the Mountain Tribes of the N.W. Frontier of India." *Journal of the Ethnological Society of London (1869–1870)* 1, no. 2 (1869): 182–93.

Ghalib, Asad Allah Khan, and K. A. Faruqi. *Dastanbuy {Storyteller}: A Diary of the Indian Revolt of 1857.* London: Asia Pub. House, 1970.

Ghalib, Mirza Asadullah Khan and Imtiyāz 'Alī Khā 'Arshī. *Makātīb-i Ghālib.* Rāmpūr: Rāmpūr Isṭaṭ Lā'ibrerī, 1949. https://dds.crl.edu/crldelivery/3313. Accessed April 10, 2017.

Graham, Lieut.-Colonel. G. F. I., BSC. *The Life and Work of Syed Ahmed Khan.* London: William Blackwood and Sons, 1885.

Giuliani, Rudy. RNC Speech. "Watch: Rudy Giuliani addresses 'Islamic extremist terrorism' in Republican National Convention speech," *LATimes.com* (video recording). July 18, 2016. Accessed November 1, 2016. http://www.latimes.com/politics/87898481-132.html.

Hunter, Robert. *The History of India: From the Earliest Ages to the Fall of the East India Company And the Proclamation of Queen Victoria In 1858.* London (etc.): T. Nelson and Sons, 1863. Permalink: http://hdl.handle.net/2027/hvd.hn3gd5. Accessed April 10, 2017.

Hunter, William Wilson. *A Comparative Dictionary of the Languages of India And High Asia: With a Dissertation. Based On the Hodgson Lists, Official Records, And Mss.* London: Trübner and Co., 1868.

———. *The Indian Musalmans: Are They Bound in Conscience to Rebel against the Queen?*, 2nd ed. London: Trübner and Co, 1872.

———. *Imperial Gazetteer: Vol. 2. Bengal to Cutwa.* London: Trübner and Co., 1881

The Indian War of Independence of 1857 by an Indian Nationalist. London, 1909.

"Jama Tafasír," *Calcutta Review.* Delhi: 1857.

Jama Tafasír, printed at Delhi 1867.

Kaye, John William. *A History of the Sepoy War in India, 1857–1858.* London: W. H. Allen, 1880.

Khan, Ghazala. "Trump criticized my silence. He knows nothing about true sacrifice," *The Washington Post*, op-ed, July 31, 2016. Accessed October 30, 2016. https://www.washingtonpost.com/opinions/ghazala-khan-donald-trump-criticized-my-silence-he-knows-nothing-about-true-sacrifice/2016/07/31/c46e52ec-571c-11e6-831d-0324760ca856_story.html?utm_term=.1c8eda7ab47a.

Khān, Sayyid Aḥmad and Jaweed Ashraf. *History of Insubordination in Bijnor District.* Delhi: Gaur Publishers and Distributors, 2012.

——— and Salim al-Din Quraishi, *The Causes of the Indian Revolt.* Patna: Khuda Bakhsh Oriental Public Library, 1995.

Khan, Syed Ahmad, principal Sudder Ameen of Mordabad. *An Essay on the Causes of Indian Revolt.* Agra: printed by J. A. Gibbons, Mofussilite Press, 1859.

———. *Risālat kher khurāfāt musalmānān ḥiṣṣah-i awwal (An account of the loyal Mahomedans of India).* Meerut: Printed by J. A. Gibbons, at the Mofussilite Press, 1860.

———. "A speech by Syud Ahmed Khan on the institution of the British Indian Association, N. W. Provinces: with the bye-laws of the Association." Allygurh: The Association, 1867.

———. *Review on Dr Hunter's Indian Musalmans: Are They Bound in Conscience to Rebel Against the Queen? The Original English Corrected by a Friend.* Benares: Printed at the Medical Hall Press, 1872.

———. *The Causes of the Indian Revolt, in Urdoo, in 1858, and translated into English by his two European friends.* Benares: Benares Medical Hall Press, 1873.

———. *Sir Syed Ahmed on the Present State of Indian Politics.* Allahabad: Printed at the Pioneer Press, 1888.

———. *Asbāb-i baghāvat-i Hind.* Karāchī: Urdū Akeḍēmī Sindh, 1957.

———. *Sir Sayyid Ahmad Khan's History of the Bijnor Rebellion.* East Lansing: Asian Studies Center, Michigan State University, 1972.

———. *Causes of the Indian Revolt: Three Essays.* Edited by Salim al-Din Quraishi. Lahore: Sang-e Meel Publications, 1997.

———. "Lecture on Islam," in *Modernist Islam: A Sourcebook, 1840–1900.* Edited by Charles Kurzman. New York: Oxford University Press, 2002, pp. 291–313.

Lāla, Jīvana and Darakhshān Tājvar. *Sarguzasht-i Dihlī: Inqilāb 1857 Kī Kahānī Jīvan Lāl Kī Zabānī.* Rāmpūr: Rāmpūr Razā Lā'ibrerī, 2007.

The Law Magazine and Law Review, Or, Quarterly Journal of Jurisprudence, March to August 1871. London: Butterworths, 1871.

The Law Relating to India, and the East-India Company; with Notes and an Appendix. 2nd edn London: W. H. Allen, 1841.

The Letters of Indophilus to "The Times." With additional notes. London: Longman, Brown, Green, Longmans and Roberts, n.d.

Lewin, Malcolm, Esq., ed., *Causes of the Indian Revolt, by a Hindu Bengali.* London: Edward Stanford, 6, Charing Cross, (October) 1857.

Lyall, Sir Alfred. *Race and Religion: An Address, May 5, 1902. The Fortnightly Review*, December 1902. Reprint. London: Social and Political Education League, n. d.

Malleson, Colonel G. B., C. S. I. *The Indian Mutiny of 1857*. London: Seeley and Co., Limited, 1891.

Minutes of Evidence Taken Before the Select Committee of the Honourable House of Commons, appointed for the purpose of taking the examination of such Witnesses as shall be ordered by the House to attend the Committee of the Whole House, on the Affairs of the East-India Company, and to report the MINUTES of such Evidence from time to time. London: by order of the Court of Directors for the information of the Proprietors, Cox and Son, 1813.

Minutes of Evidence Taken Before the Select Committee of the House of Lords, appointed to enquire into the Present State of the Affairs of The East-India Company, and into the Trade between Great Britain, the East-Indies, and China, and to Report to the House. London: Parbury, Allen, and Co., 1830.

Muhammad Bahadur Shah II. *Kulliyāt-i Ẓafar.* Dihlī: Mashvarah buk dipo, 1966.

Muir, William. "The Mahommedan Controversy," *Calcutta Review*, IV (December 1845).

———. "Biographies of Mohammed for India." *Calcutta Review* 17, no. 34 (1852).

———. *The Caliphate; Its Rise, Decline, and Fall, from Original Sources.* 2nd ed., rev. with Maps. London: Religious Tract Society, 1892.

———. *Records of the Intelligence Department of the North-West Provinces of India during the Mutiny of 1857*, vols 1 and 2. Edinburgh: 1902.

Muir, William and T. H. Weir. *The Life of Moḥammad from Original Sources.* London: Smith, 1878.

Müller, F. Max. *Lectures on the science of language, delivered at the Royal Institution of Great Britain in April, May & June 1861.* Delhi: Munshi Ram Manohar Lal, 1965.

———. *Introduction to the Science of Religion.* London, 1873.

———. "India – What Can It Teach Us? (1883)." in *Historical Thinking in South Asia: A Handbook of Sources from Colonial Times to the Present.* Edited by Michael Gottlob. New Delhi: Oxford University Press, 2003, pp. 104–7.

O'Kinealy, James. "Wahhabis in India No. III." *Calcutta Review* 51. 1870.

The Parliamentary Register: Or, an impartial report on the debates that have occurred in the two Houses of Parliament, in the course of the first session of the Fifth Parliament of the United Kingdom of Great Britain and Ireland, Vols II and III. London: Printed for John Stockdale, Piccadilly, 1813.

Prideaux, Humphrey. *The True Nature of Imposture Fully Display'd in the Life of Mahomet*, 1697.

Proclamation of the Queen to the Princes, Chiefs & People of India {giving Notice of the Transfer of the Affairs of the East India Company to the Government, and Declaring a General Amnesty for Political Offences Committed During the Mutiny}. Nov. 1st 1858. Translated into the Native Languages of British India {with a Map of India Showing the Various Tracts Where the Several Languages Are Spoken}. Calcutta, 1858. British Library Shelfmark: 14999.e.1.

Raikes, Charles. *Notes on the Revolt in the North Western Provinces of India*. London: Longman, Brown, Green, Longmans and Roberts, 1858.

Shah, Muhammad Bahadur. *Kulliyāt-i Ẓafar*. Dihlī: Mashvarah buk ḍipo, 1966.

Thornhill, Mark. *The Personal Adventures and Experiences of a Magistrate During the Rise, Progress, and Suppression of the Indian Mutiny*. London: J. Murray, 1884.

Townsend, Meredith. *The Annals of Indian Administration, Volume III*. Serampore: J. C. Murray, 1859.

Trump, Donald. "Interview with Anderson Cooper," *Anderson Cooper 360*, CNN, March 9, 2016. Full transcript, accessed April 5, 2016. http://www.cnn.com/TRANSCRIPTS/1603/09/acd.01.html.

United States Constitution. http://www.archives.gov/exhibits/charters/constituti on_transcript.html. Accessed April 5, 2016.

Urquhart, David. *The Rebellion of India. 1. – Mr. Disraeli's Speech Reviewed. 2. – Illegality of the Acts Abolishing Native Customs, and Their Consequences. 3. – The Wondrous Tale of the Greased Cartridges*. London: D. Bryce, 1857.

Wagentreiber, Florence. *Reminiscences of the Sepoy Rebellion of 1857*. Lahore: "Civil and Military Gazette" Press, 1911. http://catalog.hathitrust.org/api/volumes/oclc/13610838.html. Accessed April 10, 2017.

Wilson, Francesca H. *Rambles in Northern India. With Incidents and Descriptions of Many Scenes of the Mutiny, Including Agra, Delhi, Lucknow, Cawnpore, Allahabad, Etc. With Twelve Large Photographic Views*. London: Sampson Low, Marston, Low, and Searle, 1876.

Wilson, W. A. "The Situation in India." in *Islam and Missions: Being Papers Read at the Second missionary Conference on Behalf of the Mohammedan World at Lucknow, January 28–29, 1911* (New York, London: Fleming H. Revell, 1911). http://hdl.handle.net/2027/uc2.ark:/13960/t6542ms59. Accessed April 10, 2017.

Ya'qūb, Muḥammad, and Iqbāl Ḥusain. *Ṭilism-i Lakhna'ū*: 25, Jūlā'ī 1856–8 Ma'ī 1857. Na'ī Dihlī: Qaumī Kaunsil barā'e Farogh-i Urdū Zabān, 2012.

Secondary Sources

Abdelhalim, Julten. *Indian Muslims and Citizenship: Spaces for Jihad in Everyday*. Routledge Advances in South Asian Studies 29. Milton Park, Abingdon, Oxon: Routledge, 2016.

Abubakar, Mallam M. Bashir. "Muslim Responses to British Colonialism in Northern Nigeria as Expressed in Fulfulde Poems." *Islamic Africa*, 4, no. 1 (2013): 1–14.

Adcock, C. S. *The Limits of Tolerance: Indian Secularism and the Politics of Religious Freedom*. New York: Oxford University Press, 2014.

Afsaruddin, Asma. *Striving in the Path of God: Jihad and Martyrdom in Islamic Thought*. New York: Oxford University Press, 2013.

Ahmad, Aziz. "The Role of Ulema in Indo-Muslim History." *Studia Islamica* 31 (1970): 1–13.

Ahmad, Imtiaz, ed. *Caste and Social Stratification among the Muslims*. Delhi: Manohar Book Service, 1973.

Ahmad, Muhammad Mushtaq. "The Notions of Dār Al-ḥarb and Dār Al-islām in Islamic Jurisprudence with Special Reference to the Ḥanafī School." *Islamic*

Studies 47, no. 1 (2008): 5–37. http://www.jstor.org/stable/20839104. Accessed April 10, 2017.

Ahmad, Qeyamuddin. *The Wahabi Movement in India.* Calcutta: Cambridge University Press, 1966.

Ahmad, Syed Sami. *Sir Syed Ahmad Khan, the Saviour of Muslim India.* Karachi: Royal Book Co., 2002.

Ahmed, Kamaluddin. *Plassey to Proclamation: A Study of Indian Muslim Resistance to British Colonial Expansion in India.* Kolkata: Mudrakar, 2010.

Ahmed, Parvez. "Terror in the Name of Islam – Unholy War, Not Jihad." *Case Western Reserve Journal Of International Law* 39, no. 3 (September 2007): 759–88.

Ahmed, Shahab. *What is Islam? The Importance of Being Islamic.* Princeton, NJ: Princeton University Press, 2015.

Ali, B. Sheikh. *A Leader Reassessed: Life and Work of Sir Syed Ahmad Khan.* Mysore: Sultan Shaheed Education Trust Publication, 1999.

Ali, Md. Mohar. "The Bengal Muslims' Repudiation of the Concept of British India as Darul Harb, 1870," *The Dacca University Studies.* Vol. XVIII, Part A (June 1971): 47–68.

———. "Hunter's 'Indian Musalmans': A Re-examination of Its Background." *Journal of the Royal Asiatic Society of Great Britain and Ireland* 1 (1980): 30–51.

Ali, Parveen Shaukat. *Pillars of British Imperialism: A Case Study of the Political Ideas of Sir Alfred Lyall, 1873–1903.* Lahore: Aziz Publishers, 1976.

Aljunied, Syed Muhd. Khairudin. *Radicals: Resistance and Protest in Colonial Malaya / Syed Muhd Khairudin Aljunied.* DeKalb, IL: Northern Illinois University Press, 2015.

Allen, Charles. "The Hidden Roots of Wahhabism in British India." *World Policy Journal* 22, no. 2 (Summer 2005), 87–8. JSTOR. Accessed December 26, 2014. http://www.jstor.org/stable/40209967.

Anderson, Benedict. *Imagined Communities: Reflections on the Origin and Spread of Nationalism.* London: Verso, 1983.

Anderson, Clare. *The Indian Uprising of 1857–8 Prisons, Prisoners, and Rebellion.* London: Anthem Press, 2007.

Arjana, Sophia Rose. *Muslims in the Western Imagination.* New York: Oxford University Press, 2015.

Asad, Talal. *Genealogies of Religion: Discipline and Reasons of Power in Christianity and Islam.* Baltimore: Johns Hopkins University Press, 1993.

———. *On Suicide Bombing.* New York: Columbia University Press, 2007.

Asher, Catherine and Cynthia Talbot. *India Before Europe.* Cambridge, New York: Cambridge University Press, 2006.

———. *The Science of Empire: Scientific Knowledge, Civilization and Colonial Rule in India.* Albany: State University of New York Press, 1996.

Baber, Zaheer. "'Race,' Religion and Riots: The 'racialization' of Communal Identity and Conflict in India." *Sociology* 38, no. 4 (2004): 701–18.

Baker, David. "Colonial Beginnings and the Indian Response: The Revolt of 1857–58 in Madhya Pradesh." *Modern Asian Studies* 25, no. 3 (July, 1991): 511–43.

Bakircioglu, Onder. "A Socio-Legal Analysis of the Concept of Jihad." *The International and Comparative Law Quarterly* 59, no. 2 (2010): 413–40.

Balibar, Étienne and Immanuel Maurice Wallerstein, eds *Race, Nation, Class: Ambiguous Identities.* London: Verso, 1991.

Ballantyne, Tony. *Orientalism and Race: Aryanism in the British Empire.* Houndmills, Basingstoke, Hampshire: Palgrave, 2002.

Bandukwala, J. S. "Indian Muslims: Past, Present and Future." *Economic and Political Weekly* 41.14 (2006): 1341–4.

Banerjee, Mukulika. "Justice and Non-violent Jihād: The Anti-colonial Struggle in the North West Frontier of British India." *Études rurales* 149/150 (1999): 181–98.

"Bans on Sharia and International Law." American Civil Liberties Union. Accessed April 5, 2016. https://www.aclu.org/bans-sharia-and-international-law.

Bari, Muhammad Abdul. "A Comparative Study of the Early Wahhābi Doctrines and Contemporary Reform Movements in Indian Islām." D. Phil, diss., University of Oxford, 1954.

Bates, Crispin. *Beyond Representation: Colonial and Postcolonial Constructions of Indian Identity.* New Delhi: Oxford University Press, 2006.

———. *Subalterns and Raj: South Asia Since 1600.* London: Routledge, 2007.

Bates, Crispin, Andrea Major, Marina Carter, and Gavin Rand, eds *Mutiny at the Margins: New Perspectives on the Indian Uprising of 1857.* Vols 1–6. New Delhi: SAGE Publications, 2013–14.

Bayly, C. A. *Rulers, Townsmen, and Bazaars: North Indian Society in the Age of British Expansion, 1770–1870.* Cambridge (Cambridgeshire): Cambridge University Press, 1983.

———. *Indian Society and the Making of the British Empire.* Cambridge (Cambridgeshire): Cambridge University Press, 1987.

———. *The Raj: India and the British, 1600–1947.* London: National Portrait Gallery Publications, 1990.

———. *Empire and Information Intelligence Gathering and Social Communication in India, 1780–1870.* Cambridge: Cambridge University Press, 1996.

———. *The New Cambridge History of India.* Cambridge: Cambridge University Press, 2008.

———. *Recovering Liberties: Indian Thought in the Age of Liberalism and Empire: the Wiles Lectures Given at the Queen's University of Belfast, 2007.* Cambridge: Cambridge University Press, 2012.

Bayly, Susan. "Caste and 'race' in the Colonial Ethnography of India." in *The Concept of Race in South Asia.* Edited by Peter Robb. Delhi: Oxford University Press, 1995, pp. 165–218.

———. *The New Cambridge History of India. IV. 3: Caste, society and politics in India from the eighteenth century to the modern age.* Cambridge: Cambridge University Press, 2008.

Bayoumi, Moustafa. "Racing Religion." *CR: The New Centennial Review* 6, no. 2 (2006): 267–93.

Berglund, Jenny. "Princely Companion or Object of Offense? The Dog's Ambiguous Status in Islam." *Society & Animals* 22, no. 6 (December 2014): 545–59.

Bhadra, Gautam. "Four Rebels of Eighteen-Fifty-Seven." in *Selected Subaltern Studies.* Edited by Ranajit Guha and Gayatri Chakravorty Spivak. New York: Oxford University Press, 1988, pp. 129–75.

Bhattacharya, Subhas. "The Indigo Revolt of Bengal." *Social Scientist* 5, no. 12 (July 1977): 13–23.

Bivins, Jason. *Religion of Fear: The Politics of Horror in Conservative Evangelicalism.* Oxford: Oxford University Press, 2008.

Blankinship, Khalid Yahya. "Parity of Muslim and Western Concepts of Just War." *Muslim World* 101, no. 3 (July 2011): 412–26.

Blunt, Alison. "Embodying war: British women and domestic defilement in the Indian 'Mutiny,' 1857–8." *Journal Of Historical Geography* 26, no. 3 (July 2000): 403–28.

Bonacina, Giovanni. *The Wahhabis Seen through European Eyes (1772–1830): Deists and Puritans of Islam.* History of Oriental Studies, Volume 1. Leiden; Boston: Brill, 2015.

Bond, Ruskin. *A Flight of Pigeons.* Bombay: IBH Pub. Co, 1980.

Bonilla-Silva, Eduardo. "Rethinking Racism: Toward a Structural Interpretation." *American Sociological Review* 62, no. 3 (1997): 465–80.

Bonner, Michael David. *Jihad in Islamic History: Doctrines and Practice.* Princeton, NJ: Princeton University Press, 2006.

Bourdieu, Pierre and John B. Thompson. *Language and Symbolic Power.* Cambridge, Mass: Harvard University Press, 1991.

Boyarin, Jonathan. *The Unconverted Self: Jews, Indians, and the Identity of Christian Europe.* Chicago: University of Chicago Press, 2009.

Brah, Avtar. "Time, Place, and Others: Discourses of Race, Nation, and Ethnicity." *Sociology* 28, no. 3 (1994): 805–13.

Brufke, Juliagrace. "Ben Carson Doubles Down On Muslim In The White House Comments." *The Daily Caller*, September 22, 2015. Accessed April 5, 2016. http://dailycaller.com/2015/09/22/ben-carson-doubles-down-on-muslim-in-the-white-house-comments/.

Berger, J. M. "How White Nationalists Learned to Love Donald Trump." *Politico. com*, October 25, 2016. http://www.politico.com/magazine/story/2016/10/donald-trump-2016-white-nationalists-alt-right-214388. Accessed November 1, 2016.

Burke, Peter. "The 'Discovery' of Popular Culture." in *People's History and Socialist Theory.* Edited by Raphael Samuel. London: Routledge & Kegan Paul, 1981, pp. 216–26.

Cantarino, Vicente. "Dante and Islam: History and Analysis of a Controversy (1965)." in *Dante Studies, with the Annual Report of the Dante Society*, no. 125, *Dante and Islam* (2007): 37–55.

Carson, Penelope. *The East India Company and Religion, 1698–1858.* Woodbridge, Suffolk: Boydell Press, 2012.

Cassels, Nancy Gardner. *Social Legislation of the East India Company: Public Justice versus Public Instruction.* New Delhi, Thousand Oaks, CA: Sage Publications, 2010.

Cesari, Jocelyne. *The Awakening of Muslim Democracy: Religion, Modernity, and the State.* New York: Cambridge University Press, 2014.

Chakrabarty, Dipesh. "History as Critique and Critique(s) of History." *Economic and Political Weekly* 26, no. 37 (1991): 2162–6.

———. "Modernity and Ethnicity in India." *South Asia* 17 (1994): 140–52.

———. "Remembering 1857: An Introductory Note." *Economic and Political Weekly* 42, no. 19 (2007): 1692–5.

Chatterjee, Partha. *Nationalist Thought and the Colonial World: A Derivative Discourse?* London: Zed, 1986.

———. "For an Indian History of Peasant Struggle." *Social Scientist* 16, no. 11 (November 1988): 3–17.

Cheyette, Bryan. *Constructions of "the Jew" in English Literature and Society: Racial Representations, 1875–1945.* Cambridge; New York: Cambridge University Press, 1993.

Chidester, David. *Savage Systems Colonialism and Comparative Religion in Southern Africa.* Charlottesville: University Press of Virginia, 1996.

———. *Empire of Religion: Imperialism and Comparative Religion.* Chicago: University of Chicago Press, 2014.

Cillizza, Chris. "This Khizr Khan Ad for Hillary Clinton is Incredibly Powerful," *The Washington Post.* October 21, 2016. Accessed November 1, 2016. https://www.washingtonpost.com/news/the-fix/wp/2016/10/21/this-khizr-khan-ad-for-hillary-clinton-is-incredibly-powerful/.

Cughtā'ī, Muḥammad Ikrām. *Sir Sayyid Ahmad Khan, 1817–1898: A Prominent Muslim Politician and Educationist.* Lahore: Sang-e-Meel Publications, 2005.

———. *1857 in the Muslim Historiography.* Lahore: Sang-e-Meel Publications, 2007.

Cohn, Bernard S. *An Anthropologist among the Historians and Other Essays,* with an introduction by Ranajit Guha. Delhi: Oxford University Press, 1987.

———. *Colonialism and its Forms of Knowledge: The British in India.* Princeton, NJ: Princeton University Press, 1996.

Cook, David. *Contemporary Muslim Apocalyptic Literature,* 1st ed. Syracuse, NY: Syracuse University Press, 2005.

———. *Understanding Jihad.* Berkeley: University of California Press, 2005.

Copland, Ian. *The British Raj and the Indian Princes: Paramountcy in Western India, 1857–1930.* Bombay: Orient Longman, 1982.

———. "Christianity as an Arm of Empire: The Ambiguous Case of India under the Company, C. 1813–1858." *The Historical Journal* 49, no. 4 (December 2006): 1025–54.

Corbett, Rosemary R. "Meta-Data, Same-Sex Marriage and the Making of 'Terrorists.'" *Culture and Religion* 15, no. 2 (2014): 187–97.

Curtis, Edward E., IV. *Muslims in America: A Short History.* New York: Oxford University Press, 2009.

———. *The Call of Bilal: Islam in the African Diaspora.* Islamic Civilization & Muslim Networks. Chapel Hill, NC: University of North Carolina Press, 2014.

Dalrymple, William. *The Last Mughal: The Fall of a Dynasty: Delhi, 1857.* New York: Alfred A. Knopf, 2007.

Dar, Bashir Ahmed. *Religious Thought of Syed Ahmed Khan.* Lahore: Jadeed Urdu Press, 1957.

Datla, Kavita Saraswathi. *The Language of Secular Islam: Urdu Nationalism and Colonial India.* Honolulu: University of Hawai'i Press, 2013.

De, Sarmistha. "Marginal Whites and the Great Uprising: A Case Study of the Bengal Presidency." in *Mutiny at the Margins: New Perspectives on the Indian Uprising of 1857, vol. 2: Britain and the Indian Uprising.* Edited by Andrea Major and Crispin Bates. London: Sage Publications, 2013, pp. 165–81.

Demaria, Ed. "Ben Carson Does Not Believe a Muslim Should Be President," via "Meet the Press," *NBC News.* Accessed April 5, 2016. http://www.nbcnews.com/meet-the-press/ben-carson-does-not-believe-muslim-should-be-president-n430431.

Deshpande, Prachi. "The Making of an Indian Nationalist Archive: Lakshmibai, Jhansi, and 1857." *Journal Of Asian Studies* 67, no. 3 (August 2008): 855–87.

Devji, Faisal. *Landscapes of the Jihad: Militancy, Morality, Modernity.* Crises in World Politics. Ithaca, NY: Cornell University Press, 2005.

———. "The Mutiny to Come." *New Literary History* 40, no. 2, India and the West (Spring 2009): 411–30.

———. "Apologetic Modernity." *Modern Intellectual History* 4, no. 1 (April 2007): 61–76.

Dhanagare, D. N. "Subaltern Consciousness and Populism: Two Approaches in the Study of Social Movements in India." *Social Scientist* 16, no. 11 (November 1988): 18–35.

Dhondy, Farrukh, et al. *Mangal Pandey the rising.* Mumbai: Yash Raj Films, 2005.

Diamond, Jeremy. "Muslim Trump supporter's message amid 'no Islam' shout," *CNN.com.* July 20, 2016. Accessed October 30, 2016. http://www.cnn.com/2016/07/20/politics/american-muslim-for-trump-no-islam-response/.

Dirks, Nicholas B. "Castes of Mind." *Representations*, No. 37, Special Issue: "Imperial Fantasies and Postcolonial Histories" (Winter, 1992): 56–78.

———. *The Scandal of Empire: India and the Creation of Britain.* Cambridge, MA: Belknap Press of Harvard University Press, 2006.

Dubreuil, Laurent, and David Fieni. *Empire of Language: Toward a Critique of (Post) colonial Expression.* Ithaca, NY: Cornell University Press, 2013.

Eaton, Richard M. "The Political and Religious Authority of the Shrine of Baba Farid." in *India's Islamic Traditions, 711–1750.* Edited by Richard M. Eaton. New Delhi: Oxford University Press, 2003, pp. 263–84.

Engineer, Asghar Ali. "Muslims and Education." *Economic and Political Weekly* 36, no. 34 (2001): 3221–2.

Ernst, Carl W. *Following Muhammad.* Chapel Hill: University of North Carolina Press, 2003.

Esposito, John L. *The Islamic Threat: Myth or Reality?* New York: Oxford University Press, 1992.

Ewing, Katherine P., ed. *Shari'at and Ambiguity in South Asian Islam.* Berkeley: University of California Press, 1988.

Fanon, Franz, Jean-Paul Sartre, and Constance Farrington. *The Wretched of the Earth.* New York: Grove Press, Inc., 1965.

Farrell, J. G. *The Siege of Krishnapur.* New York: Carroll and Graf, 1973. Reprint 1985.

Feldman, David. "Conceiving Difference: Religion, Race and the Jews in Britain, C.1750–1900." *History Workshop Journal* 76, no. 1 (2013): 160–86.

Firestone, Reuven. *Jihād: The Origin of Holy War in Islam.* New York: Oxford University Press, 1999.

Fisher, Michael H. "Multiple Meanings of 1857 for Indians in Britain." *Economic and Political Weekly* 42, no. 19 (2007): 1703–9.

Foucault, Michel. *The Archeology of Knowledge and the Discourse on Language.* Translated by A. M. Sheridan Smith. New York: Pantheon Books, 1972.

Frykenberg, Robert Eric and Alaine M. Low, eds *Christians and Missionaries in India: Cross-Cultural Communication Since 1500, with Special Reference to Caste, Conversion, and Colonialism.* Grand Rapids, MI: W. B. Eerdmans, 2003.

Gaborieau, Marc. "Late Persian, Early Urdu: The case of 'Wahhabi' literature (1818–1857)." in *Confluence of Cultures: French contributions to Indo-Persian studies.* Edited by Francoise "Nalini" Delvoye. Delhi: Manohar, 1994. Reprint 1995, pp. 169–96.

Galonnier, Juliette. "The Racialization of Muslims in France and the United States: Some Insights from White Converts to Islam." *Social Compass* 62, no. 4 (2015): 570–83.

Geaves, R. A. "India 1857: A Mutiny or a War of Independence? The Muslim Perspective." *Islamic Studies* 35, no. 1 (1996): 25–44.

Geertz, Clifford. *The Interpretation of Cultures; Selected Essays.* New York: Basic, 1973.

Ghazi, Mahmood Ahmad. "The Law of War and Concept of Jihad in Islam." *Policy Perspectives* 5, no. 1 (2008): 69–86.

Ghose, R. "Islamic law and imperial space: British India as 'domain of Islam' circa 1803–1870." *Journal of Colonialism & Colonial History* 15, no. 1 (2014): 141–87.

Goldberg, David Theo, ed. *Anatomy of Racism.* Minneapolis: University of Minnesota Press, 1990.

Gottschalk, Peter. *Religion, Science, and Empire: Classifying Hinduism and Islam in British India.* New York: Oxford University Press, 2013.

Gottschalk, Peter and Gabriel Greenberg. "Common Heritage, Uncommon Fear: Islamophobia in the United States and British India, 1687–1947." in *Islamophobia in America: Anatomy of Intolerance.* Edited by Carl W. Ernst. New York: Palgrave Macmillan, 2013, pp. 21–73.

Green, Nile. *Islam and the Army in Colonial India: Sepoy Religion in the Service of Empire.* Cambridge Studies in Indian History and Society 16. Cambridge; New York: Cambridge University Press, 2009.

Guenther, Alan. "A Colonial Court Defines a Muslim." in *Islam in South Asia in Practice.* Edited by Barbara D. Metcalf. Princeton: Princeton University Press, 2009, pp. 293–304.

Guha, Ranajit. *Elementary Aspects of Peasant Insurgency in Colonial India.* Delhi: Oxford, 1983.

———. "The Prose of Counter-Insurgency." in *Selected Subaltern Studies.* Edited by Ranajit Guha and Gayatri Chakravorty Spivak. New York: Oxford University Press, 1988, pp. 45–86.

———. *Dominance without Hegemony: History and Power in Colonial India.* Cambridge, MA: Harvard University Press, 1997.

———. "A Conquest Foretold." *Social Text* 54 (Spring 1998): 85–99.

Gupta, Amit Kumar. *Nineteenth-Century Colonialism and the Great Indian Revolt.* New York: Routledge, 2016.

Habib, Irfan. "The Coming of 1857." *Social Scientist* 26, no. 1/4 (1998): 6–15.

Hadi Husain, Muhammad. *Syed Ahmed Khan: Pioneer of Muslim Resurgence.* Lahore: Institute of Islamic Culture, 1970.

Haj, Samira. *Reconfiguring Islamic Tradition: Reform, Rationality, and Modernity.* Cultural Memory in the Present. Stanford, CA: Stanford University Press, 2009.

Hall, Catherine. *Cultures of Empire: Colonizers in Britain and the Empire in the Nineteenth and Twentieth Centuries: a Reader.* New York: Routledge, 2000.

Hamidullah, Muhammad. *Muslim Conduct of State.* 7th ed. Lahore: Shaykh Muhammad Ashraf, 1961.

Hanson, John H. "Jihad and the Ahmadiyya Muslim Community: Nonviolent Efforts to Promote Islam in the Contemporary World." *Nova Religio: The Journal of Alternative and Emergent Religions* 11, no. 2 (2007): 77–93.

Haq, Mushirul. *Shah Abdul Aziz, His Life and Time: A study of India Muslims' attitude to the British in the 19th century.* Lahore: Institute of Islamic Culture, 1995.

Haqq, S. Moinul. "The Story of the War of Independence by Allamah Fadl-i Haqq of Kharyabad." *Journal of the Pakistan Historical Society* 5, no. 1 (1957): 23–57.

Hardas, Balshastri. *Armed Struggle for Freedom: Ninety Years War of Indian Independence, 1857 to Subhash.* Poona: KAL Prakashan, 1958.

Hardy, Peter. *Partners in Freedom and True Muslims. The Political Thought of Some Muslim Scholars in British India 1912–1947.* Lund: Studentlitteratur, 1971.

———. *The Muslims of British India.* Cambridge, UK: Cambridge University Press, 1972.

Harrington, Jack. *Sir John Malcolm and the Creation of British India {electronic Resource}.* 1st ed. Palgrave Studies in Cultural and Intellectual History. New York: Palgrave Macmillan, 2010.

Harrington, Peter. *Plassey, 1757: Clive of India's Finest Hour.* Westport, CT: Praeger, 2005.

Hasan, Mushirul. *From Pluralism to Separatism Qasbas in Colonial Awadh.* New Delhi: Oxford University Press, 2007.

———. *Moderate or Militant: Images of India's Muslims.* New Delhi; Oxford: Oxford University Press, 2008.

———. "The Legacies of 1857 among the Muslim Intelligentsia of North India." in *Mutiny at the Margins: New Perspectives on the Indian Uprising of 1857. Vol. V: Muslim, Dalit and Subaltern Narratives.* Edited by Crispin Bates. New Delhi: Sage Publications, 2014, pp. 103–16.

Hasan, Mushirul and M. Asaduddin. *Image and Representation: Stories of Muslim Lives in India.* New Delhi: Oxford University Press, 2000.

Hasan, Mushirul and Asim Roy. *Living Together Separately: Cultural India in History and Politics.* New Delhi: Oxford University Press, 2005.

Hasan, Tariq. *Colonialism and the Call to Jihad in British India.* New Delhi: SAGE Publications India, 2015.

Hashmi, N. A. Tajul Islam. "Maulana Karamat Ali and the Muslims of Bengal 1820–1873." *The Dacca University Studies* 23, pt A (June 1976): 123–36.

Hashmi, Sohail H. "Jihad." in *Encyclopedia of Islam and the Muslim World*, vol. 1. Edited by Richard C. Martin. New York: Macmillan Reference USA, 2004, pp. 377–9. Accessed March 23, 2015. *Gale Virtual Reference Library.*

Heck, Paul L. "'Jihad' Revisited." *The Journal of Religious Ethics* 32, no. 1 (2004): 95–128.

Hermansen, Marcia. "Wahhabis, Fakirs and Others: Reciprocal Classifications and the Transformation of Intellectual Categories." in *Perspectives of Mutual Encounters in South Asian History 1760–1860.* Edited by Jamal Malik. Leiden: Brill, 2000, pp. 23–48.

Hitchens, Christopher. *The Illusion of Permanence: British Imperialism in India.* Princeton, NJ: Princeton University Press, 1967.

Holmes, T. R. *A History of the Indian Mutiny*, 4th ed. London: W.H. Allen, 1904.

Hoover, James W. "Indian Mutiny." in *International Encyclopedia of Military History.* Edited by James C. Bradford. New York: Routledge, 2006, pp. 640–3.

Husain, Iqbal. "The Rebel Administration of Delhi." *Social Scientist* 26, no. 1/4 (1998): 25–38.

Husain, S. M. Azizuddin. "1857 as Reflected in Persian and Urdu Documents." in *Mutiny at the Margins: Volume VI: Perception, Narration and Reinvention: The Pedagogy and Historiography of the Indian Uprising.* Edited by Crispin Bates. New Delhi: SAGE Publications, 2014, pp. 170–87.

Husain, Syed Mahdi. *Bahadur Shah Zafar and the War of 1857 in Delhi.* Delhi: Aakar Books 1958. Reprint, with a new Preface by Mushirul Hasan, 2006.

Hutchinson, Lester. *The Empire of the Nabobs: A Short History of British India.* London: Allen and Unwin, 1937.

Islam, Arshad. "The Backlash in Delhi: British Treatment of the Mughal Royal Family following the Indian 'Sepoy Mutiny' of 1857." *Journal Of Muslim Minority Affairs* 31, no. 2 (June 2011): 197–215.

Islam, Maidul. "Rethinking the Muslim Question in Post-colonial India." *Social Scientist* 40, no. 7/8 (2012): 61–84.

Jafri, Saiyid Zaheer Husain. "The Profile of a Saintly Rebel: Maulvi Ahmadullah Shah." *Social Scientist* 26, no. 1/4 (1998): 39–52.

Jain, Saudamini. "At the stroke of the midnight hour: The story of India's independence." *Hindustan Times.* August 11, 2015. Accessed March 29, 2016. http://www.hindustantimes.com/india/at-the-stroke-of-the-midnight-hour-the-story-of-india-s-independence/story-m6Lp74lEyp3WWJWeUTFnPM.html.

Jalal, Ayesha. *The Sole Spokesman: Jinnah, the Muslim League, and the Demand for Pakistan.* Cambridge South Asian Studies 31. Cambridge (Cambridgeshire); New York: Cambridge University Press, 1985.

———. *Partisans of Allah: Jihad in South Asia.* Cambridge, MA: Harvard University Press, 2008.

Johnson, Sylvester. *African American Religions, 1500–2000: Colonialism, Democracy, and Freedom.* New York: Cambridge University Press, 2015.

Josh, Bhagwan. "V. D. Sarwarkar's *The Indian War of Independence*: The First Nationalist Reconstruction of the Revolt of 1857." in *Mutiny at the Margins: New Perspectives on the Indian Uprising of 1857 Vol. VI: Perception, Narration, and Reinvention: the Pedagogy and Historiography of the Indian Uprising.* Edited by Crispin Bates. New Delhi: Sage Publications, 2014, pp. 29–41.

Joshi, Khyati Y. "The Racialization of Hinduism, Islam, and Sikhism in the United States." *Equity & Excellence in Education* 39, no. 3 (2006): 211–66.

Kamali, Mohammad Hashim. "Issues in the Understanding of Jihād and Ijtihād." *Islamic Studies* 41, no. 4 (2002): 617–34.

Kapoor, Shashi, Shyam Benegal, Shabana Azmi, Jennifer Kendal, Nafisa Ali, and Ruskin Bond, *Junoon.* Secaucus, NJ: Eros International (distributor, 2000).

Kapūra, Amaranātha, V. P. Gupta, and Mohinī Guptā. *War of Indian Independence, 1857: Before and After.* New Delhi: Radha Publications, 2006.

Katz, Marion. "Pragmatic Rule and Personal Sanctification in Islamic Legal Theory." In *Law and the Sacred.* Edited by Austin Sarat, Lawrence Douglas and Martha Merrill Umphrey. Stanford: Stanford University Press, 2007, pp. 91–108.

Kaye, Mary Margaret. *Shadow of the Moon.* New York: St. Martin's Press, 1979.

Keating, Christine. *Decolonizing Democracy: Transforming the Social Contract in India.* University Park: Pennsylvania State University Press, 2011.

Kelsay, John. *Arguing the Just War in Islam.* Cambridge, MA: Harvard University Press, 2007.

Kelsay, John and James Turner Johnson, eds *Just War and Jihad: Historical and Theoretical Perspectives on War and Peace in Western and Islamic Tradition.* New York: Greenwood, 1991.

Khan, Abdul R. *The All India Muslim Educational Conference: Its Contribution to the Cultural Development of Indian Muslims, 1886–1947.* Karachi: Oxford University Press, 2001.

Khan, Iqtidar Alam. "The Gwalior Contingent in 1857–58: A Study of the Organisation and Ideology of the Sepoy Rebels." *Social Scientist* 26, no. 1/4 (1998): 53–75.

———. "The Wahabis in the 1857 Revolt: A Brief Reappraisal of Their Role." *Social Scientist* 41, no. 5/6 (2013): 15–23.

Khan, Mu'in-Ud-Din Ahmad. *Selections from Bengal Government Records on Wahhabi Trials (1863–1870).* Dacca: Asiatic Society of Pakistan, 1961.

———. "Some Reflections on Mawlana Karamat Ali's Role as a Reformer." *Islamic Studies* 4 (March 1965): 103–10.

———. "Sayyid Aḥmad Shahīd's Campaign Against the Sikhs," *Islamic Studies* 7, no. 4 (1968): 317–38.

Khan, Sanjay, dir. *1857 Kranti.* 104 episodes. Numero Uno International Limited, 2002.

King, Christopher. *One Language, Two Scripts: The Hindi Movement in Nineteenth Century North India.* New Delhi: Oxford University Press, 1994.

King, Richard. *Orientalism and Religion: Postcolonial Theory, India and "The Mystic East."* London: Routledge, 1999.

———. "Orientalism and the modern myth of 'Hinduism,'" *Numen* 46 (1999): 146–85.

"KKK leader disavows violent past, declares Trump 'best' for president," *NBC News*, May 9, 2016. http://www.nbc12.com/story/31846257/kkk-leader-disavows-violent-past-declares-trump-best-for-president. Accessed November 1, 2016.

Kohn, Margaret. "Afghānī on Empire, Islam, and Civilization." *Political Theory* 37, no. 3 (2009): 398–422.

Kolsky, Elizabeth. *Colonial Justice in British India.* Cambridge Studies in Indian History and Society 17. Cambridge; New York: Cambridge University Press, 2010.

Krishnaswamy, N. and Archana S. Burde. *The Politics of Indians' English: Linguistic Colonialism and the Expanding English Empire.* Delhi: Oxford University Press, 1998.

Kugle, Scott Alan. "Framed, Blamed and Renamed: The recasting of Islamic jurisprudence in colonial South Asia." *Modern Asian Studies* 35, no. 2 (2001): 257–313.

Lacan, Jacques and Anthony Wilden. *The Language of the Self; The Function of Language in Psychoanalysis.* Baltimore: Johns Hopkins Press, 1968.

Lahiri, Nayanjot. "Commemorating and Remembering 1857: The Revolt in Delhi and Its Afterlife." *World Archaeology* 35, no. 1, The Social Commemoration of Warfare (June 2003): 35–60.

Latour, Bruno. *We have never been modern.* Translated by Catherine Porter. Cambridge, MA: Harvard University Press, 1993.

Lawrence, Bruce B. "The Eastward Journey of Muslim Kingship: Islam in South and Southeast Asia." in *The Oxford History of Islam.* Edited by John L. Esposito. New York: Oxford University Press, 1999, pp. 395–434.

Lazare, Aaron. *On Apology.* New York: Oxford University Press, 2004.

Lelyveld, David. *Aligarh's First Generation: Muslim Solidarity in British India.* Princeton, NJ: Princeton University Press, 1978.

————. "Disenchantment at Aligarh: Islam and the Realm of the Secular in Late Nineteenth Century India." *Die Welt des Islams* 22, no. 1/4 (1982): 85–102.

————. "Colonial Knowledge and the Fate of Hindustani." *Comparative Studies in Society and History* 35, no. 4 (1993): 665–82.

————. "The colonial context of Muslim separatism: from Sayyid Ahmad Barelvi to Sayyid Ahmad Khan." in *Living Together Separately: Cultural India in History and Politics*. Edited by Mushirul Hasan and Asim Roy. New Delhi: Oxford University Press, 2005, pp. 404–14.

————. *Sir Sayyid, Maulana Azad and the Uses of Urdu*. NMML occasional paper. History and society, n.s., 35. New Delhi: Nehru Memorial Museum and Library, 2013.

Lewis, Ivor. *Sahibs, Nabobs, and Boxwallahs, a Dictionary of the Words of Anglo-India*. Bombay: Oxford University Press, 1991.

Lofgren, Mike. "Trump, Putin, and the Alt-Right International." *The Atlantic*. October 31, 2016. http://www.theatlantic.com/international/archive/2016/10/trump-putin-alt-right-comintern/506015/. Accessed November 1, 2016.

Loomba, Ania. "Race and the Possibilities of Comparative Critique." *New Literary History* 40, no. 3 (2009): 501–22.

Mahapatra, Sitakant. "The Mutiny and the Sociology of Literary Imagination." *Indian Literature* 53, no. 1 (249) (January/February 2009): 172–6.

Major, Andrea and Crispin Bates. "Introduction: Fractured Narratives and Marginal Experiences." in *Mutiny at the Margins: New Perspectives on the Indian Uprising of 1857, Vol. 2: Britain and the Indian Uprising*. Edited by Andrea Major and Crispin Bates. London: Sage Publications, 2013, pp. xv–xxiv.

Majumdar, R. C. *The Sepoy Mutiny and the Revolt of 1857*. Calcutta: Firma K. L. Mukhopadhyay, 1963.

Malik, Jamal. *Islam in South Asia: A Short History*. Leiden: Brill, 2008.

Malik, Salahuddin. *1857 War of Independence or Clash of Civilizations?: British Public Reactions*. Karachi: Oxford University Press, 2008.

————. "Popular British Interpretations of 'The Mutiny': Politics and Polemics." in *Mutiny at the Margins, Volume 2: Britain and the Indian Uprising*. Edited by Crispin Bates and Andrea Major. New Delhi: SAGE Publications, 2013, pp. 25–49.

Mamdani, Mahmood. *Good Muslim, Bad Muslim: America, the Cold War, and the Roots of Terror*. New York: Pantheon Books, 2004.

Marranci, Gabriele. *Jihad beyond Islam*. Oxford, New York: Berg, 2006.

Marshall, P. J. "British Society in India under the East India Company." *Modern Asian Studies* 31, no. 1 (February 1997): 89–108.

Martin, B. G. "Muslim Politics and Resistance to Colonial Rule: Shaykh Uways B. Muhammad Al-Barāwī and the Qādirīya Brotherhood in East Africa." *The Journal of African History* 10 (1969): 471–86.

Marx, Karl and Friedrich Engels. *The First Indian War of Independence, 1857–1859*. Moscow: Foreign Languages Publishing House, 1960.

Masters, John. *Nightrunners of Bengal, a Novel*. New York: Viking, 1951.

Masud, Muhammad Khalid, Brinkley Messick, and David S. Powers, eds *Islamic Legal Interpretation: muftis and their fatwas*. Cambridge, MA: Harvard University Press, 1996.

Masuzawa, Tomoko. *The Invention of World Religions: Or, How European Universalism was Preserved in the Language of Pluralism.* Chicago: University of Chicago Press, 1995.

——. "Our Master's Voice: F. Max Müller after A Hundred Years of Solitude." *Method & Theory in the Study of Religion* 15, no. 4 (2003): 305–28.

McCall, Bruce. "The perfect non-apology apology." *New York Times*, April 22, 2001: WK. General OneFile. Accessed December 23, 2014. http://go.galegroup.com. ezproxy.uvm.edu/ps/i.do?id=GALE%7CA73542871&v=2.1& u=vol_b92b&it=r&p=ITOF&sw=w&asid=981b6e02804883288df015fde3768f81.

McCutcheon, Russell T. *Manufacturing Religion: The Discourse on Sui Generis Religion and the Politics of Nostalgia.* New York: Oxford University Press, 1997.

McLain, Robert. *Gender and Violence in British India: The Road to Amritsar, 1914– 1919* (New York: Palgrave Macmillan, 2014).

"Memorial to be set up in memory of 1857 mutiny martyrs." *The Hindu*, May 11, 2015. Accessed March 29, 2016. http://www.thehindu.com/news/national/ other-states/memorial-to-be-set-up-in-memory-of-1857-mutiny-martyrs/arti cle7191386.ece.

Metcalf, Barbara Daly. "The Reformist 'Ulama: Muslim Religious Leadership in India, 1860–1900." Ph. D. diss., University of California, Berkeley, 1974.

——. *Islamic Revival in British India: Deoband, 1860–1900.* Princeton, NJ: Princeton University Press, 1982.

——. "Nationalist Muslims in British India: The Case of Hakim Ajmal Khan." *Modern Asian Studies* 19, no. 1 (1985): 1–28.

——. "Presidential Address: Too Little and Too Much: Reflections on Muslims in the History of India." *The Journal of Asian Studies* 54, no. 4 (1995): 951–67.

——. *"Traditionalist" Islamic Activism: Deoband, Tablighis, and Talibs.* Leiden: ISIM, 2002.

——. "Travelers' Tales in the Tablighi Jama'at." *Annals of the American Academy of Political and Social Science* 588 (2003): 136–48.

——. *Islamic Contestations: Essays on Muslims in India and Pakistan.* New Delhi, New York: Oxford University Press, 2004.

——. *Husain Ahmad Madani: The Jihad for Islam and India's Freedom.* Oxford: Oneworld, 2009.

Metcalf, Barbara Daly and Thomas R. Metcalf. *A Concise History of Modern India.* Cambridge: Cambridge University Press, 2006.

Metcalf, Barbara Daly, Rafiuddin Ahmed, and Mushirul Hasan. *India's Muslims: An Omnibus.* New Delhi: Oxford University Press, 2007.

Metcalf, Thomas R. *The Aftermath of Revolt: India 1857–1870.* Princeton, NJ: Princeton University Press, 1965.

——. *Land, Landlords, and the British Raj: Northern India in the Nineteenth Century.* Berkeley: University of California Press, 1979.

——. *Ideologies of the Raj.* Cambridge: Cambridge University Press, 1994.

——. *Forging the Raj: Essays on British India in the Heyday of Empire.* New Delhi: Oxford University Press, 2005.

——. *Imperial Connections India in the Indian Ocean Arena, 1860–1920.* Berkeley: University of California Press, 2007.

Mignolo, Walter D. *Local Histories/Global Designs: Coloniality, Subaltern Knowledges, and Border Thinking*, Princeton Studies in Culture/power/history. Princeton, NJ: Princeton University Press, 2000.

————. "The Global South and World Dis/Order." *Journal of Anthropological Research* 67, no. 2 (Summer 2011): 165–88.

Miles, Robert. *Racism*. London: Routledge, 1991.

Mittal, S. C. *India Distorted: A Study of British Historians on India*. New Delhi: M. D. Publications, 1996.

Mohammad, Noor. "The Doctrine of Jihad: An Introduction." *Journal of Law and Religion* 3, no. 2 (1985): 381–97.

Moosa, Ebrahim. "Colonialism and Islamic Law." in *Islam and Modernity Key issues and debates*. Edited by Muhammad Khalid Masud, Armando Salvatore, and Martin van Bruinessen. Edinburgh: Edinburgh University Press, 2009, pp. 158–81.

————. "Shariat Governance in Colonial and Post-colonial India." in *Islam in South Asia in Practice*. Edited by Barbara D. Metcalf. Princeton: Princeton University Press, 2009, pp. 317–25.

Morgenstein Fuerst, Ilyse R. "Sir Sayyid Aḥmad Khān." in *Biographical Dictionary of Islamic Civilisation and Culture*. Edited by Muhammad A. S. Abdel Haleem and Mustafa A. A. Shah. London: I.B.Tauris, forthcoming.

Motadel, David. "Islam and the European Empires." *The Historical Journal* 55 (2012): 831–56.

————. *Islam and Nazi Germany's War*. Cambridge, MA: The Belknap Press of Harvard University Press, 2014.

————. "Jihad 1914." *History Today* 64, no. 9 (September 2014): 41–2. Accessed January 3, 2017. http://www.historytoday.com/david-motadel/jihad-1914.

Mufti, Aamir. *Enlightenment in the Colony: The Jewish Question and the Crisis of Postcolonial Culture*. Princeton, NJ: Princeton University Press, 2007.

Narang, G. C. and Leslie Abel. "Ghalib and the Rebellion of 1857." *Mahfil* 5, No. 4, GHALIB ISSUE (1968–9): 45–57.

Narayan, Badri. "Popular Culture and 1857: A Memory Against Forgetting." *Social Scientist* 26, no. 1/4 (1998): 86–94.

Nastiti, Aulia. "Discursive Construction of Religious Minority: Minoritization of Ahmadiyya in Indonesia (July 5, 2014)." *Deutsches Asienforschungszentrum Asian Series Commentaries* 19, 2014: 1–16. SSRN: http://ssrn.com/abstract=2472294. Accessed January 2, 2017.

Nawid, Senzil. "The State, the Clergy, and British Imperial Policy in Afghanistan during the 19th and Early 20th Centuries." *International Journal of Middle East Studies* 29, no. 4 (November 1997): 581–605.

Nizami, Hasan "Delhi ki Jankani" (Delhi: Near to Death). In *1857 Majmuah Khawaja Hasan Nizami* [A Collection of Essays by Khawaja Hasan Nizami]." Edited by Muhammad Ikram Chaghtai. Lahore: Sang-e-Mel Publications, 2007.

Nizami, Taufiq Ahmad. *Muslim Political Thought and Activity in India During the First Half of the Nineteenth Century*, with a foreword by Mohammad Habib. Aligarh, India: Singh for T. M. Publications Aligarh, 1969.

Nizami, Zafar Ahmad, J. Raja Mohammad, Mujeeb Ashraf, and Shaukat Ullah Khan. *The Role of Muslims in the Indian Freedom Struggle, 1857–1947*. New Delhi: Institute of Objective Studies, 2011.

Northrop, Douglas. "Subaltern Dialogues: Subversion and Resistance in Soviet Uzbek Family Law." *Slavic Review* 60, no. 1 (2001): 115–39.

Norton, Anne. *On the Muslim Question*. Public Square. Princeton, NJ: Princeton University Press, 2013.

Oliver-Dee, Sean. *Muslim Minorities and Citizenship: Authority, Communities and Islamic Law.* London: I.B.Tauris, 2012.

Orsi, Robert A. "Snakes Alive: Religious Studies between Heaven and Earth." in *Between Heaven and Earth: The Religious Worlds People Make and the Scholars who Study Them.* Princeton, NJ: Princeton University Press, 2005, pp. 177–204.

Özcan, Azmi. *Pan-Islamism: Indian Muslims, the Ottomans, and Britain (1877–1924).* Leiden: Brill, 1997.

Padamsee, Alex. *Representations of Indian Muslims in British Colonial Discourse.* New York: Palgrave Macmillan, 2005.

———. "Ideology and Paradox in British Civil Service Accounts of Muslim 'Conspiracy' in 1857–1859." in *Mutiny at the Margins: New Perspectives on the Indian Uprising of 1857, Vol. 5.* Edited by Crispin Bates. New Delhi: Sage Publications, 2014.

Page, David. *Prelude to Partition: The Indian Muslims and the Imperial System of Control, 1920–1932.* Delhi: Oxford University Press, 1982.

Pandey, Gyanendra. *Hindus and Others: The Question of Identity in India Today.* New Delhi: Viking, 1993.

Pasha, Mohamed Abdullah. *Sir Syed Ahmad Khan: His Life and Times: a Historical Survey, Commemorating the Hundredth Anniversary of the Death of Sir Syed Ahmad Khan, 1898–1998.* Lahore: Ferozsons, 1998.

Pati, Biswamoy, ed. *The 1857 Rebellion.* New Delhi: Oxford University Press, 2007.

———. "Historians and Historiography: Situating 1857." *Economic and Political Weekly* 42, no. 19 (2007): 1686–91.

Pearson, Harlan O. *Islamic Reform and Revival in Nineteenth-century India: the Tarīqah-i-Muhmammadīyah.* New Delhi: Yoda Press, 2008.

Pernau, Margrit. *The Delhi College. Traditional Elites, the Colonial State, and Education before 1857.* Delhi: Oxford University Press, 2006.

———. *Ashraf into Middle Class: Muslims in Nineteenth-Century Delhi.* New Delhi: Oxford University Press, 2013.

Peters, Rudolph. *Islam and Colonialism: The Doctrine of Jihad in Modern History.* The Hague: Mouton, 1979.

———. *Jihad in Classical and Modern Islam.* Princeton: Markus Wiener, 1996.

Pew Research Center. "Muslim Americans," subsection "Islamic Affiliation and Converts of Islam." August 30, 2011. Accessed January 3, 2017. http://www.people-press.org/2011/08/30/section-2-religious-beliefs-and-practices/#fn-20034306-2.

Pickthall, Marmaduke William. *The Meaning of the Glorious Qur'an: Text and Explanatory Translation.* New York: Muslim World League, 1977.

Pionke, Albert D. *Plots of Opportunity: Representing Conspiracy in Victorian England.* Columbus: Ohio State University Press, 2004.

Pirzada, Syed Sharifuddin, ed. *Foundations of Pakistan: All-India Muslim League Documents, 1906–1947.* Karachi: National Publishing House, 1969.

Powell, Avril A. *Muslims and Missionaries in Pre-mutiny India.* London Studies on South Asia, No. 7. Richmond, Surrey: Curzon Press, 1993.

———. "Modernist Muslim responses to Christian critique of Islamic culture, civilization and history in northern India." in *Christians, Cultural Interactions and India's Religious Traditions.* Editors J. Brown and R. Frykenberg. Grand Rapids, MI, Cambridge, UK: William B. Eerdmans Publishing Co., Routledge Curzon, 2002, pp. 61–91.

————. *Scottish Orientalists and India: The Muir Brothers, Religion, Education and Empire*. Woodbridge, UK: Boydell Press, 2010.

————. "Questionable Loyalties: Muslim Government Servants and Rebellion." in *Mutiny at the Margins: New Perspectives on the Indian Uprising of 1857 Vol. V: Muslim, Dalit and Subaltern Narratives*. Edited by Crispin Bates. New Delhi: Sage Publications, 2014, pp. 82–102.

Procida, Mary A. *Married to the Empire: Gender, Politics and Imperialism in India, 1883–1947*, Studies in Imperialism. Manchester, UK: Manchester University Press, 2014.

Puar, Jasbir K. *Terrorist Assemblages: Homonationalism in Queer Times*. Durham, NC: Duke University Press, 2004.

————. "Reading Religion Back into Terrorist Assemblages: Author's Response." *Culture and Religion* 15, no. 2 (2014): 198–210.

Qadir, Ali. "Between secularism/s: Islam and the institutionalisation of modern higher education in mid-nineteenth century British India." *British Journal Of Religious Education* 35, no. 2 (March 2013): 125–39. Accessed January 19, 2016. *Academic Search Premier*, EBSCOhost.

Quinn, Frederick. *The Sum of All Heresies: The Image of Islam in Western Thought*. Oxford; New York: Oxford University Press, 2008.

Quraishi, Salim al-Din ed. and comp. *Cry for Freedom: Proclamations of Muslim Revolutionaries of 1857*. Lahore: Sang-e-Meel, 1997.

Qureshi, Ishtiaq Husain. *Ulema in Politics; A Study Relating to the Political Activities of the Ulema in the South-Asian Subcontinent from 1556 to 1947*. Karachi: Ma'aref, 1972.

Rag, Pankaj. "1857: Need for Alternative Sources." *Social Scientist* 26, no. 1/4 (1998): 113–47.

Raja, Masood Ashraf. "The Indian Rebellion of 1857 and Mirza Ghalib's Narrative of Survival." *Prose Studies* 31, no. 1 (2009): 40–54.

Randall, Don. "Autumn 1857: The Making of the Indian 'mutiny'". *Victorian Literature and Culture* 31, no. 1 (2003): 3–17.

Reinhart, A. Kevin. "Islamic Law as Islamic Ethics." *The Journal of Religious Ethics* 11, no. 2 (1983): 186–203.

Rex, J. "The Concept of Race in Sociological Theory." in *Race and Racialism*. Edited by Sami Zubaida. London: Tavistock, 1970, pp. 102–13.

Richards, John F. *The Mughal Empire*. Cambridge: Cambridge University Press, 1993.

Robb, Peter, ed. *The Concept of Race in South Asia*. Delhi: Oxford University Press, 1995.

Robert, Dana Lee, ed. *Converting Colonialism: Visions and Realities in Mission History, 1706–1914*. Studies in the History of Christian Missions. Grand Rapids, MI: William B. Eerdmans, 2008.

Robinson, Francis. *Islam and Muslim History in South Asia*. New Delhi: Oxford University Press, 2001.

————. *The 'Ulama of Farangi Mahall and Islamic Culture in South Asia*. Delhi: Permanent Black, 2001.

Roy, Tapti. "Visions of the Rebels: A Study of 1857 in Bundelkhand." *Modern Asian Studies* 27, no. 1, Special Issue: How Social, Political and Cultural Information Is Collected, Defined, Used and Analyzed (February 1993): 205–28.

Sachedina, Abdulaziz. "The Development of Jihad in Islamic Revelation and History." in *Cross, Crescent, and Sword: The Justification and Limitation of War in*

Western and Islamic Traditions. Edited by J. T. Johnson and J. Kelsay. Westport: Greenwood Press, 1990, pp. 35–50.

Sanyal, Usha. *Devotional Islam and Politics in British India: Ahmad Riza Khan Barelwi and his movement, 1870–1920.* Delhi: Oxford University Press, 1996.

———. *Ahmad Riza Khan Barelwi: In the Path of the Prophet.* Makers of the Muslim World. Oxford: Oneworld, 2005.

Savarkar, Vinayak Damodar and G. M. Joshi. *The Indian War of Independence, 1857.* Bombay: Phoenix Publications, 1909. Reprint 1947.

Sedgwick, Mark. "Jihad, Modernity, and Sectarianism." *Nova Religio: The Journal of Alternative and Emergent Religions* 11, no. 2 (2007): 6–27.

Segalla, Spencer D. *The Moroccan Soul: French Education, Colonial Ethnology, and Muslim Resistance, 1912–1956.* France Overseas. Lincoln: University of Nebraska Press, 2009.

Sen, Surendra Nath. *Eighteen Fifty-Seven.* Delhi: Publications Division, Ministry of Information and Broadcasting, Government of India, 1957.

Sengupta, Indra, Daud Ali, and Javed Majeed, eds *Knowledge Production, Pedagogy, and Institutions in Colonial India.* New York: Palgrave Macmillan, 2011.

Shah Ismail, *Mansab-i imamat,* passages translated by M. Mujeeb in *The Indian Muslims.* New Delhi: Munshiram Manoharlal, 1985.

Shaikh, Farzana. *Community and Consensus in Islam: Muslim Representation in Colonial India, 1860–1947.* Cambridge South Asian Studies 42. New York: Cambridge University Press, 1989.

Shani, Ornit. "Conceptions of Citizenship in India and the 'Muslim Question.'" *Modern Asian Studies* 44, no. 1 (2010): 145–73.

"Shariah in American Courts: The Expanding Incursion of Islamic Law in the U.S. Legal System." January 5, 2015. Accessed April 5, 2016. http://www.centerfors ecuritypolicy.org/2015/01/05/shariah-in-american-courts-the-expanding-incursion-of-islamic-law-in-the-u-s-legal-system/.

Sharma, Arvind. "On Hindu, Hindustan, Hinduism and Hindutva." *Numen* 49, no. 1 (2002): 1–36.

Sharma, Sanjay. "The 1837–38 Famine in U.P.: Some Dimensions of Popular Action," *Indian Economic and Social History Review* 30, no. 3 (1993): 337–72.

———. *Famine, Philanthropy and the Colonial State: North India in the Early Nineteenth Century.* New Delhi, Oxford University Press, 2001.

Shaukat Ali, Parveen. *Pillars of British Imperialism: A Case Study of the Political Ideas of Sir Alfred Lyall, 1873–1903.* Lahore: Aziz Publishers, 1976.

Siddiqui, Javed. *1857: Ek Safarnama,* 2008.

Singh, K. S. "The 'tribals' and the 1857 Uprising." *Social Scientist* 26, no. 1/4 (1998): 76–85.

Smith, Jonathan Z. "Religion, Religions, Religious." in *Critical Terms for Religious Studies.* Edited by Mark C. Taylor. Chicago: University of Chicago Press, 1998, pp. 269–84.

———. "A Matter of Class: Taxonomies of Religion." in *Relating Religion: Essays in the Study of Religion.* Chicago: University of Chicago Press, 2004, pp. 160–78.

———. "Differential Equations: On Constructing the Other." in *Relating Religion: Essays in the Study of Religion.* Chicago: University of Chicago Press, 2004, pp. 230–50.

Solomos, J. and L. Back. "Conceptualizing Racisms: Social Theory, Politics and Research." *Sociology* 28, no. 1 (1994): 143–61.

Spivak, Gayatri Chakravorty. "Can the Subaltern Speak?" in *Marxism and the Interpretation of Culture.* Edited by Cary Nelson and Lawrence Grossberg. Urbana: University of Illinois Press, 1988, pp. 271–313.

Spolsky, Bernard, ed., *The Cambridge Handbook of Language Policy.* Cambridge: Cambridge University Press, 2012.

"State Legislation Restricting Use of Foreign or Religious Law." Pew Research Center, April 8, 2013. Accessed April 6, 2016. http://features.pewforum.org/s haria-law-map/.

"The states where cow slaughter is legal in India," *Indian Express.* October 8, 2015. Accessed March 9, 2016. http://indianexpress.com/article/explained/explained-no-beef-nation/.

Stern, Philip J. *The Company-State: Corporate Sovereignty and the Early Modern Foundations of the British Empire in India.* New York: Oxford University Press, 2012.

Stokes, Eric. *The Peasant and the Raj: Studies in Agrarian Society and Peasant Rebellion in Colonial India.* Cambridge: Cambridge University Press, 1978.

———. *The Peasant Armed: The Indian Revolt of 1857.* Edited by C. A. Bayly. Oxford: Clarendon Press, 1986.

———. "Traditional Elites in the Great Rebellion of 1857." in *The 1857 Rebellion,* ed. Biswamoy Pati. New Delhi: Oxford University Press, 2007, pp. 185–204.

Strawson, John. "Islamic Law and English Texts." *Law and Critique* 6, no. 1 (1995): 21–38.

Strozier, Charles B. "The Global War on Terror, Sliced Four Ways." *World Policy Journal* 24, no. 4 (2008): 90–8.

Sturman, Rachel. "Property and Attachments: Defining Autonomy and the Claims of Family in Nineteenth-Century Western India." *Comparative Studies in Society and History* 47, no. 3 (2005): 611–37.

———. *The Government of Social Life in Colonial India: Liberalism, Religious Law, and Women's Rights.* Cambridge Studies in Indian History and Society 21. New York: Cambridge University Press, 2012.

Sullivan, Winnifred Fallers. *The Impossibility of Religious Freedom.* Princeton, NJ: Princeton University Press, 2007.

"Supreme Court will review law criminalizing homosexuality." *Reuters.* Republished in *Times of India,* February 2, 2016. Accessed March 9, 2016. http://timesofindi a.indiatimes.com/india/Supreme-Court-will-review-law-criminalizing-homos exuality/articleshow/50823515.cms.

Taban, Faruqui Anjum. "The Coming of the Revolt in Awadh: The Evidence of Urdu Newspapers." *Social Scientist* 26, no. 1/4 (1998): 16–24.

———. "The Coming of the Revolt in Awadh: The Evidence of Urdu Newspapers." In *Facets of the Great Revolt: 1857.* Edited by Shireen Moosvi. New Delhi: Tulika Books, 2008, pp. 11–17.

Tettey, Wisdom and Korbla P. Puplampu. *The African Diaspora in Canada: Negotiating Identity & Belonging.* Calgary: University of Calgary Press, 2005.

Thapar, Romila. "Imagined Religious Communities? Ancient History and the Modern Search for a Hindu Identity." *Modern Asian Studies* 23, no. 2 (1989): 209–31.

———. "Was there Historical Writing in early India?" in *Knowing India: Colonial and Modern Constructions of the Past.* Edited by Cynthia Talbot. New Delhi: Yoda Press, 2011, pp. 281–307.

Traub, James. "Is Modi's India Safe for Muslims?" *Foreign Policy.* June 26, 2015. Accessed August 15, 2015. http://foreignpolicy.com/2015/06/26/narendra-m odi-india-safe-for-muslims-hindu-nationalism-bjp-rss/.

Trüper, Henning, Dipesh Chakrabarty, and Sanjay Subrahmanyam, eds *Historical teleologies in the modern world.* Europe's Legacy in the Modern World Series. London: Bloomsbury Academic, 2015.

Tuson, Penelope. "Mutiny narratives and the imperial feminine: European Women's Accounts of the Rebellion in India in 1857." *Women's Studies International Forum* 21, no. 3 (1998): 291–303.

Upton, Charles. *The Virtues of the Prophet: A Young Muslim's Guide to the Greater Jihad: the War against the Passions, with Tafsir of the Holy Qur'an.* San Rafael, CA: Sophia Perennis, 2006.

van der Veer, Peter. *Religious Nationalism: Hindus and Muslims in India.* Berkeley: University of California Press, 1994.

————. *Imperial Encounters: Religion and Modernity in Britain and India.* Princeton, NJ: Princeton University Press, 2001.

Vann, Barry. *Puritan Islam: The Geoexpansion of the Muslim World.* Amherst, NY: Prometheus Books, 2011.

Viswanathan, Gauri. *Outside the Fold: Conversion, Modernity, and Belief.* Princeton, NJ: Princeton University Press, 1998.

Webster, Anthony. "The Strategies and Limits of Gentlemanly Capitalism: The London East India Agency Houses, Provincial Commercial Interests, and the Evolution of British Economic Policy in South and South East Asia 1800–50." *Economic History Review* 59, no. 4 (2006): 743–64.

Wolpert, Stanley. *A New History of India*, 6th edn New York, Oxford: Oxford University Press, 2000.

Yang, Anand A. "A Conversation of Rumors: The Language of Popular 'Mentalités' in Late Nineteenth-Century Colonial India." *Journal of Social History* 20, no. 3 (Spring 1987): 485–505.

INDEX

1857 Rebellion *see* Great Rebellion

Sunni, 61, 72, 78, 138, 145
Sufi, 143
texts, 47, 59, 60–1, 68–9, 77, 78,
  104, 110, 127
United States politics and, 157–62
violence inherent in, 3, 23, 35, 38,
  46, 48, 51–4, 57, 65, 91, 96–7,
  108, 126, 135–6, 154
  see also Great Rebellion; jihad;
  minoritization; Mughals and the
  Mughal Empire; racialization;
  Sepoy Rebellion; pan-Islamism;
  Wahhabi

Nana Sahib, 32
Nanautawi, Maulana Muhammad
  Qasim, 144
nationalism, Indian, 48, 50
newspapers see media
Norman, Chief Justice, 99, 134
North-West Provinces, 39, 53, 56, 110,
  138, 148
  Agra famine, 92
  Indian Musalmans and, 62

Orientalism, 77, 78
Ottoman Empire, 130–1
Oudh, India, 32, 39, 41
  see also Awadh

Pakistan, 36–7, 149
Palashi, 26
  see also Plassey
pan-Islamism, 36–7, 58, 130–1, 146
  Indian Musalmans and, 62, 101, 148
  Khan and, 137
  Wahhabism and, 133
Parliament, 16, 19, 29, 45–6
  Act XIV, 29
  Charter Act hearings, 60
  hearings, 16, 19, 21, 22, 45, 47
  House of Commons, 16–17
  House of Lords, 16, 19, 21
  see also Caste Disabilities Removal
    Act; Charter Act of 1813
Partition see Independence and
  Partition
Patna, India, 66, 68, 115–16
peasant uprising, 27, 145

Persia, 37
  language, 37, 40, 43, 44, 61, 74
  Shah, 36–7
Philindus see Müller, F. Max
Plassey, Battle of, 26–7
post-colonial, 17

Queen's Proclamation of 1858, 113
Qur'an, 53, 127, 136–7
  George Sale translation, 104
  Indian Musalmans and, 60, 69
  Review and, 104–5

race (theory), 2, 7, 23, 124–5
racialization, 3, 5–8, 11–12, 25,
  124–5, 152
  jihad and, 124–6, 132
  Khan and, 110, 136, 137
  Muslims, of, 59, 84, 124–5, 134,
    136, 146, 148, 151, 154–6,
    159, 162
Rani of Jhansi, 33, 39
rape, 41
Rebellion see Great Rebellion
religion, 2–5, 7, 10, 12, 14, 16, 18,
  20–4, 26, 30, 32, 34–5, 41, 49
  rebellion and, 46, 48, 57, 64, 91
  religious freedom, 78–9, 97
  religious studies, 47, 77, 151–2,
    155–6
  religious war, 64, 66, 69
  see also Christians and Christianity;
    Hinduism and Hindus; Jews and
    Judaism; Muslims; Sikhs
Review on Dr Hunter's Indian
  Musalmans, 11, 85, 103–5,
  111–12, 118, 120
  Islamic law in, 86, 102–3, 106–8,
    110–11
  Islamic texts in, 87, 101, 104, 110,
    115, 122
  Muslims in, 86–7, 98–100,
    105–10, 117, 136, 153
  religious freedom, 105–6
  translation and influence, 99, 101, 121
  Wahhabism in, 99, 101, 104, 108–9,
    111–16, 118–19, 121, 133–4
  see also Hunter, Sir William Wilson;
    jihad

Printed in the USA
CPSIA information can be obtained
at www.ICGtesting.com
LVHW021421081223
765922LV00004B/209